EXILED

EXILED

FROM THE KILLING FIELDS OF CAMBODIA TO CALIFORNIA AND BACK

Katya Cengel

POTOMAC BOOKS

An imprint of the University of Nebraska Press

Library of Congress
Cataloging-in-Publication Data
Names: Cengel, Katya, author.
Title: Exiled: from the killing fields of Cambodia
to California and back / Katya Cengel.
Description: [Lincoln, Nebraska]: Potomac
Books, an imprint of the University
of Nebraska Press, [2018] | Includes
bibliographical references and index.
Identifiers: LCCN 2017042817
ISBN 9781640120341 (cloth: alk. paper)
ISBN 9781640120761 (epub)
ISBN 9781640120778 (mobi)
ISBN 9781640120785 (pdf)
Subjects: LCSH: Cambodians—California.
| Cambodian Americans—California. |
Immigrant families—California. | Immigrant
families—Cambodia. | Deportees—
California. | Deportees—Cambodia. |
Cambodia—History—1975-1979—Influence.
Classification: LCC F870.K45 C46 2018
| DDC 979.4/00495932—dc23
LC record available at
https://lccn.loc.gov/2017042817

Set in Lyon by E. Cuddy.
Designed by N. Putens.

To my mother

CONTENTS

ILLUSTRATIONS

PREFACE

My father grew up in an Eastern European immigrant community outside Chicago. Much of his extended Cengel family lived nearby. The Cengel who bludgeoned his wife and two children to death before killing himself was my father's uncle. When my father told me the story, I was nine years old, or around the same age as one of his cousins, who were both girls, like my sister and I. At the time, my father was depressed, just as his uncle must have been. I couldn't help but see the similarity. At night I lay awake, wondering if the story was a warning. I pictured the girls. I saw my father as a boy. I was haunted by their fates, beaten to death with a meat grinder. Before killing himself, my father's uncle called the police. He told them he was "tired of living." He was thirty-two years old.

I don't know why my father told me this when he did. At the time I thought maybe my age reminded him of his long-dead cousins. Years later I discovered that the children were four and two years old at the time of the murder. It was my father who had been nine years old when they died. But that is how the legacy of violence was passed to me.

The stories Nheth Hak told his daughter Nalin were of a much larger magnitude; they were so immense and brutal in fact that she didn't believe him. Hak's older children survived the horrors of Cambodia's killing fields with him, but Nalin was born later, in a refugee camp in Thailand. When she was a child she insisted the stories her father told her were just that, stories. She would say, "If they traumatized you that much, how could you survive?"

Nheth didn't know how to reply. His daughter didn't believe him; she told him communism doesn't do that. But he knew it did. He lived through the Cambodian genocide; the things he endured are so horrendous he can never forget them. The Khmer Rouge ruled for only four years, but the nightmares the rebels inspired have haunted Nheth more than thirty. His six children grew up in the shadow of the violence that he could never fully shake. They in turn passed it on to their own children. And so it continues, across continents and through generations.

The belief that trauma can be passed from one generation to the next is backed not just by family legends but by science as well. As early as 2000, researchers working with the adult children of Holocaust survivors found that they were more likely to develop post-traumatic stress disorder (PTSD) after traumatic experiences than those who were not the offspring of Holocaust survivors. Since then further research has shown that adult children of Holocaust survivors with PTSD have a higher rate of PTSD themselves than those whose parents survived the Holocaust but did not suffer from PTSD. These results—and other research, much of it by Rachel Yehuda, director of the Traumatic Stress Studies Division at the Mount Sinai School of Medicine—suggest that children are at risk by inheriting changes in their parents' biology due to the parents' trauma. In short, in addition to the emotional and social stress they suffer from being raised by a parent affected by trauma, children of traumatized parents who developed PTSD actually have a higher risk of developing PTSD themselves due to physical changes.

After the fall of the Khmer Rouge, Nheth and his family were resettled in Stockton, California, in a housing complex that bore witness to its own share of violence over the years, including murders. Nheth doesn't recall any programs to help him and his family adjust to their new surroundings or any counseling to aid them in making sense of everything they had been through.

Nheth's youngest son, Touch, later ended up on the wrong side of the law. Because he is a legal permanent resident and not a citizen of the United States, and because his crime qualifies for deportation, Touch is going to be sent back to the country his family fled. We may believe by sending Touch to Cambodia we will have rid the country of a criminal, but we forget the issue is not so simple. Touch now has ties in America. He has family here and a daughter—an American—who will grow up haunted by her father's deportation and who will likely hold her country responsible for taking away her dad.

As a nation, we welcome survivors. The United States is the largest resettlement country, credited with accepting more than half of all refugees in 2013. We pride ourselves on offering a new start to the most vulnerable refugees, survivors of torture and persecution in their homelands. But too often we turn away when they don't recover and integrate quickly enough. We listen to their stories. But often unable to take in all the horror, we shut them out. And yet it is more important than ever to attempt to understand the lingering effects of trauma as the world is confronted with the highest levels of displacement on record, with a 23 percent increase in the global refugee population from 2014 to 2015. We cannot afford to abandon these people to ethnic ghettos to become radicalized, something that has happened to some Somali youth in Minnesota. We cannot overlook all they have been through and expect them to become like the rest of us Americans overnight. The physical violence they experienced may have ended, but that doesn't mean they've stopped carrying the mental and even biological residue with them.

The resettlement of Southeast Asian refugees marked the beginning of our official large-scale commitment to refugees and served as the inspiration for the U.S. Refugee Act of 1980, which established the Office of Refugee Resettlement. Prior to 1980, refugees were admitted on a more limited basis through provisions made under other laws, including the Immigration and Nationality Act of 1965. As the largest refugee group in U.S. history, the group on which our refugee program is based, the resettlement of Southeast Asians should be an example of how well our refugee system works. Instead, their later deportations highlight the increasing criminalization of our immigration policy and the holes in our refugee resettlement program. As the world tries to figure out how to handle the refugee crisis in Europe in the late 2010s, the legacy of U.S. refugee policy is being lived out in the Cambodian American community.

In 2015 I set out to tell the story of four families confronting deportation forty years after the large-scale resettlement of Southeast Asian refugees began. I continued to report in 2016, two decades after the passage of laws that are cited as the reason behind many of the deportations.

When I started reporting, I did not know how the story would end—that is, who would be sent back to Cambodia and who might be granted another chance in the United States. There are no solutions in this tale, only the words of the families living the reality. Their exact situations are unique, but they illustrate more universal issues: refugee resettlement, the legacy of violence and war, foreign involvement, and national responsibility.

I began this section with my father, and so I will end it. I was admitted to the psychosomatic ward at Children's Hospital at Stanford when I was nine. After several months I was released provisionally to my mother's care. I never lived with my father again. In researching this book I traveled to Cambodia twice, both times staying with my father, who has lived in Cambodia voluntarily on and off since the mid-1990s. We visited the tourist sites together, and he told me stories about the various coups of the 1990s. He didn't talk about his uncle unless I asked. I asked only once. He thought his uncle fought in either the Korean War or World War II. There was no recognition of PTSD back then. But that is what one psychiatrist diagnosed me with as a child, PTSD. We never talked about that.

Our family's legacy of violence is nothing compared to what the Cambodians endured. In modern times, few communities have experienced violence to quite the extent that Cambodians have. While the phenomenon is present in many families, it is more obvious in extreme cases such as that of the Cambodians and Cambodian Americans.

From their darkest stories, it is possible we may discover a way forward. It is also possible, by refusing to consider their past and our role in it, we will continue to darken the future for us all.

COMPLETE CAST OF CHARACTERS

TOUCH AND FAMILY

NHETH HAK AND MOM KHAT Touch's parents, who were adults under the Khmer Rouge, now live in Stockton, California.

CHAMROEUN HAK The brother born between Puthy and Touch, and who still lives with his parents.

LISA HAK Touch's youngest sister, who was born in the United States.

NALIN HAK (NOW CHHIM) Touch's sister, who was born in Thailand.

PUTHY HAK Touch's eldest brother, who suffers from kidney failure.

SOPHAL HAK Touch's eldest sister.

TOUCH HAK On the list to be deported, he wants to donate a kidney to his brother Puthy. He lives in Santa Ana with Puthy and is the father of Priscilla Hak.

SRIM (CURLY) AND EMILY CHRIM Touch's friends, Emily is an immigration attorney, and Curly is on the list to be deported. They live in Stockton.

JACQUELINE DAN Touch's lawyer.

ONNA OUM Touch's cousin, who lives in Stockton.

SAN AND FAMILY

SAN TRAN CROUCHER Born in Vietnam but ethnically Khmer, she moved to Cambodia before the Khmer Rouge takeover. She is Khmer Krom and was an adult under the Khmer Rouge's rule. She later resettled in Long Beach, California.

TOM CROUCHER San's American husband.

SITHEA SAN San's middle daughter and one of the founders of Cambodia Town in Long Beach, she lives in Cambodia with her husband, Richer San.

SITHEA VY (JENNIFER DIEP) San's youngest daughter.

SITHY YI San's eldest daughter, who is on the list to be deported.

RINH San's older sister, who is a Buddhist nun in Vietnam.

LAUREN THOR Sithy's elder daughter and mother of Jocelyn, Madelyn, and Makayla.

LAUREL THOR Sithy's daughter.

JAMES TRAN San's younger brother, who was out of the country when the Khmer Rouge came to power. He eventually resettled in Long Beach.

KC Sithy's boyfriend.

KIM LUU-NG Sithy's lawyer.

PHAN San's relative and good friend during the Khmer Rouge years.

DAVID AND FAMILY

CHANTHAVETH ROS David's mother, an adult under the Khmer Rouge, who lives in Long Beach.

DAVID ROS On the list to be deported, he served nineteen years for murder. He lives in Long Beach, California, and is active in the anti-deportation movement.

NATHAN ROS David's younger brother, who is a youth pastor.

DEBBIE KEODARA David's girlfriend, a Laotian refugee who resettled in Seattle, Washington.

ALAYSIA Debbie's daughter.

SOLOMON David and Debbie's young son.

HARENE CHAU One of David's older sisters.

SECONDARY CHARACTERS

MARY BLATZ Long Beach community activist.

CHEA BOU AND SAMBATH NHEP Husband and wife, they are dealing with Chea's deportation. They have five children and live in Oakland, California.

SONG CHHANG Former Cambodian senator now living in Long Beach, California. Song studied in the United States in the 1960s. Before the Khmer Rouge came to power, he served as the minister of information in Lon Nol's Khmer Republic. After the Khmer Rouge, he served as a senator and adviser for the current Cambodian People's Party.

KATRINA DIZON MARIATEGUE Southeast Asia Resource Action Center's immigration policy manager in Washington DC.

MIA-LIA KIERNAN Cofounder and organizer of the 1 Love Movement.

CHANPHIRUN MEANOWUTH MIN Nephew of Lon Nol, the prime minister of Cambodia before the Khmer Rouge took over. He was on the list to be deported. He lives near Long Beach with his wife, Terry Min; their son, Max; and Terry's daughter, Pearl.

LINDA TAM Chea's lawyer.

CAMBODIA CAST

SARITH "RITH" CHAN Touch's childhood friend, who has a tour business in Battambang.

BUN ENG CHOU Cambodia's secretary of state for the Ministry of Interior.

SARITH KEO Codirector of Returnee Integration Support Center (RISC) in Phnom Penh.

BILL HEROD Adviser to RISC.

MEAN IN Bun Eng Chou's assistant.

KHE KHOUEN A mentally ill female deportee living outside of Battambang.

SOPHEA PHEA A female deportee living in Phnom Penh and active in 1 Love Cambodia.

SNA A deportee living in Battambang who grew up with Rath Koy.

CHANDARA "ZAR" TEP David Ros's friend, who is a deportee living in Phnom Penh.

NHEB THAI Sarith Chan's cousin, who is a deportee living in Battambang.

EXILED

INTRODUCTION

This story begins long before the Khmer Rouge came to power in Cambodia in 1975 and continues long after the party was ousted by the Vietnamese four years later. American involvement runs almost as deep, starting far earlier than the massive resettlement of Cambodian refugees in the United States in the 1980s. To understand the lives of the families chronicled in this book, it is necessary to understand the historical context—and for that we must go to Cambodia. The history here is dense and convoluted. As is often the case, the line between victors and victims is muddy. That between criminals and saviors is even less clear. This is not unique to Cambodia, but the degree to which it happened in Cambodia's recent history is notable—and in some ways underappreciated. The leaders of the Khmer Rouge, a communist regime responsible for one of the worst genocides of the twentieth century, were monsters. But often lost in our condemnation of them is that those who preceded them and those who replaced them were no heroes. In fact, they were not always even the enemy of the Khmer Rouge; occasionally they were even allies.

At different times, the Vietnamese, the Americans, and the Cambodians all fought against—and with—the Khmer Rouge. They supported or fought the Khmer Rouge not because its rule was good or bad for Cambodia but because of how its support or opposition played out on the larger world stage. Whole books have been written on this topic. *Exiled* is about individual families, so I will keep the background where it belongs, in the background. Still, it is important to understand some basic recent history, which I introduce here along with the families whose daily lives are still haunted by the events outlined in this book. The history comes from a variety of sources, most notably journalist Elizabeth Becker's book *When the War Was Over: Cambodia and the Khmer Rouge Revolution*.

The historical period upon which much of Cambodian identity and culture is based is that of the Angkor Civilization, which ruled from the ninth to the fourteenth centuries. Some consider the most famous of the Hindu temples constructed during this time, Angkor Wat, to be the seventh wonder of the world. The empire was destroyed in part by two things that continue to haunt Cambodia—foreign conquest and the Cambodian ruling family. Both factors played a part in French colonial rule. In 1860 Cambodian king Norodom signed a treaty with the French to protect Cambodia from its neighbors, Vietnam and Thailand. Relations between Cambodia and Vietnam are similar to those between rival princes fighting for the same throne; even when they are united against a common enemy they never fully trust one another.

In its rule of French Indochina—Vietnam, Laos, and Cambodia—the French tended to favor the Vietnamese over the Cambodians. The French were the ones who transferred land inhabited by the ethnic Khmer minority, the Khmer Krom, to the Vietnamese in 1949. To be fair, both Vietnam and Cambodia have historical ties to the land, located in what is now southern Vietnam, and it is difficult to determine whose claim is stronger. The French simply chose their favorite. Ever since, the Khmer Krom have struggled to find a place to call home, falling victim to the deep distrust that both countries hold for each other.

San Tran Croucher experienced this firsthand as a child in the Mekong Delta of South Vietnam and later as a young woman in Phnom Penh, Cambodia. Her earliest memories are of fleeing ethnic attacks in her village in Vietnam. She remembers the endless teasing her Vietnamese accent inspired in Cambodia. I met San when she was seventy-five years old and living in California. She had survived the Cambodian genocide. So had her three daughters: Sithy, Sithea, and Jennifer. But after being resettled in California, Sithy struggled. As a preteen and teenager under the Khmer Rouge, Sithy had been the family's savior, the strong one who learned how to steal food for them and keep them alive. In the United States, Sithy's survival skills were best suited for a life of crime, and she was locked up for drug possession and threatened with deportation. San hadn't been able to protect Sithy from beatings, starvation, and worse under the Khmer Rouge. Now she wants to be the mother she never could be and has hired a lawyer to fight Sithy's deportation case. Only time will tell if she is too late.

To understand Sithy's struggles in the United States, you must first understand what happened to her under the Khmer Rouge. To understand the Khmer Rouge, we have to look at the beginnings of the communist movement in French Indochina. Under French rule, a select number of talented Southeast Asian youth studied in Paris in the mid-twentieth century. There they were introduced to French politics, including Marxism-Leninism. Among these students were future Khmer Rouge leaders Saloth Sar, later renamed Pol Pot, and Ieng Sary. In this way French education helped inspire movements against French rule. For Cambodians, further inspiration came when the French failed to keep Thailand from taking Cambodian territory. In 1945 the Cambodians allied themselves with the Japanese and overthrew the French.

The French did not give up easily. When Japanese rule proved disruptive, the Cambodian royalty once again made a deal with the French. This time Norodom's grandson Prince Norodom Sihanouk, who had been put in place by the French, helped the French regain power from the Japanese. Meanwhile, Vietnam was fighting to gain its freedom from the French in what came to be known as the First Indochina War. Pol Pot was among the Cambodian communists who joined the Viet Minh in the battle against the French. The Vietnamese and Cambodian communists were working together, but their relationship did not last. According to Becker, the Vietnamese viewed the Cambodian communists as part of a larger communist movement in the region and not so much as a national power unto themselves. The Cambodians resented this characterization and fought for recognition in their own right. Meanwhile, several different groups in Cambodia were fighting the French. After the groups frayed and fell apart, the Khmer Rouge absorbed members from all these groups.

As the communists became more of a threat, King Sihanouk murdered and disappeared many leftists and convinced others to leave the movement.

The survivors were forced to go underground. Some fled to the jungle; others, to Vietnam. At first, the Americans provided aid, but fearing too much U.S. involvement, Sihanouk later refused their aid. As a result, his military budget shrank. The amount paid to peasants for their rice fell. Sihanouk's power slipped away. In 1970 the king's pro-American military chief, Lt. Gen. Lon Nol, and his first deputy premier, Prince Sisowath Sirik Matak, overthrew him. Lon Nol was known for fighting the communists in Vietnam, the same people who were helping the communists in his own country. This earned Lon Nol the support of the United States, which was now trying to withdraw from Vietnam, where it had been fighting communism since 1955.

As so often happens when one tyrant is exchanged for another, life did not improve for the Cambodian people under Lon Nol. To sustain the army, farmers were now forced to sell their rice to the government at very low prices. People literally starved. Lon Nol and the leaders of his armed forces became known for corruption and incompetence, and the regime survived only thanks to strong U.S. support.

Meanwhile, Sihanouk teamed up with his former enemy, the Khmer Rouge. Despite having been helped by the Vietnamese communists when Sihanouk was persecuting them, the Khmer Rouge rebels now began purging Vietnamese nationals in Cambodia and Cambodian communists who had earlier sought refuge and trained in Vietnam. Each side was lying to the other, but all of them were lying to the people.

Chanphirun Meanowuth Min wasn't really one of those people. Supplied with a bodyguard and a military vehicle bearing diplomatic plates, he was a sheltered student about to start university. Lon Nol, his uncle, not only protected him but also put him in danger. When Lon Nol began to lose power, Chanphirun was whisked off to the United States. Lon Nol also escaped. But Chanphirun's parents and sisters stayed behind. The guilt of surviving while the rest of his family perished ate at Chanphirun. He sought solace in the oblivion made possible by drugs, a habit supported by small crimes.

When Chanphirun was ordered deported to Cambodia in the early 2000s, a stranger, a former politician who had served under his uncle, came to his rescue. Their tale is that of second chances not everyone believes they deserve. Neither of them is blameless. The man who helped Chanphirun,

Song Chhang, admits he simply picked the lesser of two evils by serving under Lon Nol. He chose the Lon Nol regime in part because of its backing from the United States, which he had grown to respect after an earlier stint studying there. Others chose the Khmer Rouge because they believed anything would be better than the corrupt Lon Nol government.

In the early 1970s, according to Becker, few knew the true leaders of the Communist Party of Kampuchea, better known as the Khmer Rouge, or their plans for what they called Democratic Kampuchea. Only those who found themselves already under Khmer Rouge control understood what was to come, but having been cut off from the rest of the country, they had no real chance to warn the others. In the territories the Khmer Rouge controlled in southern Cambodia, people were placed in cooperatives and then grouped in smaller work crews to farm the land. Khmer Rouge party members oversaw the cooperatives. The people had no money or markets and no way to leave. Those who protested Khmer Rouge policies began to disappear.

The rest of the country was still under Lon Nol's rule, supported by U.S. humanitarian and military aid. Cambodia became critical to the U.S. government's fight against communism in Southeast Asia after the Americans signed the Paris Peace Accords with Vietnam in 1973 and an agreement with Laos soon afterward. The United States began a bombing campaign with Lon Nol's support. Along with earlier U.S. bombings, its bombing of civilian villages and a Khmer Republic military base caused much death and destruction. All the fighting brought streams of refugees into the cities. The five-year-long civil war left the country a mess, destroying four-fifths of its industrial factories, damaging the majority of its rubber plantations, and leaving most of its roads, railroads, ports, and docks unusable. Thus passed the Second Indochina War. There would still be another. But when the Khmer Rouge captured Phnom Penh on April 17, 1975, the Cambodian people didn't know this and thought peace had finally come to Southeast Asia and Cambodia. They met the Khmer Rouge invaders with hope more than fear.

The hope was short lived. Almost at once the cities and towns were evacuated. Contact with the outside world was silenced, international mail and telephone service shut down, the borders closed and mined, and flights severely restricted. Barracks and canteens replaced family homes. The country was split into zones and their people formed into work brigades and armies, all aimed at the goal of transforming Cambodia into a wealthy modern country by 1990. Yet anything modern was abolished, with the few factories and enterprises that survived the war then destroyed. There was nothing but work and political education. Schools and Buddhist temples became storage places and prisons. The Khmer Rouge was implementing a modern utopia from scratch, literally starting over at what it called Year Zero.

At first many people trusted the new rulers and took them at their word. Some of Lon Nol's soldiers willingly gave themselves up, believing the Khmer Rouge's promise that they would be spared. Instead, they were slaughtered en masse, becoming the regime's first victims. The elite and the leaders of the Lon Nol government came next, followed by the educated. Teachers, engineers, and doctors were singled out and killed. The goal was a rural classless society, but although the Khmer Rouge did its best to obliterate the educated and wealthy classes, it simply created new classes to replace them. Those who had been under Khmer Rouge rule before Phnom Penh was taken were known as "old people"; those who came under the party's rule afterward were "new people." In the beginning, old people were relatively safe from destruction; new people were not.

Leaders were chosen based on their loyalty and military service, not for skills that would prove useful to their jobs, according to Becker. Children were turned into spies, their youth making them easy to mold into some of the regime's strongest supporters. The goal was increased rice production, which was to be achieved through unrealistic production goals that required that rice be grown and harvested year round and that people work longer than twelve-hour days. Unable to meet the goals, leaders doctored their results. When the falsification was discovered, the leaders were punished. Once it was revealed that the goals actually had not been met, a scapegoat was needed to blame for the failure. In this way the party turned on itself, targeting group after group until the accusers became the targeted.

The Khmer Rouge ruled through fear and instability; no one, even its own members, knew where he or she stood with the party. The danger faced by different groups varied at different times and in different zones. Tuol

Sleng (S-21) prison, one of almost two hundred such prisons, is estimated to have received from 12,273 to 20,000 political prisoners. The number of estimated survivors ranges from 7 to 179. Zones were targeted for not meeting quotas or just because they could be. Entire villages were emptied as their residents were slaughtered. When the Western Zone was targeted, some sought refuge in Thailand, and their reports were some of the first to come out about the Khmer Rouge. Not everyone believed them.

In addition to fighting its own people, the Khmer Rouge was convinced the Vietnamese were going to invade and engaged in battles with the historic enemy along the border. When the Eastern Zone failed to beat the Vietnamese, Eastern Zone leaders were arrested. Some of the leaders were able to escape to the jungle and cross the border to Vietnam, where they joined forces with the Vietnamese troops fighting the Khmer Rouge. That is what Hun Sen did, the man who would go on to rule post–Khmer Rouge Cambodia. And so, in 1977, began the Third Indochina War. Though the war was fought between Cambodia and Vietnam, it was orchestrated in part by the world's great powers of the day: the United States, the People's Republic of China, and the Soviet Union.

The Vietnamese communists had originally been supported by China, but fearing China's expansionistic tendencies, the Vietnamese now sought support from the Soviet Union. The United States, which fought the Vietnam War in part to contain communist China, now sided with China against the Soviet Union. After Vietnam invaded Cambodia in 1978 and captured Phnom Penh in 1979, China invaded North Vietnam in retaliation. In turn, the United States gave China, Thailand, and the Khmer Rouge aid to fight the Vietnamese occupation of Cambodia.

As a result, although the Vietnamese overthrew the Khmer Rouge in 1979, the Khmer Rouge remained active thanks to foreign funding and support. Sanctions were imposed on Cambodia because of the Vietnamese occupation, and the United Nations (UN) gave a seat not to Cambodia's new rulers but to the ousted Khmer Rouge rulers. In part because of this support, the Khmer Rouge leaders were not tried for their crimes. Some attempts were made, but they were ineffective as they came too late. When the Vietnamese finally withdrew in 1989, they left Hun Sen in power, where he has remained ever since. Four years later, the UN transitional authority oversaw an election. By the beginning of the twenty-first century, defections and the death of Pol Pot meant the Khmer Rouge was no longer a threat. Although in power for a relatively short period, during its era 21 to 25 percent of the Cambodian population is believed to have died of starvation, disease, torture, execution, and forced labor.

Many of the survivors fled to Thailand. At first they were considered displaced, not refugees. Some ended up in camps run by members of the Khmer Rouge who had sought refuge from the Vietnamese invaders in the border region with Thailand. The Royal Thai Army forced more than forty thousand refugees back to Cambodia. It is estimated that at least 10 percent of them died, killed by Thai soldiers, land mines, and sickness and disease.

Nheth Hak made sure it was safe before he led his family to Thailand. His youngest son, Touch, remembers night robberies at the refugee camp in Thailand and finding dead bodies in the compound. His eldest son, Puthy, remembers being taken from his family and put to work under the Khmer Rouge. They spent years in refugee camps waiting to be resettled in one of the countries taking the majority of the Cambodian refugees: France, Canada, Australia, and the United States. The Hak family ended up in Stockton, California. Puthy was almost grown by then. He struggled to learn English and barely managed to graduate from high school. Touch joined a gang, dropped out of high school, and got into gambling and drugs. He spent almost a decade in prison on drug charges and was about to be deported to Cambodia when he learned Puthy had kidney failure. Touch was granted a stay of removal so he could donate a kidney to his brother. Now the stay is almost up, and Puthy still doesn't have a new kidney. Time is running out for both of them.

Puthy and Touch are among the 158,000 Cambodians who came to the United States, mainly as refugees, during the tail end of the last century. Most of them arrived after the fall of the Khmer Rouge in 1979 and were granted permanent resident status. Many of them didn't understand they needed to undertake another lengthy and costly process to become citizens. The Office of the United Nations High Commissioner on Refugees has criticized the United States for this extra step, accusing it of failing to respect international law.

"I often say these folks aren't being deported because of some crime they committed; they're being deported because of the paperwork they didn't complete," said Bill Herod, an American who works with the deportees. Members of the older generation probably feel very guilty now, he added, "because if they had gotten citizenship, their children would have gotten derivative citizenship, and this whole mess would have been avoided."

But they didn't. In some cases they were scared to deal with the government after their experience with the Khmer Rouge; in others, they simply did not understand the process due to language and other barriers. In general, the Cambodians who came after 1979 were poorly educated farmers who needed more help than preceding Southeast Asian immigrants, but they received less as a result of an economic downturn and a new emphasis on preventing government dependency.

Of those surveyed for a 2005 *Journal of American Medical Association* article, almost every one of the refugees had experienced near death due to starvation, and 90 percent had a family member or friend who had been murdered. Community stigma attached to mental health meant few, aside from those who were not functioning well at all, sought treatment. Seattle social worker Tracy Harachi, who has studied Cambodian youths, said that they had more trouble adjusting to life in America than their Vietnamese counterparts had, as evidenced in the formers' higher dropout and criminal detention rates. The Cambodian community, said Harachi, "is typically resettled in sort of what one would term [a] ghetto area, often with a parent who has mental illness or is severely depressed."

The larger Southeast Asian American community has some of the lowest high school graduation rates and some of the highest rates of poverty, arrests, and incarceration. They are also subject to some of the strictest sentencing punishments. This might not have been noted if it were not for harsh immigration laws passed in 1996 that greatly increased the deportation of noncitizens, including Southeast Asian "criminal aliens" who were ordered to be deported to the countries they had fled. The Illegal Immigration Reform and Immigrant Responsibility Act and the Antiterrorism and Effective Death Penalty Act—passed in reaction to the World Trade Center (1993) and Oklahoma City (1995) bombings, respectively—both greatly changed how the United States treats legal permanent residents. The laws expanded the list of deportable offenses and limited the power of immigration judges to review and, in some cases, prevent deportations. Under the new laws, some crimes that do not qualify as felonies under state law are classified as aggravated felonies under immigration law. The laws were also made retroactive.

According to a Human Rights Watch report, more than three-quarters of the legal permanent residents deported between 1997 and 2007 had been convicted only of nonviolent crimes. Marijuana and cocaine possession and traffic offenses are some of the most common crimes for which people were deported. The tough laws enacted during the "War on Drugs" mean even minor drug offenses can result in deportation. Another Human Rights Watch report found that between 2007 and 2012, one out of every four noncitizens deported had a drug conviction as his or her most serious conviction. (It is not clear how many deportees are legal permanent residents, as Immigration and Customs Enforcement [ICE] would not break the numbers down, according to Human Rights Watch.)

Any drug offense, aside from the conviction of possession of thirty grams or less of marijuana, can result in the deportation of a legal permanent resident. While those with convictions for possession can apply for "cancellation of removal," they often have to do so while detained, according to a 2015 report by Human Rights Watch. Drug diversion programs and even pardons do not remove the immigration consequences of a drug crime. Although attorneys are required to advise their noncitizen clients about immigration consequences, criminal defense attorneys do not always do so, according to immigrants and immigration attorneys. It is not done so much out of malice as from a lack of knowledge; even immigration lawyers report being overwhelmed by all the nuances of immigration law. Defendants who may not be native English speakers have an even harder time understanding and often plead guilty to avoid immediate incarceration, not realizing the long-term consequences of such a decision.

According to ICE, legal residents have been sent to Cambodia after being charged with felony crimes including homicide, rape, assault, burglary, robbery, larceny, drug offenses, and fraud. "ICE is focused on smart, effective immigration enforcement that prioritizes the removal of criminal aliens," said ICE spokeswoman Nicole Navas.

There were misgivings about the laws even when they were passed, but efforts to revise them have been derailed by increased anti-immigration sentiment following the terrorist attacks of September 11, 2001, said Grace Meng, a researcher for the U.S. Program at Human Rights Watch. Those who support the laws, like Ira Mehlman, spokesperson for the Federation for American Immigration Reform, argue that too many people are waiting to come to this country to keep those who do not respect its laws. "The idea that we are going to allow people who have come here and committed crimes, whether they're violent or nonviolent, to remain, it's simply objectionable," said Mehlman.

Others argue that these people have already served time for their crimes, and it is unfair to punish them again. Deportation also means punishing their families, often including their children, who are U.S. citizens. Subjecting them to mandatory immigration detention pending their removal proceedings is unjust. Although they can no longer be indefinitely detained and must be released after a certain number of months if their journey is not soon, they are not eligible to apply for release on bond.

Since the passage of the 1996 laws, more than fifteen thousand Cambodians, Vietnamese, and Laotians have been ordered deported. The orders cannot be executed, however, unless the countries they are ordered deported to accept them. In its 2008 repatriation agreement with the United States, Vietnam stipulated that the United States could not deport those who arrived in the country prior to 1995, basically excluding those who came as refugees following the wars in Southeast Asia. The repatriation agreement Cambodia signed with the United States in 2002 had no such stipulation.

Today there are more than five hundred deportees from the United States living in Cambodia. The majority of them are men, and many have families of their own in the United States. Sambath Nhep's husband is one of them. Alone in Oakland, California, for the first time since she was married in the seventh grade, Sambath is struggling to raise her eight-year-old daughter and keep her two surviving sons out of prison. Her husband, Chea Bou, has already been deported. They talk several times a day, whenever Sambath isn't working or sleeping. Their daughter thinks her dad is away visiting family. Soon they will have to find a way to move on. What that means, though, is unclear.

Chea's adjustment to life in Cambodia has been difficult. More than a decade after the first deportees began arriving in the country, little help is available for them. In Phnom Penh the Returnee Integration Support Center (RISC) does its best to help deportees secure housing, employment, and identification. While most deportees can speak Khmer, the local language, few can read and write it. As a group, they suffer from high rates of substance abuse and emotional distress, according to Bill Herod, a RISC adviser. He estimates that 10 percent are doing okay. The others are in jail, dead, or barely holding it together.

"These are people who are completely shaped by their time in the States, good or bad," said Bill. "And if they're drug addicts, or got addicted in the States, and they were in gangs in the States, it's because of the failure of refugee resettlement programs in the United States."

Hun Sen and his Cambodia's People Party have ruled Cambodia for more than three decades, a feat he has accomplished through violence and corruption. Those who have lived under Hun Sen's rule and never had the chance to escape to America are suspicious of the deportees.

"They are thought of as criminals who did some terrible thing to have gotten kicked out of the golden land of America, a dream of all Cambodians," said Anida Yoeu Ali, a Cambodian American artist who spent time living in Phnom Penh voluntarily.

David Ros did do something terrible—he murdered a man—and served nineteen years in prison for it. Then he was ordered deported. Still, more than half a decade later he hasn't been taken. He isn't so much worried about what will happen to him when he is deported but what will happen to his young son, Solomon. Every six months David checks in with ICE. The next time could be his last.

PART 1

YEAR ZERO

1

THE DIPLOMAT AND THE DEPORTEE

They were all youngish, in their thirties and forties, and all men. All people he used to know. They didn't tell him their crimes, and he didn't ask. All they told him was that they were on the list to be deported to Cambodia. Then they asked for his help.

They sought him out because he used to be like them, a tough, streetwise, bad boy. But now he had his own picture-framing business next to a nail salon and a cluster of other small shops on a busy corner in Long Beach, California. Inside the one-story brick building, he was surrounded by a history different from his own in hundreds of historical photos of Long Beach; they were quaint black-and-white beach scenes from the previous century, including one of a smartly dressed fire chief and his staff headed to work in an early automobile. It wasn't the Long Beach Chanphirun Meanowuth Min knew, but it was the Long Beach he sold. Then there were the custom framing jobs he did: abstract paintings, athletic jerseys, American flags. This was his life now. The men who came in off the street asking for help did not belong in it.

But it hadn't been that long since Chanphirun had been a part of their world. Like them, he had been a convicted noncitizen felon on the list to be deported. That was in 2003, early on, just after the deportations became a reality. Only Chanphirun had been allowed to stay. They wanted to know how. He told them the first thing that came to mind: "Get down on your knees and pray."

He remembers telling them to pray a lot and to try not to get in any more trouble. Become a good person. Do what I did, and, just maybe, there will be a miracle. If you are lucky, it will work at the very last minute, as it did for me, and you won't be deported to a land you haven't known for decades, a land your families fled, often before you were old enough to remember.

He never saw them again. They vanished, swallowed by the streets from which they had emerged. That was a decade ago. They don't come anymore. Maybe they are okay. Maybe they are in trouble again. Chanphirun doesn't know. He doesn't want to. He has a wife and son now.

In early 2015 he is fifty-six, although he looks younger, is still trim and fit, and is dressed stylishly but not outlandishly. He has black tortoiseshell glasses and wears tight shirts that reveal his flesh has yet to soften and sag. He has a thick accent but not so thick that he can't be understood. A photo of his wife and son decorate his office.

One wrong move and he could lose it all: the wife he met on the internet, the four-year-old son he plays Power Rangers with, the framing shop he used to work at and now owns. If he gets in trouble with the law, he could be deported to the country he fled decades ago. In his nightmares he sees it vividly—Cambodia.

Sometimes he is in the jungle. Sometimes there is a firing squad with soldiers. Sometimes he is in the city. In the last scene he is wandering, trying to find his family—not his wife and son but the family he lost after he came to the United States in 1975, just months before the country fell to the Khmer Rouge: his mother, his father, and his four sisters. The family who had been leaders in the previous U.S.-backed government, which was overthrown when the communist Khmer Rouge took control. The family who had sent him to Washington DC, promising they would be right behind him.

They weren't. Other Cambodians came, refugees of the regime under which almost a quarter of the country's population died.

The refugees sought Chanphirun out, wanting him to know his family's fate. They wanted him to know they were really sorry. They told him his uncle Lon Non (not to be confused with Lon Nol) had been beheaded and his parents slaughtered. They didn't say anything about his sisters, the older one or the three younger ones. They didn't have to. He knew they were dead. A family such as his did not survive the Khmer Rouge. He was alive only because they had sent him away.

He was nineteen. His past had been erased. His future was empty. Too timid to kill himself but lacking the will to live, he got into drugs: marijuana, cocaine, speed, quaaludes. He did time for reckless driving, driving under the influence, and selling drugs. In 2001 he was convicted for trying to defraud Medi-Cal (the California Medical Assistance Program) by selling blood and stolen medical identification cards and was ordered to pay $25,000 in restitution and to spend sixteen months in prison. Two years later he was on the list of convicted U.S. legal permanent resident Cambodian felons to be deported to Cambodia.

But because of who he was, and who his uncle had been—Lon Non's brother, Lon Nol, the prime minister of Cambodia before the Khmer Rouge took over—Chanphirun was not returned to Cambodia. The Khmer Rouge were no longer in power, but those in the government at the time had close links to the previous rulers. A former Cambodian government official testified that Chanphirun would likely face torture or worse if he was sent back to Cambodia. Chanphirun was not deported, but as a convicted felon, he is no longer eligible for citizenship and thus is still deportable should he face further legal troubles. The man who saved him from deportation in 2003 was the same man who helped fly his uncle Lon Nol out of Cambodia days before it fell to the communists in 1975—Song Chhang.

Song chuckles when I ask him how he convinced an American judge not to deport Chanphirun. "I tell them a story," he says.

It is several hours before he returns to that story. In the meantime, he tells me half a dozen other stories. The story of how he helped Lon Nol escape Phnom Penh days before the city fell. The story of his return to his native village half a century after he left. The story of nine CBS and NBC journalists killed during the civil war.

He talks over the noise of the city drifting in through his open window—the ubiquitous leaf blowers of Southern California and the sounds of traffic coming from the busy Long Beach intersection below. A seventy-five-year-old man with the physical reminders of a recent stroke, Song is a storyteller who understands he doesn't have a whole lot of time left to talk.

"I was born in a poor village," he begins. "Nothing different [from] an African village, except we not that black."

He smiles playfully. A white-haired man with swollen, almost lifeless legs, Song has little: no car, no wife, not much of a relationship with his grown children. He isn't bitter, merely realistic.

"I learn that term 'decrepit,'" he says. "I say, 'I'm old, I'm handicapped, but I am not decrepit,' yet."

He came from little, and that is most likely how he will leave this world. In between, there was more. In the early 1950s he left his little river village to attend the French high school five miles away. It wasn't far, but it was far enough that poor village children lacking transportation didn't go home once they left for high school. Instead, they lived in the "French Village," small bamboo barracks they built next to their French teachers' bungalows. The French were still clinging to power in the region, and at night Song and his companions would study the French Revolution while fishing for their dinner. Those same friends later went on to serve in the government that replaced the French one. Song served beside them. He was the minister of information in Lon Nol's pro-American military government before the country fell to the communists. Others from their school became leaders in the Khmer Rouge, the communists. Khieu Samphan was one of them. Song remembers the former Khmer Rouge head of state telling him that he had chased the Vietnamese out of Cambodia. Song replied, "We tried to chase Vietnamese. You kill us."

Song chuckles again. It is easy to do from the safety of his second-story apartment. The United States is his home now; it has been for decades. He sees Cambodia on visits, as he did in December 2014, when he returned to his childhood village for the first time in more than half a century.

He found his relatives telling stories, the same stories they were telling when he left. It was as if nothing had changed. But so much had. The French were gone. The Americans had come, bombed the country, and gone. The Khmer Rouge had come, committed mass murder, and gone underground. The Vietnamese had come and bombed, but they were still around.

Song experienced the changes from outside the village: first in a provincial town, then in the country's capital of Phnom Penh, and finally in the

United States. His relatives experienced the changes from within. Which group was dropping the bombs made little difference; all they knew was that the fighting had taken the lives of many in their village. Communists, American-backed governments, French rulers—all had fought over the land they called home. The Khmer Rouge ruled for a time. Now there was someone different.

They chided Song for not being there to help them when the Khmer Rouge came. They blamed him for the bombs that were dropped on them, even though he told them he had nothing to do with that. It didn't matter. He had been the most powerful person they knew, so they held him responsible. Song asked if the Khmer Rouge had come looking for him.

"Oh yeah, they ask for you all the time. Anybody related to you would be killed," his cousins told him.

"Why you not killed?" Song wanted to know.

"Because we good people. Because we join the Khmer Rouge."

The Khmer Rouge came to their village looking for recruits. The recruits were told they would be fighting the people who had bombed them. They joined because Song wasn't there to protect them, and they wanted to survive. By staying put, his relatives in the village were forced to change. Song changed by leaving.

The first time he left his country was to study at Louisiana State University (LSU) in 1962. Song chose LSU because of the location's French connection. A product of his country's former French rulers, Song speaks French and writes French poetry. He considers himself a specialist in French literature and brags that as an undergraduate student at LSU, he instructed graduate students in French literature. His own major was agriculture. His passport to America was a United States Agency for International Development (USAID) program that provided funding for Cambodian students to study agriculture and technology in the United States and was largely responsible for what little Cambodian migration there was to the country at the time. Crawfish, beer, and a white girlfriend followed.

Song returned to Cambodia in 1968. He worked for King Norodom Sihanouk until the king was ousted. Lon Nol took over, and Song enlisted in the Cambodian military. Within the military and larger government, his English skills earned him rapid promotions, and soon he was a spokesman for the military and then minister of information for the Khmer Republic. It all happened very, very quickly.

The downfall happened almost as quickly, so quickly he never had time to tell his mother he was leaving his homeland. He thought he would be back in three months. Instead, it was fifteen years before he was able to return.

There were signs, of course. There always are. In 1970 Song was supposed to travel with a team of nine CBS and NBC television journalists to his childhood province. He had agreed to help them in their reporting on the killings being done by the Khmer Rouge. As a military press briefer, Song spent much of his time hanging around journalists. Too much time, probably. The night before he was supposed to travel with them, he became very drunk. He overslept the next morning, and the journalists went without him. They never came back. All nine were killed—four by a rocket-powered grenade, the rest beaten to death by the Khmer Rouge.

While holding a female journalist Song knew captive, the Khmer Rouge asked her why the Vietnamese received more favorable press coverage than the Khmer Rouge did. She told them it was because the Vietnamese released their captured journalists; the Khmer Rouge killed them. They ended up letting her go. For the nine who died, Song planted a tree in Phnom Penh in their memory. He helps arrange and attends reunions of the old war correspondents. Their numbers are dwindling now, not because of war, but because of age, the one killer no one escapes. Justice, if there is any, is now finding the Khmer Rouge for the most part not in the courts but in failing bodies and minds. Song is lucky enough to suffer the same fate, having escaped the Khmer Rouge on April Fool's Day 1975. It was a Tuesday.

For three months the Khmer Rouge had been blasting the capital of the Khmer Republic with rockets and artillery. Major highways were blocked, and access to the Mekong River, which was the conduit for most of the food, ammunition, and petrol supplies for the capital, had been cut. Political infighting and corruption plagued the Lon Nol government, and civilian and military branches fought each other daily. The plan to remove Lon Nol from the country was hatched in secrecy. A week before it happened,

Song was appointed ambassador at-large. It was his job to work on a peace settlement. Getting Lon Nol out of the country seemed a good place to start; it would take away one of the excuses the Khmer Rouge might use for not agreeing to a peace deal. That is what Song believed. Others believed it was a way to ease Lon Nol out of leadership. Still others thought the president was leaving for a medical checkup with his American doctors. Song came up with the phrase "smooth and orderly transfer of power" to describe the whole operation. And it was smooth: before leaving, Lon Nol officially gave Senate chairman Sokham Khoy the power to act as president pro tempore of the Khmer Republic.

Lon Nol left his country with tears in his eyes. Song left with a small suitcase of clothes, photos, and notes. Before boarding the helicopter, he greeted government officials who would not be going. Some winked, others cried. The rest simply got on with their work. Song spent more time with the president's brother, Gen. Lon Non. He told him about the travel plans that would take those leaving first to Bali, Indonesia, aboard a helicopter and then to Honolulu, Hawaii, aboard a U.S. Air Force jet. Lon Non was Chanphirun's unlucky uncle, the one who didn't make it out, the one who was beheaded.

Just before they left, Song's former military chief briefer reached out to him. "He got us all to rise up and fight," the man said of Lon Nol. "Now he's deserting us."

In a way, the same could have been said of Song.

About five thousand Cambodians—most of them members of the military, diplomats, and those already outside the country—were evacuated to the United States around the same time. They would become early leaders among the Cambodian diaspora and, along with the few Cambodians already in the country, would play a role in advocating for the large number of Cambodian refugees that followed. Song was among those who helped.

"I was not a lobbyist," he says. "I just talk to people."

It is a talent that has not diminished with age and that was well honed from his time serving as an information minister. He knew how to bring attention to an issue and fill a press conference. Invitations to U.S. Senate meetings followed. He spoke with senators in Kansas City and New York

City. He told a Jewish congressman that the genocide in Cambodia was like the Holocaust. The senator was not convinced. Song provided his reasoning.

It was 1977, halfway into the brutal Khmer Rouge regime that would result in the deaths of around two million people. Pol Pot, the regime's leader, forced Cambodians to work on communal farms in the countryside. Execution, starvation, and disease killed whole segments of the population. Money, private property, and religion were abolished and the date set back to Year Zero. Wearing glasses or otherwise showing supposed signs of education could get you killed. Some managed to escape to Thailand, and Song was advocating on their behalf.

His arguments worked. Soon the Jewish community was asking him to give talks. He was invited to speak on the radio, to attend more meetings. Something, maybe everything, was having an effect. In 1979 the Khmer Rouge were forced from power, and many more refugees flooded Thailand. Due in part to the efforts of Cambodians living in the United States like Song, and news about the growing humanitarian and refugee crisis in Southeast Asia, the United States passed the 1980 Refugee Act. By the time the official U.S. Cambodian refugee program ended in 1994, more than 150,000 Cambodians had been admitted, with the majority of them as refugees.

Getting them admitted was the first part. The second part was resettlement. The several thousand Cambodians originally admitted were initially sent to empty military bases, including Camp Pendleton near Long Beach, California. The few Cambodians living in the region, some of whom were former participants in the USAID college program Song took part in, helped the refugees resettle. In this way those at Camp Pendleton were brought to Long Beach, thanks to the existing Cambodian community willing to sponsor them. Efforts were later made to resettle the refugees in different areas, hoping that by dispersing them throughout the country they would more easily assimilate. But many of those sent elsewhere made their way to Long Beach, an area with an established Cambodian community, a warm climate, entry-level jobs, and relatively inexpensive housing.

As early as 1981, Long Beach was being called the Cambodian capital of the United States. In 2007 the Long Beach City Council officially recognized

Cambodia Town, a few blocks in Long Beach centered on Anaheim Street. Today Long Beach is one of the cities with the largest population of Cambodians outside Cambodia with around twenty thousand people of Cambodian descent living in the city.

Economically, says Song, the Cambodians aren't as resilient as their Chinese and Vietnamese counterparts. Chinese and Vietnamese immigrants come from cities where they are used to hustling, explains Song. Cambodians always had land passed from one generation to the next. They had security because of their land and thus did not develop the "killer business instinct." It is the same problem they are facing today in Cambodia, he argues, with the Vietnamese taking over. Cambodians simply are "not good at business," says Song. That the Khmer Rouge did such a good job killing off educated Cambodians probably didn't help. Because many of the refugees who survived the Khmer Rouge were not literate in their own language, it was extremely hard for them to learn English and fully integrate in the United States, including starting their own businesses.

Their surroundings, often in public housing complexes, also didn't exactly lend themselves to entrepreneurship. Gang violence between Latinos and Cambodians became an issue. It was a violent time for America's inner cities, and the state and federal governments responded with punitive measures. When it came to legal permanent residents who had broken the law, the government found an easy way to get rid of the problem—deportation. Two 1996 laws dramatically increased the number of people being deported—the Antiterrorism and Effective Death Penalty Act and the Illegal Immigration Reform and Immigrant Responsibility Act.

These laws largely took away judicial review, leaving judges almost powerless to stop individual deportations. Because criminal defense lawyers are not always aware of possible immigration outcomes, they do not always advise their clients correctly. Once they get to immigration court, noncitizens are not entitled to a government-appointed attorney.

At the same time, the definition of an aggravated felony was expanded and mandatory detention came into practice. Local law enforcement was encouraged, and often provided with monetary incentives, to help the federal Immigration and Naturalization Service. Although the number of criminal deportations increased, the majority of deportations were for nonviolent offenses.

Since the passage of the 1996 laws, small victories have been won in the Supreme Court that allow certain deportation waivers and place limits on the amount of time a person can be detained. Otherwise, things have gone mostly in the other direction, with budgets for enforcement steadily increasing.

Song was in Cambodia at the time, advising Prime Minister Hun Sen's government. Song's organization, Save Cambodia, worked on government reforms and was cited for a presidential award by U.S. president Ronald Reagan in 1983. Song tried to convince the Cambodians not to accept the deportees. They didn't listen, and in 2002 he found himself trying to help a group of people deported to a country where they knew no one. He visited them in prison cells as they waited for someone to pick them up. But no one came.

Save Cambodia has since disappeared, says Song, "because I don't care anymore about it." It isn't that he doesn't care so much as that he cares too much. He had told the Cambodians what to do: "Refuse to accept the deportees. Just don't take them." But they did. He doesn't get into the immense pressure the U.S. government was putting on Cambodia, including threatening the visa program for Cambodians wishing to visit the United States.

His girlfriend interrupts him with a plate of fresh fruit. She is younger than he is, and her English is limited. The disruption distracts him. He launches into a speech about the Vietnamese. Vietnam and Cambodia have a contentious relationship. When Song helped Cambodian refugees resettle in the States, some accused him of doing so to make it easier for the Vietnamese to take over Cambodia. He supports current Cambodian prime minister Hun Sen, a long-serving dictator who is accused of being a puppet of the Vietnamese. He defends his support of Hun Sen by arguing that the Vietnamese are the only ones who can win over the Khmer people, the only ones who can unite the various factions.

"I know what's going on. I've been minister [in] three governments, three generations," he says.

Now he addresses his followers from his bedroom via Facebook, slippers on his feet. He returns to the topic of the Cambodian government's acceptance of the deportees abruptly. "They want to do something, okay, screw it."

He doesn't want to tell the story of the deportees because it doesn't end how he feels it should have. "I'm not supposed to tell like that."

The story he will tell is Chanphirun's. Song was in the United States when Chanphirun was ordered deported. The story Song told the immigration judge in the case was not made up, was not lies; it was just a new story, he says. And yet it really wasn't. Song's closing statement, the one he is so proud of, is simple: he argued that it would be against U.S. policy to deport convicted criminals to a country with no means to handle them, thereby endangering the people.

"That's my final remark: 'You send these people over there, you don't help them, and you don't help anybody. You don't correct them, you create problems for them, and you run against U.S. policy not to do these things in another country.'"

He thinks that is what saved Chanphirun from deportation. Chanphirun thinks it is because Song spoke about Chanphirun's family, reminding the judge of what happened to those who remained in Cambodia and of how vulnerable Chanphirun might be should he be sent back to Cambodia.

The reasoning is no longer important. Chanphirun got to stay. He got to marry and have a son. Now his greatest worry is not being exiled to a country that took his family from him but that his son will follow in his footsteps, make the same mistakes he did and join the criminal world. That is why, despite the real chance his son could fight in a conflict and could engage in the very types of things Chanphirun has seen too much of already in his life, he wants his son to join the military. His son is like him, only wilder. Chanphirun believes the military would provide his son with discipline, a chance to "change his destiny." It could also get him killed.

Chanphirun knows this, but he feels it is better for his son to die serving the country, and the people he loves and cares about, than some other way. Because, he says, either way death will find him. And when it does, there is nothing Chanphirun or anyone else can do to stop it.

"I believe strongly that each one of us, God watch[es] over us, and if his time comes, there's nothing I can do about it," he says.

Song has come to a different kind of acceptance. He can't change the fate of the deportees, so he no longer tries. It is too painful, and he has known pain. He and Chanphirun have that in common—the pain of losing their heritage. They cheated death by abandoning their homeland and their families. That was the price they paid for survival. The legacy of violence still haunts them and the larger Cambodian community, both abroad and at home.

2

"IT WAS A MASSACRE"

Cleveland Elementary School, Stockton, California, January 17, 1989.

Touch Hak needs to go to the bathroom. He opens the door to exit his portable fifth-grade classroom.

Boom! Boom!

A teacher at the school will later describe hearing what she thought were firecrackers. Touch knows better. It is gunfire.

His teacher calls to him: "Touch, come back here! Get down! Get down!"

Touch hears screaming. Before he shuts the door, Touch sees a gunman on the roof of the sixth-grade classroom. The gunman, Patrick West, makes wide swoops with an AK-47 rifle, shooting dozens of children. It is midday and hundreds of first-, second-, and third-grade students are at recess, including Touch's sister and several of his cousins. Touch sees teachers running and blood everywhere. In addition to the AK-47, West, who is outfitted in a flak jacket and military fatigues, has two handguns. Written on one of the guns is the word "Victory."

West is calm as he launches about sixty rounds at the students. The scene below is utter chaos. Children run in every direction. Teachers scramble to pull youngsters to safety.

Helicopters and ambulances load the victims. Panicked parents, many of them residents of a nearby apartment complex, arrive on the scene. Touch's mother is crying. Terrified family and friends surround him, demanding answers.

"Where's my kid?"

"Where's your cousin?"

"Where's this, where's that?"

Touch tells them he doesn't know.

He is young, eleven years old. But it isn't the first time he has seen a dead body. As with four of the five children killed, Touch is Cambodian. He was born during the bloody regime of the Khmer Rouge. When his older brother Puthy was his age, he was carrying boulders in a children's work camp in Cambodia. Their parents brought them to Stockton in 1985 to start over. Four years later, Patrick West—a twenty-four-year-old loner, drifter, and alcoholic with a criminal record for drugs, weapons, and soliciting sex—came to Touch's school. West killed five children and injured thirty people, many of them critically. Then he shot himself in the head.

Santa Ana, California, June 2015.

"It was a massacre," says Touch.

His brother Puthy adds that the shooting particularly traumatized the older generation. They are sitting in the living room of Puthy's Santa Ana home. Touch is going bald now and shaves what is left of his hair. Puthy wears loose black pants, a gold chain around his neck. It is a warm southern California morning, but Puthy is wrapped in a blanket.

If the school shooting had happened in Cambodia, Puthy thinks the older generation would have been able to understand; they had seen many people die in Southeast Asia. But the random killing of children was not supposed to happen in California, in Stockton, in the yard of their children's elementary school a few blocks from their homes. That such violence would find them here was almost unfathomable.

"They thinking, 'We are safe place now, we are safe place now . . . ,'" says Puthy. Was it bad luck? That is what Puthy wonders.

Touch thinks the opposite. His family was lucky because despite his sister and cousins being outside at recess during the shooting, none of them were killed.

But they didn't come out unscathed. Even now, more than a quarter of a century later, Touch can diagram the layout of the school, recalling exactly where everything was: the fifth- and sixth-grade buildings, the soccer field, the place where they played dodge ball. He had nightmares for weeks, months, years.

"I still have nightmares," he says.

"Same thing like me," adds Puthy. "After I see the movie *The Killing Fields*, I couldn't sleep for a couple days."

That is why, when Touch says the trouble started with his deportation, Puthy corrects him. The trouble, Puthy says, started in childhood.

Puthy is fifty and lives on a flat, tree-lined street in a Southern California suburb. Most of the houses in the neighborhood are single-story, ranch-style homes. American flags and garage sale signs are common. There is more than one sport utility vehicle parked in Puthy's driveway, and his living room features an expansive leather couch set. It is all very American. Even the shoes piled by the door are common in certain California households. But the mural-size paintings decorating the home take you to a different place. Rice fields welcome guests in the front hall. In the living room the Angkor Wat temple complex covers most of one wall. In the dining room a traditional Cambodian dancer catches the eye and holds it.

Puthy was a teenager when his family escaped Cambodia in 1979 and, following a lengthy stay in refugee camps, was an adult by the time they resettled in the United States. His accent is thick; his English, imperfect. The first time he went to school was in the refugee camp. It was there that he learned to read and write Khmer, the official language of Cambodia.

There were no schools in his village in northwest Cambodia during the troubled times of his childhood, just long days spent taking the cows to graze while his parents worked in the rice fields. They had two cows and three children at the time. Puthy is the second of the children but the first boy. The fourth child, Touch, was born in 1977, after the Khmer Rouge came to power. Two more followed—one born in Thailand and the last in the United States. Compared to their older siblings, the last two had it easy.

Not Puthy. "My childhood is not that great," he says.

It is a clear understatement, highlighted by the comparison he makes next to war-ravaged Iraq. He explains that as in Iraq in the twenty-first century, there were two forces fighting each other in Cambodia in 1970—the

Khmer Rouge and the military government of Lon Nol. There were two main forces maybe, but in both Cambodia and Iraq, more than two groups were fighting. Regardless, Puthy's point is clear: no matter how many factions there were, the people were trapped between them.

Puthy and his family lived in the countryside near the border with Thailand. Their village was outside Battambang, Cambodia's second-largest city. During the day, government soldiers would come. The Khmer Rouge arrived at night.

Both asked the same question: "Did you see anything happen?"

The answer was always the same: "No."

Then they did whatever the opposing forces asked them to do. The Khmer Rouge rebels, who were living in the forest at the time, needed supplies, mostly medical items. Puthy's parents bought the guerrillas what they needed and gave it to them when they visited at night. During the day, his parents ran errands for the government soldiers. The duplicity left them continually on edge and unsure of "who's going to guard you, who's going to kill you," says Puthy.

In 1975 the Khmer Rouge grabbed power and ruled for four bloody years. Puthy was ten years old when they took power. His family members survived the initial massacres because they were poor subsistence farmers and not members of the hated bourgeoisie. Still, that didn't save them from the work camps. Eventually almost everyone was sent to work camps: men to one, women to another, and children of different ages to still others. For a year Puthy didn't see his parents.

"You can't go home," he says. "Nobody go home."

Instead, the adolescent boys hauled stones for construction projects. Pieces of rock were chipped from the hillside and hand carried to another location. It was an endless cycle of walking and carrying from morning to night. Those in charge did not accept excuses. The stones were never too heavy; the boys, never too weak to lift them. They survived on watery porridge, which was served twice a day. It was enough to keep them from starving, no more. They slept bunched together on a bamboo bed or, if they were lucky like Puthy, in a hammock brought from home. At night, they took turns on guard duty. Puthy didn't know what they were guarding against, only that he had to spend an hour watching over his comrades. No one tried to run back home. There was no home to run to.

Justice was swift for those who ran afoul of the Khmer Rouge regime. Puthy believes he witnessed his first execution in 1976, but he isn't sure. Having never gone to school, days, months, and years meant little to him. The Khmer Rouge also abolished the old system of time, starting over at Year Zero. The exact date may be lost, but the crime—adultery—and the punishment are two things Puthy will never forget. There was no judge, just "a group of village people say, 'This is what happened. This is what you do to show people don't do it again.'" The punishment was carried out by a mob. They beat the adulterer to death with pieces of wood. Puthy decided he never wanted to see anything like it again and did not attend any other executions after that. There were more. People were always dying under the Khmer Rouge; you couldn't escape it. They were also disappearing. Once they disappeared, he said, "that's it, they're done." Puthy slaps his hands together to emphasize his point.

One of his mother's friends disappeared around 1978 or 1979. She was there one night, gone the next morning. By then Puthy was back home in his village. When the Vietnamese captured the Cambodian capital of Phnom Penh in 1979, the Khmer Rouge fled, and the people in the work camps returned home. Those who left the camps and had the misfortune of running into Khmer Rouge on the road were killed on the spot, no questions asked.

The country was in chaos. There was no government, nothing. People relied on their own wits. Puthy's parents decided they would be safer in the city Battambang. Their own village was close to the Thai border, where the Khmer Rouge were hiding. On the road to Battambang they saw burned tanks, dead bodies, and spent bullets. They didn't stay long in the city. They needed food and heard the United Nations was at the Thai border and that there was food there. They turned around and walked back toward the Thai border.

Touch was a toddler at the time, the youngest of four children, but Touch was not the brother Puthy carried when they walked toward Thailand. Instead, it was the brother born between them, Chamroeun, a sickly, skinny child who seems to have suffered the most ill health effects from the famine years of the Khmer Rouge.

"He's so skinny at that time, you can see him. He couldn't carry a cup of water or something," says Puthy.

At the refugee camp there was food, shelter, and schooling, but it was all rudimentary. Dwellings—calling them homes would be a stretch—were built from bamboo and palm. The food was rationed. English lessons cost extra. Then there were the soldiers. The Thai people were nice, says Puthy, but not the Thai soldiers, who were meant to protect the refugees. When Cambodians tried to leave the camp or return with something to sell, the soldiers would beat them.

It is at the refugee camps—there would be several—that Touch's memories begin, although he isn't very clear about what happened at which camp. Two recollections stand out; both feature dead bodies. In the first memory, Touch is four years old, maybe five. He is studying Khmer, the Cambodian language, in school. He walks to and from school with his brother Chamroeun. They have to cross a small creek. On the walk home one day there is a flash flood. Touch and Chamroeun cross the creek. Another boy attempts to cross right afterward. The brothers make it across. The other boy is swept away. His body is later found several miles from where the brothers crossed.

"It was just that quick," says Touch. "It was just, boom! And he was gone. Me and my brother was just kind of lucky on that one."

Again, he uses the word "lucky." Some would consider growing up in a refugee camp and watching a schoolmate drown unlucky. Not Touch. He survived. He is lucky.

Another time he saw two bodies in the road, left there by the camp guards who killed them. Puthy fills in the details Touch was too young to understand. Not all the refugees stayed in the camp. Some wanted the freedom to come and go as they pleased. Because they didn't live in the camp, they didn't receive food rations. Instead, some stole from camp residents.

After the fall of the Khmer Rouge, two main kinds of camps were along the Thai-Cambodian border—border camps inside Cambodia and refugee camps set up by the international community in Thailand. The situation in both sets of camps was far from ideal. Food shortages were frequent in the

Cambodian camps as were battles between the different military groups, including the Khmer Rouge, controlling the different camps. In Thailand at least one of the refugee camps, Sa Kaeo, was known to be controlled by Khmer Rouge who had fled the fighting while using civilians as shields.

Touch remembers armed robbers entering almost every night at one of the camps where they stayed. Usually camp residents were left on their own to defend themselves. But one night there was a shootout between the camp guards and the robbers. Two robbers ended up dead. Their bodies were left in the street until the next afternoon, a reminder for residents of what would happen if they ever left and turned to robbery. Touch and Puthy heard and saw everything.

"I go to school. I come back, people still gather [around the bodies]," says Puthy.

The family dug a sort of basement in their house where they could hide from robbers. "That's like our plan B," says Touch.

He and Puthy laugh. When someone broke into the camp, a siren would sound. That was the sign for residents to go inside their houses and unlock their doors and wait for the robbers. They were supposed to let them in, not fight them. They didn't have much choice.

"Door's not a door anyway, really," says Touch.

"Piece of wood, something like that," adds Puthy. "Then they just come in, take the thing out. 'Okay, you want to come in, come in.' You can't stop them."

But one time Puthy did. He was sleeping by the front door. His father was in the house with him. Touch was in the basement with his mother and siblings. He heard the robbers ask for money. Then he heard Puthy respond that he didn't have any.

"I thought my brother was dead," says Touch.

But for some reason when Puthy told the robbers he didn't have any money, they believed him. They had a gun, but they didn't use it. Instead, they left without taking anything and continued to the next house. Puthy was the family hero that day.

In Stockton it was harder to be a hero. The first thing Puthy said when he stepped into his aunt's Stockton apartment on October 23, 1985, was that he wanted to go back to Thailand. It is Touch who remembers the exact date as it is listed on his deportation orders.

Puthy grew up in Thailand, and although he had little there, he knew how to do a lot with not much. In the United States he had expected more, but the home they first stayed in was crammed with people, three related families in a two-bedroom apartment. They had no furniture and felt as if they were illegal migrants who had been smuggled into the country in a huge group and housed in a dump. They were not the first in their family to arrive. An aunt preceded them and sponsored their resettlement. They lived with their aunt and her family in the beginning.

When they first landed in San Francisco, though, they were impressed. Touch and his brother Chamroeun couldn't get enough of the moving walkway at the airport. They ran on it and stopped, ran and stopped. Puthy watched, wondering how it was able to move on its own. They marveled at the huge buildings and laughed at the puffy "Eskimo" jackets they were given by a representative of a refugee resettlement agency. An uncle and his friends picked them up and whisked them off in a fleet of cars.

Eventually they got their own apartment in the same complex where their aunt lived, an apartment building that quickly filled with Cambodian refugees. Puthy was almost twenty years old, but he was placed in ninth grade. He had learned some English in Thailand, but it wasn't enough. He struggled to keep up. He watched his compatriots drop out and listened to his classmates' taunts: "How many times you fail, at your age, you still in ninth grade?"

He stuck it out for four years and received his diploma. Then he told his father he was done. He couldn't go any further. His English was not good enough for college. His father understood. They had received government aid when the family arrived, and as part of the program his father had been encouraged to attend courses on living in the United States and on English for non-native speakers. Some of those who took the courses found jobs. Puthy's father was not one of them. He never mastered English. In Cambodia he had studied only until middle school; then he had gone to work to help support his family.

Puthy took his first job in 1989, after he finished high school. He was a pick-up and delivery driver for a printing company. Today he is an inspector at a machine shop. In between there were other jobs: "I quit here and there, go back here and there." He never had children. His parents chose his wife. He remembers her from his childhood in Cambodia. She is a refugee too. It was for her that Puthy moved to Santa Ana after high school. He was there, almost 370 miles away, when Touch started getting into trouble in Stockton.

Although he started school in the United States at a younger age and at a lower grade—second grade—than Puthy had, Touch still found life in Stockton difficult. He had trouble learning English and was constantly teased about his accent. By fourth grade he had given up on correcting teachers when they pronounced his name Touch, as in how it is spelled, and not Too-ch, or how it should be pronounced.

"Touch Hak?"

"Here."

"That was it," says Touch. "From that point on it was just 'Touch.'"

In seventh grade the teasing had become more physical. Not all the Cambodian kids appreciated being pushed around, and they began to form neighborhood gangs to protect themselves. Touch joined a group when he was twelve or thirteen years old. It was hard to resist. The kids would say, "You have to get in there, man, because we know you from way back." That was the turning point. Before high school Touch made mostly As and Bs. In high school he started getting Ds and Fs and smoking weed. He stopped attending classes and was expelled. His father sent him to Tennessee to live with an uncle.

Somewhere along the way Touch came to the realization that gang life wasn't for him. He didn't want to be violent, but he also didn't know how to turn his back on his friends. He decided, as the young so often do, that marriage was the best escape. At eighteen he married his high school sweetheart, and they moved to Florida to live with her brother.

Without a high school diploma, his options were limited, but he did okay. He says he was able to support his wife and daughter by working in shipping and handling. Everything was good. Until, suddenly, it wasn't.

"I started doing a little bit of gambling and lost some money," says Touch. "And then there was people there, and they really got me hooked on drugs."

The first time he tried "ice," the purest form of methamphetamine, he became obsessed with it. Soon he was spending $300 to $400 a week on ice. It grew harder and harder to support his habit. When he learned that the ice he was smoking came from California, he got to thinking about how he could use friends back home to help him make money by importing ice to Florida. He did that for a while. Word spread. Someone asked him to obtain ecstasy. He decided to order even more and sell it himself. He made a call and asked for five thousand pills. Unbeknownst to him, the phone was tapped, and he was charged as part of a larger group with conspiracy to manufacture ecstasy. Later, the individual charge of possession and intent to sell ecstasy was added. He pled guilty to one count—conspiracy to possess with intent to distribute—was sentenced to nine years, and served eight, beginning in February 2005.

"The feds want me to talk, but I can't," says Touch. "I'm from the street too. I have my own code. I say, 'Nah, I cannot help you.'"

It wasn't the first time Touch had been in trouble with the law. When he was in his twenties, he received two years of probation, five hundred hours of community service, and a monetary fine for aggravated assault with a deadly weapon. He admits he hit a man with a beer bottle but claims he was not the one who initiated the fight.

While he was incarcerated, Touch earned his General Educational Development (GED) certificate. He also got divorced. Before he got out he learned he was being investigated for deportation to Cambodia, something he qualified for because he was a noncitizen felon. Puthy and the rest of the family had become citizens, but Touch and one of his sisters had never bothered to change their status from legal permanent resident to citizen. That decision now meant instead of being freed when he finished his sentence, Touch was handed over to Immigration and Customs Enforcement. It was then that Puthy decided to tell Touch the secret he had been keeping from him for the last fourteen years. Puthy's kidneys were failing him.

"Suddenly I think they deport [him] without seeing me, so I just tell him what's going on," says Puthy, who has been on dialysis since 2012.

Touch promised Puthy that he would be his donor as soon as he was released from immigration detention, but the only way he knew to get out of detention was to sign a paper agreeing to his deportation to Cambodia. This is how Touch and many other deportees understand the paperwork. It is likely he signed a stipulated order of removal, waiving his procedural rights or basically agreeing not to contest his removal and not appeal the judge's decision to remove him. Immigration lawyers say many people sign the paperwork without understanding the consequences due to the lack of translation, the lack of legal counsel, and the misinformation from deportation officers. In his book *Aftermath: Deportation Law and the New American Diaspora*, Daniel Kanstroom writes that the number of these orders increased from around five thousand in 2004 to thirty thousand in 2007.

At first, Touch says he resisted. But after a judge told him that he had little chance of fighting his deportation, Touch says he decided to go ahead and sign. At the time, Touch did not have a lawyer. He thought after he signed, he would be released back into the community until his deportation. That is what happened to the other Cambodians he knew who had been in similar situations. They were out for months and sometimes even years, which was more than enough time for Touch to give Puthy one of his kidneys.

Deportees often think they have to sign the papers to get out of detention, said Jacqueline Dan, the lawyer now representing Touch, but that is not the case. Instead, what they are doing is allowing ICE to start the process of deportation.

"There are no papers that you sign to get out of detention; they just decide to let you go," said Jacqueline.

But they didn't decide to let Touch go. Instead, he was flown to Tacoma, Washington, where he found himself in a holding cell with several dozen other Cambodians. Clearly they were going to be deported very soon. He called Puthy.

"'Bro, this is it. I'm leaving. . . . I'm sorry I can't help you."

The Cambodian consulate came to interview the group. They began to issue travel documents. Word spread that there was a Cambodian man who might be able to help. A number of the detainees called him.

"Hey, man, help me."

"Help me."

"Help me!"

There were many calls, and they all went the same way. Touch was almost the last to talk to Seattle activist and fellow Cambodian refugee Many Uch. Touch told Many about Puthy and how all he wanted was enough time to give his brother his kidney. His story was different than the others', so Many got behind it. Puthy also wrote to ICE and a state senator in Stockton. Touch wrote to Attorney General Eric Holder and then to President Barack Obama. Newspapers ran sympathetic pieces. In press accounts, Touch is pictured with his only child, a fifteen-year-old daughter with glasses and dimples. In the photo she is smiling, and Touch has an arm around her. It isn't clear if she is hugging him back.

Touch was granted a year's release on September 5, 2014, two days after Puthy's fiftieth birthday. He was released on September 11. He flew straight to Los Angeles (LA) to be with Puthy. Months of tests and procedures followed. In May 2015 they finally learned whether they were a match.

"They tested my blood," says Touch. "The only thing is, we're not compatible."

Puthy had never thought of asking any other family member for a kidney. Touch was his brother and, so he thought, his best chance. Their other brother, Chamroeun, was never an option.

"He's not well," says Touch. "He's not like a normal man now."

"He got a little bit slower than us," adds Puthy.

Chamroeun still lives at home with their parents in Stockton. According to the family, he is unable to take care of himself.

None of the Hak siblings survived their childhood unscathed. Puthy believes that the physical brutality his own body was put through under the Khmer Rouge has contributed to his health problems. He may be onto something. Rates of diabetes, hypertension, and hyperlipidemia (all related to kidney disease) in Cambodian refugees are far higher than in the general U.S. population, according to recent research. Touch and his parents blame the schoolyard shooting in part for Touch's bad choices and legal troubles later in life. Until relatively recently, none of them received any counseling.

It is mid-June 2015, and Touch is supposed to be deported to Cambodia, a country he barely remembers, in less than three months. One last possibility might buy him time and his brother a kidney. Although the brothers aren't matched, together they could find Puthy a kidney through an exchange between incompatible donor-recipient pairs. The process of matching Touch's kidney to a recipient and finding a donor match for Puthy takes time, though—three years by most estimates—and time is something the brothers don't have. Unless, of course, Immigration and Customs Enforcement grants Touch another extension. But Touch is scared to ask for fear that when he tells the agency he isn't a match, ICE will automatically deport him, deeming it no longer necessary for him to be in the country. Puthy believes ICE will be more sympathetic. After all, he says, the agency granted the first extension.

The truth is, neither knows what will happen.

"They have mercy, they do it. They don't, they don't," says Puthy. "We can't do anything about it."

3

THE MOTHER

When she forgets, the nightmares return.

So she forces herself to remember. Remember how her malnourished body swelled until her belly looked like a balloon. Remember how her nieces and nephews were executed. Remember how she used to take clothes off of the dead. She remembers it all, so she will never forget that she needs to take an anxiety pill before she heads upstairs to bed each night in her suburban Southern California home. Because if she forgets to take the pill, the nightmares will return.

They are always the same. She has lost her children. She may be a great-grandmother now, but in the nightmares she is simply a mother, a woman running around "this [way] and that," trying to find her kids. "Where are they?"

Sometimes she is in the United States. Sometimes she is in Cambodia. Wherever San Tran Croucher is, her three daughters are not.

The nightmares started in 2011, when San's adult daughter, Sithy Yi, pleaded no contest to possession for sale of methamphetamine, a crime that would place Sithy in deportation proceedings. Ever since then, San has been forced to remember everything. Relive the killing fields over and over and over again. Remember how Sithy, her eldest daughter, helped her survive. Remember that her nightmares will become reality if Sithy is sent back to Cambodia.

Under the Khmer Rouge, it was Sithy who learned to steal in order to feed her mother and sisters. It was Sithy who saved San and in the process destroyed herself. San knows the behavior that got Sithy in trouble in the

United States is the same behavior that enabled her to keep them alive in Cambodia.

"She's only doing what she learned to do to survive, to stay alive in the killing fields," says San. "That's how she knows."

San is old now, seventy-five. She has raised three daughters and five grandchildren. The grandchildren are grown. They have relationships, jobs, and independent lives. They no longer need her. But Sithy does. Sithy needs San to save her from Cambodia, to protect her in a way San never could when Sithy was small.

Phnom Penh, Cambodia, April 17, 1975.

Paper bills float in the air. Money of all denominations is crushed underfoot, torn by the crowds being forced out of the city. San and her daughters follow the rest of the capital's residents. Before being taken from her home earlier that morning, San stuffed her purse with Cambodian bills and gave it to her nine-year-old daughter, Sithy, to carry. Now San wonders why others are discarding their cash and asks those around her.

"Didn't you know? They don't use money anymore."

San didn't know. If that is true—if the country's new rulers, the Khmer Rouge, don't use money—then, San realizes, she has nothing. Nothing to keep her and her three young daughters alive on this forced exodus.

Different parts of Phnom Penh were evacuated by different groups of Khmer Rouge. The various factions did not always get along and did not follow, or issue, the same orders. In the Northern Zone the use of money was abolished in 1974. In his book *The Pol Pot Regime*, Ben Kiernan reports that on April 18, 1975, Northern Khmer Rouge troops threw bills in the air and declared money would no longer be used. Thus, it is possible San saw the money in the air. It is also possible she mixed up two different memories and did not see the floating money until later, after the currency was no longer used in any of the zones into which the Khmer Rouge had split the country. I have chosen to tell the story as she remembers it.

San turns and heads toward home, hoping to retrieve the dried fish and other food she prepared but forgot to bring. It is then that she notices the bodies lying on the curb, near the side of the street. There are two.

A soldier notices her hesitation: "You cannot go back, only forward." He points at the lifeless figures. "If you not listen, you end up like them."

San continues forward, out of the city, away from her home. The bodies are behind her now. They are the first she has seen under the new rulers. She didn't expect the killing to continue. After all, the Khmer Rouge have won; the rebels have taken the capital and ousted the government. The fighting is over.

The beginning of the end started that morning when the rockets pounding down on Phnom Penh began to ease up. In their wake, the first of the rebel Khmer Rouge forces entered the city. Soon afterward a handful of soldiers pointed their guns at San's house. The soldiers were just boys, twelve or thirteen years old. They carried guns that each had a huge bullet stuck on the muzzle, earning the weapons the nickname "Banana Blossoms." They ordered San and her daughters to leave the house. The girl's father wasn't there; he was working outside the country. In the confusion, San forgot the dried food she had prepared. Phan, a relative and good friend who had come the night before after being forced out of her own home, had packed two mosquito nets. San hadn't thought of that either.

The soldiers told them they would only be gone three days, enough time for the Khmer Rouge to "take care of the American enemy." San believed them. She thought they were going to rebuild the country, not destroy it. Most people did. The Khmer Rouge forces had done a good job keeping their intentions and their leadership secret. The areas of the country already under their control were isolated, with the people unable to come and go freely; so news of how the Khmer Rouge governed was slow to reach the capital. In Phnom Penh there were refugees and food shortages, but people of the middle and upper classes such as San were more isolated from these happenings. The corrupt Lon Nol government made sure of that.

And that is why San hadn't left the month before, when her mother came to visit. Her mother had heard that the Khmer Rouge were going to kill people when they took power and wanted to bring her daughters and grandchildren back to the family home in Vietnam. San's younger sister left, but San and her older sister stayed.

"Mom, it's just a rumor," San said. "Nobody knows exactly what's going on."

What San did know was that in Cambodia she had a good government job, a maid to watch the children, and a middle-class existence. In Vietnam she used to wake at three o'clock in the morning to work in the rice fields. She vowed as a child not to be a farmer like her father. But what else was there for her to do in Vietnam? She had no partner there, no job, nothing but family. And that family included an authoritarian father whose control she resented.

San was only sixteen years old when she left Vietnam in 1959. Between fighting with her father and the persecution of her people, the Khmer Krom, San had few pleasant memories of the country. What she remembered was hunger, hardship, and struggle.

San was born in the village of Prey Chop in Bac Lieu Province in southern Vietnam in 1943, the fourth of eight children. World War II was still being fought, and Vietnam was trying to negotiate its independence from France. It was a volatile and unpredictable time, especially for the Khmer Krom, who are ethnic Khmer from an area in southern Vietnam known as Kampuchea. Both Vietnam and Cambodia claim historical ties to Kampuchea, and during San's early childhood she remembers the tension between the two groups and the fighting that resulted. The sound of gunfire was constant.

The worst of the fighting seems to have happened in 1945 and 1946, with both the Khmer and Vietnamese accused of looting and killing. The Khmer are said to have beheaded their Vietnamese victims; the Vietnamese, under the Vietnamese pro-independence coalition Viet Minh, were accused of drowning and burning their Khmer victims and setting fire to their villages. San remembers only being under attack, a situation that continued until she was at least five years old and her younger brother, James, was a baby. When the family fled into the jungle at night, San would ride on her father's shoulders while her mother carried James. They would make the journey nightly, hiding from potential attackers under the cover of the trees. They slept outside without beds or a roof, returning home only when it was light. As the fighting continued, refugees fled to Prey Chop, and the once quiet village of around twenty families became far larger. The newcomers told stories of babies being bayoneted and monks being imprisoned. The Khmer Krom fought with knives. San was terrified.

43

"And I kept thinking, 'When I grow up, any place is better than this.'"

In the 1950s and '60s, legislation was passed in Vietnam aimed at forcibly assimilating the Khmer Krom. Public schools no longer taught Khmer, and it became necessary to have a Vietnamese name to get a job or attend school. More disruptive methods of forced assimilation included the arrest and imprisonment of Khmer Krom Buddhist monks and the confiscation of ancestral Khmer Krom lands.

It was a scary time to be Khmer Krom. Yet San remembers the hunger of her childhood almost as strongly as she remembers the bullets and bayonets. San's father was a farmer but a relatively wealthy one. The family had income and sustenance from their rice fields, but San's father invested most of it in gold instead of using it to feed his family. Within his family, he was "like a king." His decisions were never questioned. He was also highly regarded among his fellow villagers, having received some education in Cambodia in his youth. None of this worked in San's favor, though, when it came to her family's nutrition.

The family lived near the South China Sea, in the Mekong Delta, a region crossed with rivers, swamps, and islands. Fish were abundant, but unless San caught them, her family did not eat them. As practicing Buddhists, they were not allowed to kill. San felt a pang of guilt whenever she caught a fish, but it was better than the hunger pangs. Although he refused to fish, her father had no problem eating the fish San caught. The contradiction was not lost on San, and she later abandoned Buddhism. The monks were even more coddled. The village women, including San's mother, would not kill farm animals to feed their families, but they would slaughter them to feed the monks.

San struggled against all these perceived injustices, but there was one she fought more than the rest—the idea that girls didn't need to be educated. San spent three years at the community school, carrying her lunch in a box made from coconut shells. The school, held at a Buddhist pagoda, did not go past third grade. When San graduated, her father told her that her education was over. Khmer Krom girls did not need to be educated because they would never be anything other than farmers' wives.

That was not the life San wanted. Since she was young, her father had woken her at three o'clock every morning to work in the rice fields with her mother and siblings. He seldom joined them. It was cold, wet, exhausting work. San hated it and figured out early on that education was her escape from farming. To continue her education, San would need to bike to another community about nine miles away. Her father had not allowed San's three older sisters to make the journey, and he saw no reason to treat San differently. But San kept at him, and eventually he relented. The first year she biked with her friends. The second year, she traveled with James, her sole brother and the sibling born directly after her. San would bike, and James would ride on the bike's handlebars. During the rainy season, they frequently made the trip in the pouring rain. The unpaved road would flood from the downpours and far-reaching waves from the nearby sea.

After two years, San again ran out of options as the school only went to fifth grade. To continue studying, she would have to travel even farther from home, so far in fact that she would need to stay at the school and only return home every few months when she ran out of money or food. She did this for four years, three of them with James, until she completed ninth grade. Although San has three younger sisters, none followed her example and attempted to study past third grade. San was the only one. She had done what none of the other girls in her family had been able to do.

But that was not enough. San's goal had always been to escape farming and her father. Because she was Khmer Krom, Cambodia seemed the perfect alternative to Vietnam. She noticed that villagers who moved to Cambodia and came back to visit were always nicely dressed and seemed "respectable." What they did, San did not know; she only knew that they were not farmers. They did not wake at three in the morning to work in a rice field, enduring rain, cold, and exhaustion. San dreamed of working in an office or somewhere else indoors. She did not speak to her parents about her plans. Only when she was ready to leave did she tell her father, asking his permission to move to Cambodia. He refused.

"As a girl you have to be with your parents," he told her. "You cannot go."

She begged. He remained firm. So did San. She was going to Cambodia whether her father gave her permission or not. It took all her courage to tell him this. She prepared herself for a spanking or worse. The abuse seemed less painful than staying put.

"If you don't let me go, I still go," she told her father. "But I don't feel comfortable because I go without your permission." She pleaded with him: "Please, give me your permission."

Her father said nothing. For a week he didn't speak to her.

San waited.

Finally he called her back to talk: "Are you sure you want to do that?"

"Yes."

And that was it. She was going to Cambodia with her father's grudging acceptance if not permission. Her fresh start coincided with Cambodia's. Six years before, after ninety years of French rule, Cambodia had gained independence. King Sihanouk ruled the kingdom. Both their futures seemed filled with possibility.

Unbeknownst to San, the Khmer Krom would become pawns in the fighting that engulfed the region. The United States trained some of them to fight against the communist Viet Cong during the Vietnam War. That group was known as the White Scarves. Another group, the Khmer Serei, focused on fighting the Cambodian communists. Having fought against communist movements in Vietnam and Cambodia, the Khmer Krom were trusted by neither country after the communists took over. Although Vietnam initially helped the Cambodian communist movement, once the Khmer Rouge took power, those with Vietnamese connections—especially Cambodian communists who had lived in exile in Vietnam—were some of the first to be slaughtered.

That came later, though.

It was arranged that San would make the journey with Chris, the son of her eldest sister, Rinh. The boy was fifteen, just a year younger than San. The teenagers would live in an area of Cambodia near the Thai border, where Chris's father was then living. What they hadn't realized was that Chris's father had married another woman. His new wife was around the same age as San and treated San as a maid, not as a relative. San left and moved to Phnom Penh. From there she wrote her sister Rinh, telling her that her husband had married a much younger woman. San knew her family wouldn't allow her to stay in Cambodia on her own, so she asked Rinh to join her. Rinh agreed and brought her three younger children with her. They moved into a small thatched hut on the outskirts of the city. Rinh made cookies and sold them in local stores.

At the time San arrived in Cambodia, the communists were largely absent from the capital, with government persecution having forced them into the countryside and underground. The group that King Sihanouk nicknamed the Khmer Rouge officially formed the year after San moved to Cambodia. Three years later, in 1963, the rebels launched an armed rebellion, naming Pol Pot their leader. Unrest was brewing, but on the surface, in the capital of Phnom Penh, it was easy to ignore.

Unable to find a job, San decided to return to school so she could obtain a Cambodian diploma. Later she found work as a live-in babysitter. She had to wake three times in the night to feed the baby and make sure its cloth diapers were washed and ready for the next day. She was so tired she often struggled to stay awake at school. She also struggled to understand her lessons. Although San could speak Khmer, she could not speak French, the language still used in Cambodian schools. Vietnam had already stopped teaching in French, and San's education had been entirely in Vietnamese. San decided to repeat the ninth grade before moving on to tenth grade, a grade that Vietnamese schools did not include at the time.

It was not easy. At school, when the teacher called on her to read something in Khmer, the other students would laugh and tease her because she spoke the Cambodian language with a Vietnamese accent. The teacher didn't scold them. San kept reading, despite her embarrassment. As it had been her decision to come to Cambodia and to study in Cambodia, San reminded herself there was no one really to blame for the teasing but herself. Her accent may have hindered her initially, but in time her Vietnamese-language skills proved an asset. While still in school, she landed a job as an evening radio news broadcaster for the government broadcasting station's Vietnamese-language program. It was a job she kept until the Khmer Rouge took over. It was a job that should have spelled her death under their control. But again that was later.

Meanwhile, San focused first on completing tenth grade and then on finding work. After graduating she took a daytime job as a receptionist in the government's Finance Ministry. Along the way she fell in love. His name was Len Diep, and he was studying to be an engineer. They met while in school, and San continued to support his studies after she completed her own. They had three daughters: Sithy, born in 1966; Sithea, born in 1967; and Sithea Vy, who goes by Jennifer, born in 1970. Len traveled frequently for work, and the relationship ultimately didn't last.

"That is life. Hurt. Pain. Life."

Still it was better than farming. San worked inside. She had enough money to hire a maid to watch her daughters while she was at work. Most of the maids she hired didn't last long. They would quit, and she would have to ask the older woman next door to watch her daughters in the evening. Her night job didn't last all night, as she only worked for the evening broadcast. She would come home from her day job, cook dinner for the girls, and then go back and make sure she knew her script before going on the air at 9:00 p.m. She worked two weeks on, two weeks off, sharing the position with another woman.

"It's tough for me. That's why I feel like I don't have close relationship to my children, because I work all the time, day and night."

It was exhausting but worthwhile. She had a television and a refrigerator, luxuries not many Cambodians had at the time. Her daughters had plenty to eat and were always well dressed. Her youngest, Jennifer, even went to a private school. The eldest, Sithy, looked out for her younger sisters, especially Sithea. Even back then, Sithy was the tough one, fighting at school so timid Sithea didn't have to. Other family members also helped out as several of San's siblings had joined her in Cambodia. Together they learned how to mask their accents.

Cambodia had become home. Unfortunately, Cambodia had also become a war zone. The year Jennifer was born, 1970, was the year San was finally able to find a maid who would stay with the family and the same year Sihanouk was ousted as head of state. Cambodian general Lon Nol and his pro-American military colleagues staged the coup. As a result, many of Sihanouk's supporters joined the Khmer Rouge. The Vietnamese initially aided the Khmer Rouge rebels in their fight against Lon Nol and his American backers, but by the end of 1972 the Vietnamese had withdrawn from the country.

By 1973 most of Cambodia was controlled by the Khmer Rouge. To regain territory Lon Nol's Khmer Republic government, with help from the United States, dropped about 2.7 million tons of bombs on Cambodia. The U.S. government's goal of the bombing campaign was tangled with its fight against communism in Southeast Asia. The death toll from this and earlier U.S. bombings reached anywhere from 150,000 to 600,000, a figure that turned many to the Khmer Rouge side. Fighting in farming areas caused food shortages and resulted in large numbers of refugees fleeing the countryside for the city. The agricultural situation became so bad that Cambodia had to import rice in 1972. The economy was almost completely destroyed and only survived largely because of U.S. aid. Rice riots and malnutrition were common.

In early 1975 San's faithful maid quit. Not long afterward, the markets closed. As food became scarce, San tried to stock up what she could. Her family spent time in the bunker below the house as the war that had been raging between the rebels and the government for five years approached the capital. Several houses were burned and people killed. The man San had once loved, the father of her three girls, was not in the country. Neither was her brother, James, but his wife and two young children were. James was working in Thailand and had sent his pregnant wife and children back to Cambodia so his sisters San and Rinh could look after them.

That was the life San was living when the Khmer Rouge took over. It was not an easy life. But it was a life she had worked hard to make for herself and one she enjoyed, with dinners in restaurants, trips to Vietnam so her daughters could see her family, and time spent with her older sister.

Neither San nor her daughters slept the night of April 16; the bombing and shooting were too intense. In the morning, they raised the white flag of surrender as they had been advised. There were shouts of joy in the neighborhood as people celebrated what they believed was the end of the war. After five years of fighting, peace had finally come. They were told they needed to leave their homes because the Americans were going to bomb the city. San's two older daughters were excited, for they relished the idea of spending time in the countryside, away from school and chores. Sithy thought it would be like a vacation. She saw the bodies, but she thought the people were just sleeping. San knew better.

San had come to Cambodia to escape the terror of Vietnam and the attacks on the Khmer Krom. Later she would long for the days of Vietnamese brutality over what she experienced under Cambodia's Khmer Rouge. At least the Vietnamese didn't kill their own people without reason, she thought. The Cambodians did. The problem for San was that she had never considered herself either fully Vietnamese or Cambodian. When a boat taking Vietnamese people to Vietnam came to their area, San and her daughters did not get on board.

4

THE MURDERER

Long Beach, California, August 2016.

The agents showed up at Chanthaveth Ros's Long Beach home early in the morning. They had a picture of her eldest son, David Ros. Her son had coached her over and over again that she was never to let Immigration and Customs Enforcement agents into her home.

"Make them get a search warrant," David told her. "You don't have to let them in. You don't even have to open the door."

But she panicked when she saw the armed and uniformed ICE agents on her doorstep. And she did both things: She opened the door, and she let them in.

Chanthaveth Ros's first son is a former felon. Her second son is a pastor. It was her second son, Nathan, whom she had tried to abort. It was the mid-1970s; the Khmer Rouge were in power. She had four children already and didn't want to bring another child into the world only to watch it be beaten, starved, and tortured. She drank stuff and did stuff, but for some reason she remained pregnant. The baby, Nathan, lived. Many others in her family did not. Eight of her sixteen siblings died during the genocide.

If Chanthaveth had stayed in Phnom Penh, she believes she would have also died. But after getting married in 1967 she moved to Battambang with her husband. They had five children together. Nathan was six months old when her husband disappeared. David always thought the Khmer Rouge took his father because he was ethnically Chinese. Chanthaveth laughs at the suggestion. The Khmer Rouge didn't only target the Chinese. They "didn't like anybody, even Cambodian," she says.

She is sitting in a plastic chair in her backyard. She is sixty-eight years old and has only one kidney and no breasts. She has spent much of her life in America on public assistance. She knows poverty, but she didn't come from it. The daughter of a colonel in Cambodia, she grew up with chauffeurs and maids. She was a rich girl who married a businessman. The Khmer Rouge, she says, "don't like rich people. They like poor, poor people live in the jungle or something."

Her husband knew he was a target of their hatred and went into hiding. Later she heard the Khmer Rouge had found him and killed him. She never saw him again after he fled. As the widow of someone who had been killed by the regime, she was tainted, guilty by association for whatever "crime" her husband had committed. After her husband left, she and the children were taken to a distant village. The former occupants of the village had starved to death. The family and other undesirables were left in the village to starve. In her telling, the village never has a name. They survived by eating whatever they could find in nature. It wasn't much, and they knew they couldn't last long. Many of them didn't.

"At nighttime I heard they take the people to kill," says Chanthaveth. "I heard the yell[ing] and screaming, one by one."

Chanthaveth knew one night they would come for her and her children. She was lucky, though. Before they came, the Vietnamese invaded and the Khmer Rouge fled. In 1979 she crossed into Thailand with her children. The next year she was in Indonesia. Two years later she was resettled in Oklahoma City with her mother and stepfather, her five children, and her niece. But she had trouble settling down. She married a younger man, divorced him, moved to Boston, then got back together with him, and moved to Chicago. Her children, she says, got lost in all the moving around. She didn't have time to take care of them. In some ways she feels they raised themselves. They had to. She didn't speak English. She didn't drive. She didn't know how things worked. She did not question when her fourteen-year-old daughter was put in high school even though her daughter's English-language skills were too limited to comprehend high school–level classes.

In the almost two decades David was behind bars, Chanthaveth saw him five times. For twenty years, she says, she lost him. During that time, she survived a cancer of the female reproductive organs and had one of her kidneys removed. She lost both her mother and stepfather, neither of whom David was able to see while he was in prison. In the early 2000s, she was diagnosed with breast cancer, so both of her breasts have been removed. She has high blood pressure, and with a single kidney, she does not expect to be healthy enough to travel to Cambodia to visit her son when he is deported.

"If he go, he cannot see me again," she says. "I am going to die here, and he not come back."

Long Beach, California, Summer 2015.

David Ros doesn't hide much. His identification documents say he is forty years old, but he isn't positive that is accurate. His age, he explains, is based solely on his mother's memory, which is questionable at best due to the torture she suffered under the Khmer Rouge. Regardless, David is old enough to belong to a generation that largely favors tattoos, like chest and bicep tats, that can be covered by clothes. In contrast, the first tattoo David got in prison is on the back of his left hand. It is a Khmer symbol. His black medical scrubs cover some of the other tattoos. And there are others. David was in prison for almost twenty years, so he had lots of time to get inked.

It is a weekday afternoon and David is sitting in his mother's backyard in Long Beach. He starts our conversation with a warning: "This is my conviction. You don't get a lot of sympathy for this." It is what he tells reporters at the start of any interview. He pauses for only a second before continuing: "So, um, I had a second-degree felony murder."

He isn't sure a layperson knows what that means, so he explains: he killed somebody. It wasn't premeditated; he didn't plan on murdering anyone. Instead, somebody died because of his negligence or thoughtlessness. That is how he puts it, with the technical terms shielding him from the emotional reality.

David is cool and calm, a well-spoken and well-mannered middle-aged man with wire-rim glasses. He was sixteen years old when he fired the shots that killed a man. Although he was a juvenile at the time, he was convicted as an adult because of the severity of the offense.

"Because it wasn't one person," says David. "It was two people that got shot. One died as a result of a gunshot wound. The other one did not."

It happened quickly, as calamities so often do. David had a gun. He was at a party, "jibber jabbering" with another guy. The jabber turned to threats; the threats, to actions. David pulled a gun. Then he pulled the trigger, twice—once for the man he was arguing with and once for the man's friend who had come to the man's aid. It was the friend who died. His internal bleeding couldn't be stopped.

That is how David tells it. He says it wasn't his intention to kill anyone. He says the man he was arguing with grabbed the gun, and while they were fighting over it, the shots were fired. A bullet went through the friend's hand and then through his side. Court documents describe a very different scene, including an additional charge of assault in the first degree. But this is David's story, so you won't hear the court's version until later.

It is four o'clock in the afternoon, and David has just finished his shift as a biomedical technician at a dialysis clinic. Basically he operates the machines that clean the blood of desperate people awaiting kidney transplants. He starts his shift at two-thirty in the morning and gets off at three o'clock in the afternoon. Now he is sitting in a plastic lawn chair in a yard full of activity. His two grandnieces, toddling twin girls, play in front of a bright blue bungalow from which his sister occasionally peeks out. In the shade of a covered deck, a man works on an old-fashioned sewing machine; his presence remains unexplained. The ubiquitous Southern California swimming pool has long since been bricked and cemented.

"It's tragic," says David. "My grandmother died in the pool. My grandfather died soon after. My mom had it bulldozed over."

She needed to hide the memory, avoid the reality of her loss. David tried a similar tactic. After he killed a man, he ran. He got in a car and sped off, ditching the gun along the way. He was actually already on the run. He was pretty much always on the run back then. Multiple states, multiple crimes, he kept busy breaking the law and not for little things. Armed home invasions were his specialty. Jewelry, cash—he took whatever he could get. He was no Robin Hood; he was a punk kid taking from his own struggling community. Most of the time he didn't think about his victims. It was the 1980s, and Long Beach was infested with gangs, including the Asian American street gangs Asian Boyz and Tiny Rascal Gang, the latter being a Cambodian enterprise.

David was one of the youngest in his crew. He quit school in ninth grade, and he could barely read and write. It was only later, when he was in prison, that he continued his education by obtaining his GED certificate and reading up on whatever interested him. Back then it was mainly material about the Khmer Rouge, something he had never understood.

"A lot of kids my age did not understand it, either," he says. "They still don't."

The older generation didn't talk much about the brutal years under Pol Pot. David has tried to piece together what he can from his own memories, his mother's stories, and his research. He wants to learn about his homeland because that is where he is headed. Both he and his sister are on the list of people to be deported to Cambodia. Almost everyone in the Cambodian community in Long Beach knows someone who has been or will be deported. David points to a man who has just entered the backyard, a cousin.

"We're the same age. We came at the same time. Committed almost the same offense but in different states." He lowers his voice. "But somehow he got lost in the system."

David's cousin is not required to report to ICE. He is essentially free except his green card is no longer valid, and he is scared to apply for a new one for fear that attracting government attention could end his freedom. Without a valid green card or other documentation, the list of things he can't do is long and includes working in the country legally and traveling overseas.

David has a different set of restrictions. He must check in with ICE every six months. The agency could hold him for deportation at any time. Before he is deported, he believes the Cambodian consulate will interview him. In his experience, that is usually what happens. Sometimes it happens while potential deportees are still in detention. David was lucky. He got out of detention.

He has been out since 2009. He has been preparing for his forced return to Cambodia even longer. In prison he wrote his mother letters in Khmer, learning a language he had known until then only orally. His mother wrote him back. Initially she planned to travel to Cambodia to be there to greet him when he arrived, but now she does not think her declining health will allow her to make the trip. She talks about finding him a Cambodian wife. David has already found some of his own friends among the deported. He knew them before—from prison, from the streets—and will meet them again when he goes to Cambodia. Until then he communicates with them via Facebook and on the phone. He follows one friend's Facebook posts. Most of the posts are about how much he misses his family in the United States.

David thinks about it sometimes—going back: "Just get this over with." He laughs at the situation: his wanting to go back while his friend wants to come here. Laughing is something he does often—not angry, nervous, hateful laughter but genuine amusement at the absurdity of life. And at the ludicrousness of his desperately wanting to see Cambodia and to understand his heritage while being forced to do so at the same time and on terms that won't allow him to return to the United States. That is when he thinks about his son, Solomon.

David and Solomon. In the biblical story Israel's warrior king David battles Goliath, and his son, Solomon, is the wisest man in the world. David Ros also thinks about Solomon's mother, his girlfriend Debbie Keodara, and his girlfriend's daughter, Alaysia. The uncertainty of the situation is hard on Debbie, hard on their relationship. Every time David checks in with ICE, he wonders if he will make it back. He brings someone with him so he can give that person his keys, credit cards, and cash—just in case. When he can, he also tries to bring along Solomon. At almost four years old, Solomon is too young to understand. He just goes along because he is a daddy's boy.

David was only about a year older than Solomon is now when his family fled Cambodia. He has a single baby picture of himself. The next childhood shot was taken when he was about six years old. He is in a refugee camp in Thailand lined up with his younger brother, three older sisters, and a cousin. They are all wearing yellow shirts with red crosses, a gift from the Catholic organization that was sponsoring their resettlement in the United States.

The younger kids all have short hair and skinny arms, making it hard to tell the boys from the girls.

David's memory of what occurred in the time between when the photos were taken is almost as limited as the visual trail. His family lived in a village. Where it was located or what it was called are not things he has ever asked. He did ask about his father, a Cambodian of Chinese ethnicity. The story he remembers hearing is that the Khmer Rouge was targeting ethnic minorities in their village. His mother told his father and his uncle to run and hide. She hoped they would be able to meet up later.

David knows from his studies that the Khmer Rouge did not treat ethnic minorities well. It goes back to colonialism and postcolonial rule. Social structures were rigid under the French and later under King Norodom Sihanouk. According to journalist Elizabeth Becker, Chinese émigrés ended up working mostly in commerce, an activity considered beneath Cambodian elites. In her book *When the War Was Over*, Becker writes that in time the Chinese developed a near monopoly on business, trade, and informal banking. The Chinese ran many big businesses, and the money lenders were also often Chinese. The Vietnamese largely worked as middlemen, while Cambodians worked in government, education, or agriculture.

In their war on the educated and the wealthy and on capitalism in general, the Khmer Rouge also waged war on ethnic groups, including the Vietnamese and Chinese. The Chinese were seen as members of a postimperial capitalist class that was acting in the interests of China. At the same time, the Khmer Rouge had some respect for China's communist leaders. The contradiction was typical of the Khmer Rouge rebels, who were expert at making enemies of friends and friends of enemies. On which side of them you stood, and often whether you lived or died, depended on timing and location as much as on official policy.

The grudging recognition shown to the communist government in China did not extend to Cambodians of Chinese ethnicity. David's father and uncle ran from the village in the middle of the night. Their family never saw either of them again. They could have survived. But if they had, David believes that someone in their extended family—in China, in Cambodia, in Canada—would have heard from them. And no one ever did. So the family assumes they are dead. They believe that after the brothers fled the village, they were ambushed and killed.

The Khmer Rouge targeted David's maternal relatives for a different reason—they really were the enemy. David's grandfather was a high-ranking member of Lon Nol's army. He fought against the Khmer Rouge but died of cancer before they took over. Some might say he was lucky. Many of his children, David's aunts and uncles, also served in Lon Nol's military and were later "totally wiped out" by the Khmer Rouge. According to David, the whole family was slated for execution. His mother was tortured. She and her children were saved because of his grandmother's second husband.

The relationship seems to have begun before the death of David's grandfather, a man who had multiple wives. Over time David's grandmother drifted away from her first husband, exchanging her role as one of several wives of a prominent man for that of the sole wife of a simple farmer. It proved to be a wise decision. The marriage meant David's grandmother was a peasant, or an "old person." She was no longer a member of the despised urban elite, who were referred to as "new people." This change in her status is what saved David, his mother, and his siblings from "imminent execution."

They may have escaped immediate death, but slow starvation was still a definite possibility. Hunger is what David remembers most clearly—lying on the ground, crying, begging his mother for food—and there being nothing she could do because there wasn't any food. She tried. There were times she stole potatoes, corn, and even a chicken from those lucky enough to be favored by the rulers and to have access to such things. There was also a time when she was caught and beaten.

David remembers another time as well, during a regime celebration, when there was food, so much food, that the hungry people couldn't stop eating. David ate so much he almost died. Others did die. After being starved for so long, their bodies no longer knew how to digest the food, and they choked and became bloated. David could barely breathe.

There isn't much else he recalls. He was too young. His eldest sister could say more, but he doesn't trust her memory, her mind. She was old enough to be separated from the others, sent to a camp where she was brainwashed to be Khmer Rouge, and trained to spy on her family and on her mother.

"It has affected her," says David. "You can tell."

He doesn't elaborate. Instead, he launches into a talk about Vietnam, about politics, about the Khmer Rouge's war mentality. At the time, there were separate camps for girls and boys where they learned how to be soldiers, how to fight the Vietnamese. The Khmer Rouge both predicted and ensured their biggest fear, a Vietnamese invasion. The Vietnamese communists saw the Cambodian communists as a subgroup of their own movement and not as a separate power in their own right. That was one of the main tensions. It was also the reason the Khmer Rouge didn't trust the Cambodian communists who had fled to Vietnam to escape the persecution of previous Cambodian rulers. From the moment it took power, the Khmer Rouge fought the Vietnamese and kept fighting until the Vietnamese forced the party from power. At that point David and his family headed to Thailand along with countless other civilians.

Hunger is also what David remembers most about the three years he spent as a refugee in Thailand. The rations were small, and his young body craved more food, more nutrients, more everything. He started to wander, looking for food wherever he could. He was six or seven years old. There were little shacks in the camp—small "restaurants" and shops. David would sneak behind the shacks, where people put out the food they didn't use. He snatched the food and took it back to his grandmother, who cut out the rotten parts—the brown spots from the carrots, the eyes from the potatoes—and then she would cook it.

As the oldest boy, David felt responsible; he scavenged whatever was edible, stole what he found. "The hunger drives you," he says.

He was one of the youngest in his family, but he remembers more than some of his siblings do. Close to two decades in prison gave him a lot of time to reflect, to recall, to relive. When he first went in, David was in a room by himself for twenty-three hours a day. The prison called it protective custody. He was only sixteen years old, and the other inmates were adults. The prison kept him apart for his own safety, allowing him out only for an hour a day to shower and use the phone. He lived like that for fifteen months. Then they moved him to the general population. Out there, as the young guy, he thought he needed to prove how tough he was, so he did. He got into fights, got sent to isolation, got out, got into more fights, got sent back to isolation. All the alone time gave him plenty of time to study, mostly about Cambodia. Thus, his memories are colored by his research. He remembers some things, fills in the blanks for others. David's mother is vague when she speaks about her past, so David's version is the one being told.

There was a school at the refugee camp, but he didn't learn much. His education didn't really begin until he was in prison; that is when he grew up. Not at first, but later. Before that he was the rebellious one, the class clown, the kid who had to hold out his hand so teachers could hit it with a ruler, the one who was always having to write stuff on the board. That happened even back in Thailand.

He was eight years old when the family arrived in Oklahoma City, where a local Catholic organization had agreed to sponsor them. They were Christian, largely because David's father had been Christian, but the elderly white couple who welcomed them was Baptist. David remembers the drive through downtown Oklahoma City. He had never seen such big buildings and called out, "Look at these giant huts!" They were all he knew; he had not seen many buildings before.

He spoke in Khmer. None of them spoke English back then. No one except the man his mother married just before they came to the United States, a man David never learned to call Dad, a man his mother separated from three years later. That man spoke a few words of English.

Maybe ten or twenty Cambodian families were living in the area back then. All the Christian ones went to a local Baptist church; it was where they met up. The rest of the time they were the outsiders in what had previously been a community of blacks and whites. As Cambodians they were teased, picked on. So they left, moving to other places where there were more Southeast Asians. This double resettlement was one of the failures of the anti-cluster movement, which had sought to integrate the Cambodians better into American society by spreading them around. But instead of integrating them, it often ended up isolating them.

David's mother moved David and his siblings to Massachusetts. She was separated from her second husband by then and wanted to be closer to her sister and other relatives. From there they went to Rhode Island, then

Chicago, and back to Massachusetts. The lack of a stable physical home during much of her children's childhood is something David believes his mother now regrets.

"I think she blames herself a lot about my incarceration and about my mistakes," he says. "I try to reassure her. I chose my path."

He lowers his voice. He isn't sure how to say what he wants to say next. There are several "maybes" and at least one "because." The truth is, he says, "I don't know why I turned out bad."

At one time he played sports and liked school. If he hadn't been uprooted from his old white friends in Oklahoma—good kids who kept him in school—he thinks he might have turned out differently. Then again, he also talks about how he was always rebellious and getting in trouble at school.

By the time they returned to Lowell, Massachusetts, David was in high school. Lowell was a densely populated hub of the Cambodian community. For the first time since he came to the States, David was surrounded by people who looked like him. Instead of white friends, he had Cambodian friends, good and bad ones. All of a sudden he was "Mr. Popular." Cambodian girls thought he was cute, so he started dating. The Cambodian boys thought he was cool, so he did what they did: smoked weed, skipped class, attended parties. He stopped coming home. His mother would go looking for him and would show up at parties. She would be standing there in her coat in the middle of the night with his little brother at her side.

Smoking weed led to stealing cars, which led to worse and worse. There were a bunch of kids, not a gang so much as a group of kids that were turning bad. After David's third run-in with the law, he was sentenced to thirteen months at juvenile hall. His mother came to visit him and make sure he was settling in okay. She could have bailed him out. She had done it before. But she didn't. It wasn't that she wanted him locked up; she just wanted him alive.

He did three months before escaping. It was an open-door kind of place—no bars—so escaping was pretty easy. He was about fifteen years old and on the run. He made his way to Long Beach, where his grandmother was living. His mom was terrified. She didn't understand the law and didn't want her elder son locked up for the rest of his life. David reassured her and told her if he stayed out of trouble until he was eighteen, then he would be okay. His childhood crimes would be forgiven, wiped free. He would be able to start over. All he had to do was lay low in Long Beach for a few more years.

Only that isn't what happened. In Long Beach David's behavior was even worse after he met members of Asian Boyz and the Tiny Rascal Gang. In Massachusetts the Cambodian kids hadn't been targets. Maybe they had faced some racial things in school but just normal school stuff, David remembers, not gang stuff. In Long Beach it was different. In Long Beach it was gang stuff; it was Hispanics against Southeast Asians.

As David tells it, the gangs were there before the Cambodians arrived. His cousin grew up in Long Beach after being dropped down in the East Side—the middle of the ghetto—surrounded by drugs, violence, and crime. The ghetto was where all the Cambodians ended up; the environment pretty much guaranteed to lead some kids to crime. So that's what happened: kids went where they felt comfortable, where they felt protected. They gravitated toward others who spoke the same language, shared the same culture. That's how it started—not out of offense but out of defense as they sought to defend themselves from getting teased, to protect themselves from being jumped, beaten up, and taken advantage of. Then there were the bad ones, the ones who said they had to fight back, and—just like that—gangs were formed.

Asian Boyz—comprising mostly Cambodians, Laotians, Vietnamese, and Filipinos—was founded in Long Beach in the 1990s largely in response to harassment from the preexisting Hispanic gang, East Side Longos (ESL). The Tiny Rascal Gang was founded by Cambodians, but according to law enforcement sources, it was heavily influenced by the ESL. The Tiny Rascal Gang learned how to dress, write graffiti, and generally be gang members by copying the ESL. In time, the gangs, which began as a form of protection for the Southeast Asian community, started taking advantage of and preying on their own community.

It didn't happen just in Long Beach. The Cambodian refugee community of the 1980s was settled basically in ghettos, says Tracy Harachi, a social worker who has studied the Cambodian American community. A 2010 report by the Walter Leitner International Human Rights Clinic at Fordham

Law School came to a similar conclusion, stating that many Cambodian communities "were riddled with crime and poverty." The report goes on to chronicle the difficult economic and cultural circumstances the refugees found themselves in—an economic recession and unfriendly government policies in the United States. In Long Beach almost three hundred Cambodians signed up for a vocational training program in 1981 that had seats for only thirty. Refugee assistance agencies were able to do little more than take the refugees from the airport and deliver them to an apartment. Left on their own for days in a completely foreign environment, the refugees often went without heat or food. When they finally ventured out, the youths faced discrimination and harassment. All of this led to Cambodian youths feeling isolated and in need of a support system that would allow them some protection. Plainly speaking, they formed gangs.

It wasn't something the Cambodian community wanted, insists David. But "if you were Cambodian" in Long Beach back then, you couldn't "walk down the street without getting beat up or shot at," he says. When you have a little brother or cousin who is beaten up, you become vindictive. You want revenge, and you get it by going to a group that can provide that kind of support, that kind of violence. Then the other side does the same thing, and before you know it, everything is escalating. A lot of innocent people get shot, and each time an innocent person gets shot, another innocent person joins a gang. That wasn't exactly how it happened with David. He claims he was never really in a gang; he just hung out with gang members and did a lot of the things they did. The distinction is unclear.

When he first came to California, David stayed with family in Fresno, another hotbed of Southeast Asian gangs, before making his way to Long Beach. From there, his mother sent him to Chicago to live with his stepfather. In Chicago David dated a woman whom he eventually followed to Seattle, Washington. By that time he had warrants for his arrest in Massachusetts and California. He was supposed to be lying low. But that wasn't the kind of lifestyle he was leading, not with the kind of friends he had. A month, two months seemed like forever. Lying low for years seemed impossible. He didn't think about repercussions.

On the night of the murder, David went to a party. He brought a gun because he was a big shot. He pulled it out because he was a foolish teenager. He fired it because his finger was on the trigger. That's how he explains it.

The cops caught him for speeding. Then someone identified the car he was driving as the vehicle that had fled the crime scene. Someone else found the gun he had tossed when he ran. David was the one who told his mother. After the shock wore off, she scraped together whatever money she could and hired David a lawyer. The lawyer didn't have a lot of wiggle room. David was a fugitive running from state to state, his girlfriend was eight years older than he was, and his friends were gang bangers. He wasn't a teenager who took one wrong turn. He was someone who had already done considerable damage in his short life.

David was tried as an adult and sentenced to 251 months, just shy of twenty-one years. He ended up serving eighteen and a half years. It would have been less, but in the beginning he was still fighting the system and lost a lot of good behavior time. After seven years he asked to be transferred to California so he could be closer to his grandparents, whose health was deteriorating. In California, prisons were crowded, and prisoners policed themselves along ethnic lines. It was organized and rigid. You couldn't opt out, or say "that's not my beef" and stand aside. If something happened you had to go with your people; if you didn't, you would be dealt with afterward. Each group had its own workout area in the yard, its own shower area, its own dayroom area. The Asians were the smallest group, so they had to be especially cohesive. It was more violent than in Washington but also more consistent. In Washington, says David, you could go up to a Mexican guy and get in a fistfight. In California, if you had a problem with a Mexican guy, you went to his people, and they dealt with it. Because of that, there were no little fights, just big stuff.

Toward the end of his sentence, David was sent back to Washington. He started to think about life after prison. Instead of learning a skill of questionable outside value, he focused on skills he knew he lacked and needed. He joined committees, groups that included prisoners and non-prisoners, so he would become comfortable interacting with "respectable people." He wanted to be able to communicate with people whom society viewed as successful without being nervous. He also practiced reading and writing in Khmer because he knew he faced deportation to Cambodia. Wherever he ended up after prison, he was determined to succeed.

Toward the end of David's imprisonment, his case was returned to the courts. David's case was one of a number of cases affected by a Washington State Supreme Court opinion dealing with the felony murder law. Quite a few first-degree and second-degree murder cases that were felony murder versus premeditated murder were reduced to manslaughter, according to a Washington judge. That didn't happen with David's case. In 2005 the court ruled that his previous sentence was consistent with the sentencing reform, and he continued to serve out his original sentence.

A year before he was released, ICE agents paid him a visit. He had been expecting them. After he was released from prison in 2009, he spent three months in immigration detention. If he had to choose, David would take prison over detention any day. In prison there are programs, things to do. In detention there is a room with a bunch of people and a pack of cards. It is like jail, "very, very, very boring." While in detention he signed a paper allowing for his removal from the States to go forward. Like Touch, he thought he had to sign the paper to get out of detention, but that isn't exactly correct, as we know from Touch's lawyer, Jacqueline Dan.

A stipulated order of removal means only that you aren't contesting removal, that you aren't going to fight it. Jacqueline says most people sign the order because they are worn down, because they believe incorrectly that by doing so they will be released from detention, and because there is still a misconception in the Southeast Asian community that their respective country of origin isn't going to take them. At one time Cambodia didn't take them, but that isn't the case any longer. It may take people slowly, but it does takes them.

Before 2001 detainees could be kept in detention indefinitely, and many were. It wasn't only Cambodians who were detained; Cubans, Laotians, and all sorts of other people whose countries of origin did not accept them for deportation were detained indefinitely. It was Kim Ho Ma, a Cambodian, who challenged the practice. The U.S. Supreme Court sided with him and so ended indefinite detention, a practice that immigration enforcement had justified under the harsh 1996 immigration laws. Immigration is now only allowed to hold deportees for 90 to 180 days, after which time they get out if their deportation isn't imminent.

But being released doesn't mean they will avoid deportation; it just means they can wait outside instead of in detention. After he was released, David had to stay in Washington for two years on probation. He originally stayed with an Irish American couple he met through his involvement in a prison committee activity. Not long after he was out, they drove him to Long Beach so he could visit his family. Back in Washington, he met Debbie Keodara, a Laotian refugee with a five-year-old daughter. Initially he didn't tell her about his crime or impending deportation. When she got pregnant, they started living together. A few months after Solomon was born in 2011, they moved to Long Beach.

Gangs aren't much of a problem in Long Beach anymore, at least not as they were in the 1980s and 1990s. It took time, but the gang task force got rid of many of them by cracking down on anyone it suspected was a gang member and by doing everything it could to keep the people off the street. Most of the "Original Gangsters" got locked up. Some are getting out now, like David, but being older, many don't want to be involved in that lifestyle anymore. Not having been with family in a long time, they want to be with a woman and have a family of their own. They get married, have kids, take life seriously; they do what David did. They have a lot to prove to their families; they need to show that they aren't the same person they used to be. David certainly doesn't seem to be. According to the law, he is rehabilitated.

And yet, because David is not a citizen, he is viewed differently. He is forever a teenager who shot a man and not a father who serves as the main support for his family. The double punishment—that is what got David involved in the anti-deportation movement. He was big into the social movement at first, helping grassroots organizations to publicize the issue and to try to convince the U.S. government to change the laws. He has toned it down in recent years. With work and family, he doesn't have much spare time. He also has come to a sort of peace with the idea of his deportation. Debbie complains that he talks about it as if it isn't important to him.

"It's not that it's nothing to me; it's just that I've accepted it," he says. "But she has not."

5

SITHY AND SITHEA

San didn't want to tell her story. It was Tom Croucher, her husband, who insisted she talk. On the surface, they seem almost a cliché. He is a self-possessed American businessman with blue eyes and a briefcase full of ideas. She is a petite Southeast Asian woman who loves to cook and lets her husband do the talking. Tom is eighty years old and needs a walker to get around. His pale skin is covered with liver spots. Five years his junior, San is still agile. She has thick black hair and what look like stenciled-on eyebrows.

That is where the white man–Asian woman cliché ends, and it becomes another—that of an elderly couple who have been together so long their existence has become interdependent. San jokes that together they can get around, so long as she does the walking and he does most of the driving.

It is not a first partnership for either of them. Both Tom's children and San's daughters were grown when the couple got together. Then San's eldest daughter, Sithy, proved unable to care for her children. San and Tom raised five of Sithy's six children in a three-bedroom townhouse in Bellflower, near Long Beach. Their last grandson's paternal family is raising him.

By his telling, Tom took to his second fatherhood graciously, converting his home office into a bedroom for San's four granddaughters and encouraging San to enroll the children in activities so they would stay out of trouble. A fifth grandchild, a boy, came later. Tom hadn't been as eager to take on yet another young child but eventually relented.

San signed the girls up for ice skating and spent her afternoons chauffeuring them from school to practice and her evenings cooking in the townhouse's cramped kitchen. Tom promised her that one day she would have a big kitchen. Around 2004, he delivered. There is nothing tiny about the two-story suburban home they live in now in Eastvale, about an hour inland from Long Beach. There are no walls to confine or separate the kitchen from the sitting room; it has an open floor plan. The countertops are wide and numerous, and the kitchen island is so far from any wall it really is an island unto itself. Two small birds and a cockatoo can freely roam the area. San has three stoves to cook on: one in the kitchen, one in the garage, and one on the enclosed back porch. San and Tom spend most of their time on the porch, listening to the hummingbirds outside. It is a nice change from the police sirens they used to hear in Long Beach.

San never expected something this nice. "God gave me more than I ever dreamed of," she says.

But it came late in life and, as it turns out, would be taken all too soon.

The house would have been perfect when San first arrived in the United States in the early 1980s and was raising her three daughters in a studio apartment in Long Beach. It would have been nice even later, when she and Tom were raising her grandchildren in the Bellflower townhouse. But it is too big for two elderly people. Still they do a good job of occupying the space. They installed an electric stair climber so Tom, who can no longer climb the stairs, can ride a chair to the second floor. San also gets a kick out of transporting the laundry basket on the device.

The front room is filled with boxes of Tom's work. An engineer who has yet to retire, Tom is an expert in metallurgy and the author of several technical books. A highchair for visiting great-grandchildren is kept by the dining room table located on the enclosed porch. Family photos—school pictures, wedding pictures, graduation pictures, studio shots, spontaneous shots, sports shots—cover the downstairs walls and continue up to the second floor. Almost hidden among them is a small black-and-white print of Sithy and Sithea, San's older daughters. The picture was taken on a trip to Vietnam before the Cambodian genocide. In the photo, the sisters, only a year apart in age, look like twin little dolls, tiny and delicate in short dresses and bobbed hair.

In more recent photos Sithea has the same neat and tidy appearance; only now she's more commanding and less innocent. Sithy looks rougher and beautiful but in a worn-down sort of way. They are both petite, like their mother, but Sithy has more curves and plays them to her advantage. She wears her hair long, with chunky bangs and blonde highlights.

The sisters share many of the same childhood memories. Jennifer, who is three years younger than Sithea, doesn't figure as prominently in their recollections. Sithea describes the Cambodian genocide as something she experienced with Sithy. She tells about how she and her sister were at first excited when the Khmer Rouge evacuated Phnom Penh because they were eager to see the countryside. It is the same story Sithy and San tell. But it begins differently.

In Sithea's TEDx Talk, a community version of the more famous TED (Technology, Entertainment, Design) Talks, her father and mother are still together. Her version is neater, more black and white. Before the Khmer Rouge take over, her father has to leave the country and wants to take them with him, but her mother refuses. In San's version, she is already separated from the girl's father. The rest of the story is the same.

In 1981 San and her daughters arrived in Orange County, California. They had $10, which to them at the time seemed a fortune. They had saved the money in case San's brother was not at the airport to greet them. But James was there and took them home to Long Beach, a city linked to Cambodia since the 1960s, when several Cambodian students attended California State University–Long Beach and other nearby colleges under a USAID program. Later, quite a few of the refugees processed at Camp Pendleton, only ninety miles south of Long Beach, ended up settling in the city. After that period, refugees usually ended up in Long Beach the way San did, because they had friends or family there.

After living with James for a few months, San and her daughters moved into an unheated studio. San's $500 welfare check and $50 worth of food stamps didn't leave enough money to pay the heating bills, so they used electric blankets to keep warm at night. When they walked they crushed slugs underfoot. In time San found temporary work that paid $400 a month through an AmeriCorps Volunteers in Service to America poverty reduction program. The work eventually led to a full-time receptionist position at the United Cambodian Community of Long Beach.

The girls, none of whom spoke English, were placed in school based on their age. Sithy was put in eighth grade; Sithea, in seventh. At their junior high school, a group of African American girls began to pick on the sisters. At first, not understanding what the girls were saying, Sithy and Sithea smiled. Then someone translated the taunts: "Fuck you! Go back to your country!"

The kids who translated the taunts taught the sisters what to say in response. The next time the girls yelled at them, Sithy and Sithea shouted back: "You too!"

That's when the fighting started. Both sisters were suspended. The next year Sithy was moved to high school and Sithea to eighth grade. Then their journeys begin to diverge. When Sithea graduated from junior high, Sithy made her graduation dress. She modeled it after the dress Sithea wanted but San could not afford. Sithea went on to graduate from high school and college. She married a fellow Cambodian refugee, Richer San, and has played a role in the revitalization of both her homeland, where she has lived since 2012, and her adopted city. Sithea and Richer have a habit of making the news in both Phnom Penh and Long Beach. In 2007 they helped establish Cambodia Town, a few blocks of shops on Anaheim Street in Long Beach. More recently, in 2014, Richer was briefly jailed in Cambodia on a fraud case. An American citizen, he was released after the U.S. Embassy intervened, a move Cambodian prime minister Hun Sen supported.

Once Sithy visited Sithea in Cambodia. She was supposed to stay two weeks but left after only two days, too haunted by memories to remain. Sithy never escaped the poverty and violence of their childhood. For her Cambodia is still home of the Khmer Rouge; Long Beach, the crime-ridden inner city. Sometimes she wakes up feeling as though a ghost is lying beside her.

Today she has woken from a nap at her mother's house following what she describes as a mild bout of food poisoning. She is moving slowly and speaks softly. She takes a seat at the table on the covered porch, somehow managing to look sexy even in sweatpants and a T-shirt. Tom moves to the main house to watch football with Sithy's boyfriend. The boyfriend has a shaved head and tattoos but doesn't beat Sithy, and for that San and Tom are grateful. In separate declarations made to help Sithy's legal case, she,

Tom, and San all cite the abuse Sithy has suffered at the hands of various boyfriends. Tom keeps her legal records on his computer. It is only October 2015, but he is already preparing for her next hearing in February 2016. The family is fighting her deportation, something not many do because they cannot afford a private attorney and believe they cannot win.

It is Tom who pays the lawyer and organizes meetings between the lawyer and the family. He has always handled the legal work. San is feisty and tough, but her English is limited and her knowledge of the U.S. legal and tax system lacking. Unfortunately Sithy didn't consult Tom or her mother before she pleaded no contest to the possession and sale of a controlled substance, methamphetamine, in 2011. She did not have an interpreter and says that her court-appointed attorney did not tell her that by pleading guilty she would be subject to deportation proceedings. All she understood was that if she pled guilty, then she could go home; if she didn't, then she could be locked up for quite a while.

She did do time—not long but long enough to experience the boredom and stress of incarceration. Her mother keeps the letters Sithy wrote the family from inside. They are decorated with cartoon Betty Boops, teddy bears, and baby carriages. Sithy boasts that while other prisoners had to trace drawings, she was able to simply copy the images by looking at them. She has always been good at art. In Cambodia, before the Khmer Rouge, she was also good in school, she says, and smarter than either of her sisters.

When Sithy arrived in the United States, she was thrilled to be studying again. Pleasure quickly turned to frustration when she discovered she couldn't understand anything that was being said. San remembers a science test Sithy brought home. The only marking on it was Sithy's name; that was all Sithy understood. San couldn't help, as her knowledge of English wasn't much better.

Sithy had the added problem of suffering seizures, which started during the genocide in Cambodia. The seizures continued in California and grew worse when Sithy was stressed. There were tests and medicine, but the medicine made Sithy sleepy and the results never changed. Sithy only made it through a few months of high school before her seizures became so bad the school sent her home. A teacher came to work with Sithy twice a week, but Sithy didn't like studying at home so she stopped being there when the teacher showed up. Then, one day, Sithy didn't come home.

A policeman showed up later. San couldn't understand what he was saying and asked him to write it down so she could show someone at work the next day. In the morning, her colleague translated the note for her. Sithy had been found trying to jump off a pier into the ocean and had been taken to a mental hospital. Sithy had to stay in the hospital for a few days of observation before San could take her home. Soon after she returned home, Sithy met her first boyfriend and moved out. She never returned to school and never learned to read or write in English. She still has trouble asking for help. Americans, she explains, tell you what they feel, but Asians keep quiet; and when you keep quiet, people don't know how to help you.

"That's what happened," she says. "I wanted to tell them what happened, but I couldn't."

Instead, she stayed silent and went from one bad relationship to another. In the mid-1980s San bought a run-down duplex in Long Beach. San lived in the front unit and let Sithy live in the back unit. At the time, Sithy had a boyfriend and two young daughters. Once, around two o'clock in the morning, the little girls knocked on San's door.

"Help Mommy!" they cried. "Daddy beat Mommy up, and Mommy fell down."

San went and tried to rescue her eldest daughter. Sithy's boyfriend threatened to kill the whole family if anyone called the police. San believed him. The Khmer Rouge had said the same thing, and she had seen them follow through. San was too scared to do anything, so she watched him beat her daughter in front of her.

"I come here, I afraid," she explains. "I don't know the law. I don't know what to do."

Sithy finally kicked that boyfriend out after he pointed a gun at her and threatened to kill her. She was working at a video store, trying to support her then three young daughters when she met her next boyfriend, a "gang banger." Soon he was living with her. A fourth daughter followed, and so did the beatings and threats. This time San called the police. The boyfriend was arrested in 1992. That is when the family's legal problems began. Several months later, after the boyfriend was no longer in custody, cops raided their home, looking for him. It turns out he was wanted for a murder in Northern California. The boyfriend was later found and convicted, and Sithy was arrested for harboring a fugitive. Sithy was picking her daughters up from school when the police took her. The little girls called San at work, and San called Tom, whom she was then dating. Tom hired a lawyer to get Sithy out on bail. The case dragged through the system before eventually being dismissed.

Meanwhile, the raid brought attention to San's duplex and the modifications she had made. Before long she was fighting a court case related to code violations for building codes she had no idea existed and issues she thought the contractor she had hired had handled. Tom spent his spare time researching the case. Three years later, with the help of a lawyer, most of the charges were dismissed. In between, in 1994, San and Tom married, and San moved in with Tom in Bellflower. She kept the duplex in Long Beach.

When San discovered Sithy was leaving the children unattended, she reported her daughter to the county. Tom agreed to take in the children if San quit her job to care for them. At first it was just the four girls, but in 1995 Sithy had a new boyfriend and a son. This boyfriend was a drug dealer, and Sithy started using cocaine. San once again reported her daughter to authorities and gained custody of the boy. Instead of saying her children were taken from her, Sithy says she let her mother have them.

"I told government, I give my kid to my mom," she says. "Not about I don't want my kid. No. I don't want my kid see my life."

She didn't want them to witness the string of boyfriends, the abuse, and the drugs. But another abusive boyfriend and another son followed, with this son being cared for by her boyfriend's family. She hasn't seen her youngest child in a decade. Yet another boyfriend followed. He beat her for working at a bikini bar.

Somewhere in there one of her abusive boyfriends was jailed and later deported to Cambodia. He blamed Sithy for getting him locked up and starting his path to deportation. Sithy's eldest daughter, Lauren, the one who most resembles her, spotted on Facebook a picture of him in the uniform of the Cambodian military.

All of this is in the written declaration Sithy has made to submit with her application for immigration relief before the immigration court. Regarding the drug charges, she says she had the drugs because her friends sometimes paid her with drugs when they lost while playing card games at her house. In person, she says she kept the drugs to keep people playing; if there were drugs on hand, they had less reason to leave. She didn't sell them; she just gave them away. She had formerly worked as a cocktail waitress at a gambling house and opened her own home gambling operation after being let go from her job.

San interrupts: "Okay, I explain something to you, Sithy. Not the 'open the gambling.' Like you have some friends to come sit down and play around, doesn't mean you 'opened a gambling.' That different."

"For me, I call it that," says Sithy.

"No. No. Don't call that. It's wrong."

San has never stopped being her eldest daughter's protector. When Sithy couldn't pass her written driver's license test because she can't read English, San helped her understand the questions at home beforehand. Now she patiently tries to explain to Sithy why the words she uses matter. Sithy isn't interested and continues her story the way she wants to tell it, not understanding that the meaning of the words she uses can be easily twisted.

Sithy points to a scar above her eye, a mark left by stitches she had after a particularly bad beating. The police took pictures of her afterward, but now she tells San the photos were taken so long ago the police no longer have them. They want to use the photos as evidence in her case and prove the danger she faces if she is deported to Cambodia, where the man who is responsible for that particular injury is now serving in the military.

San has trouble listening to the stories of abuse. She is impatient. She doesn't understand why Sithy didn't have all her abusers locked away. San would have. Sithy tries to explain. She talks about how the laws are screwed up and how jailing her abuser doesn't really help her.

"I tell my daughter, 'If at some point my boyfriend kill me, don't do nothing,'" she says. "'Even you put in jail, I not going to come back.'"

"No!" interjects San.

"Even [if she says to him,] 'I lock you up,' I told my daughter, 'I not going to live back. I die, I die, so let the God punish them.'"

Reading Sithy's declaration, her death seemed assured on more than one occasion. There were numerous suicide attempts with pills and alcohol, with knives, with jumps from high places. There were also accounts of plenty of abuse at the hands of various boyfriends. The descriptions are frustratingly repetitive: cuts, bruises, hospital visits, threats. Then there was the name-calling: "whore," "bitch," "slut." It is hard to understand how she kept coming back for more of the same, from one man to the next. Then, at the end of the declaration, Sithy writes that the beatings reminded her of what she endured under the Khmer Rouge.

"I came to believe that if I listened [to] my boyfriends they would not beat me. This was how I survived with the Khmer Rouge."

And maybe that is the answer—what she endured under the Khmer Rouge. It is why San finally decided to tell her story. With her daughter facing deportation, Tom convinced San that the whole family history of hardship and suffering needed to be recounted. It was time. San agreed. She shares with her daughters the memories of torture. After dinner Tom shows a video of Sithea's TEDx talk about the genocide. It is then that Sithy and her boyfriend head home to Long Beach.

Not long afterward, San's brother, James, stops by with his wife. James lives nearby, and San often invites him and his new wife over to pick up food when she cooks. His wife heads to the kitchen to pack up some Thai chicken curry. She is James's third wife. His second wife is dead. His first wife was lost during the genocide. Or so he thought.

James was not in Cambodia during the genocide. He left his pregnant wife and children in Cambodia under the care of San and his other sister while he was working out of the country. During the genocide San became separated from her sister-in-law. After the nightmare ended, San found James but not her sister-in-law. James remarried, but San continued her search. Years later she tracked down her sister-in-law. James was reunited with his first wife briefly, and after his second wife died young, he thought of living with his first wife again. San urged him not to after seeing how they fought whenever they were together. She knew her sister-in-law could not forgive James for not being there during the genocide. Even San is sometimes frustrated with her brother for having escaped the suffering.

"Sometimes James doesn't understand me when I talk about what [we] went through, because he wasn't there," she says.

Not long ago San and Tom attended a concert at which one of the singers told a story. The singer's mother had been in Europe during the Holocaust. At one point she was placed in a line and her sister was placed in another. The sister told her to join her line. At first she refused, but later she snuck to her sister's side. Neither of them knew it, but the line they were in was for the living. The other line, the line the singer had been in, was for those being sent to the gas chambers. The singer and her sister survived, but the horror stayed with them.

San cried when she heard the story. Her tears were of sadness and relief. She was grateful that there were others who understood what she had experienced. But as with the different lines, even those who experience genocides and other atrocities do not experience them the same way. The Khmer Rouge separated families, and San wasn't with Sithy and her other daughters during the worst years. She would see them sometimes, but they all lived apart in different work groups. San was able to hold Sithea when she was close to death. Sithea and Jennifer were both extremely ill during the Khmer Rouge years. But for Sithy, it was even worse, because Sithy had survived by cooperating with the Khmer Rouge.

6

"IT'S NOT WHAT YOU THINK"

The Khmer Rouge knew the trick. The rebels knew how to keep people from trying to escape. They separated families. Without her daughters, there was no way San would try to leave Cambodia. Sithy was older, so they put her in one place. They put her youngest, Jennifer, in another place. Sometimes they put the children together but not with a parent, never with a parent. Only in the beginning, and then on special occasions, was San with her daughters.

"Once a year, I get to be with them for two or three days," she says.

In between, when she had a chance, she would try to sneak away to see Sithea or Jennifer or even her eldest, Sithy. She could never stay long. But at least she got to see them, to know what had happened to them. She doesn't say it, but it is clear what she means when she says "know what happened to them." She wanted to make sure they were still alive.

Several months after the Khmer Rouge's takeover of Phnom Penh, when San was still with her daughters, she remembers seeing a ship. They were living near the Mekong River then, and as the ship was a little way out in the water, people had to jump into the river and swim to reach it. People said the ship was going to Vietnam, and anyone who could claim ties to Vietnam was allowed on board.

Vietnamese people living in Cambodia were not so much welcomed back to Vietnam as encouraged to leave Cambodia. In September 1975 an estimated 150,000 Vietnamese either were forced out of or chose to leave Cambodia. San spoke Vietnamese and had a Vietnamese last name. She was ethnically Khmer, but she had been born in Vietnam and could have easily left on the ship. The water was high and the current was strong, but San had grown up near the river and knew how to swim.

"I look at the river and think, 'If my kid can swim, or doing something, we going to jump too,' because if we jump to the ship, we would be taken."

But her daughters couldn't swim.

Sithy tried once. She and Sithea had been washing a cooking pot in the Mekong River, the same river where San had seen the ship. It may have been around the same time of year, the rainy season, because the water was high and fast, just as when San watched people swim out to the ship. Sithy went under quickly. Sithea jumped in to save her, momentarily forgetting she could not swim. They would have both died if other people hadn't rescued them.

That was the kind of family they were, risking their lives to help each other. As the oldest child, Sithy felt it was her job to protect and care for the others. During the Khmer Rouge years, she was constantly looking for ways to improve her family's situation. It began during the exodus from Phnom Penh, when little Jennifer, only five years old at the time, had trouble keeping up with the others. Sithy found an abandoned bicycle with flat tires in a village along the way and managed to push Jennifer on it. Later Sithy fished for the family, adding protein to their meager rice rations. One holiday, when the children were given a bite of pork as a treat, Sithy saved some for her mother.

The Khmer Rouge broke apart families. The breakdown of San's happened slowly, but it happened all the same. Sithy fought it hard. And for that she was punished.

Phnom Penh, Cambodia, April 17, 1975.

Khmer Rouge farmers line up alongside the road. As the Phnom Penh refugees make their exit, they exchange their valuable necklaces, watches, and rings for food. San trades her Rolex watch for a pot and some rice. With her relatives' help, she builds a small fire in a nearby rice field and cooks the food. After resting for a bit, she gets up and joins everyone else on the road.

The first person San sees is her neighbor Nget, who works at the military hospital. Nget was trapped at the hospital during the bombardment of Phnom Penh. For four days she couldn't go anywhere. Afterward, when the Khmer

Rouge rebels came, they kicked everyone out of the hospital, even patients who were being operated on at the time. Nget thought many of the patients probably died. Survivors later reported seeing family members pushing the sick on hospital beds out of the city. The gesture may have extended the patients' lives slightly, but Nget was right; most of them did not make it.

Nget joins San, and they take turns carrying Jennifer, who has trouble keeping up with them before Sithy finds the bike on which to put the little girl. A little farther on, San's sister Rinh spots some cousins pushing a car loaded with food. Their cousins tell them the rebels were lying when they said they would be able to go home in three days. "We will probably never go home again," they say.

That night they sleep in a rice field. In the morning they continue walking, reaching the airport later in the day. Bodies and pieces of bodies—hands, feet, arms, legs, heads, torsos—are strewn everywhere. The smell is unbearable. In time, San will become accustomed to the stench of death, and it will no longer bother her. But in those first few days, she was still human. She had yet to watch her youngest daughter devour a dog's liver, the girl's face smeared in blood, her extreme hunger masking the foul odor of the half-cooked animal's innards.

The dead at the airport were members of the Cambodian Army, the institution to which San's brother, James, belonged. That night his first son is born on a porch in a village where the family knows no one. They name the boy Sam. Mother and newborn ride in the cousins' car the next day.

Nget is no longer with them. After finding her brother, she decides to accompany him to their hometown. She invites San to come with her, but San stays with the cousins, who are headed toward the Mekong River, where they hope they might be able to make an escape. Initially San hopes that by following the Mekong, she can reach her parents in Vietnam.

The emptying of the capital had been chaotic. Some evacuees were told to head to their ancestral villages. Others were told only to leave Phnom Penh. Some stopped when they found a place that would accept them. Others kept walking. Their orders varied depending on which faction or zone of the Khmer Rouge was carrying them out.

Although the Khmer Rouge had only just taken the capital, the rebels had been ruling other parts of the country for some time and had split it up into administrative zones. The new people who had not yet lived under the Khmer Rouge were referred to as "April Seventeenth people," reflecting the date when they began living under the Khmer Rouge. They were also sometimes called new people in contrast to those of the rural peasant class, many of whom had been already living under the Khmer Rouge and were called old people.

There is no road to the river, so they push the car through rice fields, hoping they are headed in the right direction. The car makes slow progress. San and her good friend Phan decide to go ahead to scout out a place for them to stay. They take San's daughters with them. While they are walking, they hear a bomb explode in the distance. The Khmer Rouge have mined the Mekong, making it largely impassable. They see more bodies, as the sick and elderly fall from exhaustion and the young and middle aged from disease. The Khmer Rouge kill others, especially former soldiers.

When San, Phan, and the girls reach a road, they wait. It grows dark, and still their party does not arrive. They spend another night in a rice field, expecting the rest of the group to join them before morning. They do not. Without food, San, Phan, and the girls can wait no longer. They continue walking, looking for something to eat and hoping the others will find them soon. They never do.

San learned later that the Khmer Rouge killed all the cousins. It would be years before she learned what happened to Rinh and Rinh's children and more than a decade before she found James's wife and his children. The Khmer Rouge had been in power less than a week, and already San's family had been torn apart. The regime would take the concept further, later implementing communal eating in cafeterias so families no longer ate together. This also made it hard for families to cook whatever small edibles they were able to collect on their own, adding to the mass starvation that would occur under the Khmer Rouge. The term "comrade" would replace most familial titles, and the government would arrange most marriages.

San kept walking, not really knowing where she was going. She stopped when she was hungry or too tired to move anymore. One night she found a pagoda where many people were also looking for food. The monks had been kicked out. The Khmer Rouge were running things. Before distributing any food, the Khmer Rouge gathered everyone together and questioned them about their former occupations. Those who worked for the government and the military or showed signs of being educated were put on one side. Everyone else, what the Khmer Rouge called the regular people, were put on the other side. When asked what she did, San answered truthfully, telling the rebels she worked as a Vietnamese-language radio broadcaster and as a receptionist for the government broadcasting station. She gave them her government identification card. Then she took a seat next to the other educated people.

After everyone had been separated, San's group was moved to a school-room, where they were given rice and told to sleep. In the morning, a local Khmer Rouge woman approached San.

"Why are you in that group?" she asked.

"I used to work for the government, and they promised to send us back to Phnom Penh to work," San replied.

The woman shook her head. "That's not what I heard."

The woman was Khmer Rouge, but her son was not. She had not seen him since he had fled from the Khmer Rouge. She whispered a warning to San: "It is not the way you think. If you can get out of here, get out of here. Do not stay here."

San didn't understand what she was hearing. "The Khmer Rouge promised that we could return to Phnom Penh to work," she said.

The woman shook her head and repeated the same thing she had told San before: "It is not what you think. Get out of here if you can." Then she left.

San found Phan and told her what she had heard. They decided to listen to the woman and leave. They slipped away not long afterward. San doesn't know what happened to those who stayed, but she is pretty sure the educated people, the group she had been with, were killed.

Promising a return to Phnom Penh and their previous jobs was a tactic the Khmer Rouge employed to trick those they deemed "enemies" to go quietly to their death. They did bring some people, mainly those who worked in factories, back to Phnom Penh to work but not former government workers like San. Along with soldiers, doctors, lawyers, and teachers, government workers were some of the first to be killed. Later the Vietnamese, or anyone who had spent time in Vietnam, became suspect. Still later, the party began to turn on itself, with paranoia destroying it from the inside out. A killer one day was a victim the next.

San didn't know any of this yet, but she was starting to learn. When she arrived in the next village, Cheur Khmao, she gave the rebels a different name, one that couldn't be linked to her government identification card, which was now in the hands of the Khmer Rouge. That is when she became San.

When she could, San tried to hold on to the person she had been before, the life she had lived. It was hard. She went to work pulling weeds in the cornfields at 3:00 a.m., when the big morning star was in the sky. She came home at 7:00 p.m. to a one-room hut. It was the life her father had trained her for, the life she thought she had left behind. Now she escaped it by daydreaming.

"I bring shovel and everything go to work, but my mind is not myself. I have daydreaming, imagination," she said. She would think about "what I was, what I'm doing, enjoying inside of me instead of reality I working right now."

San thought about the path of her life, how it had come full circle in some ways now that she was back working in the fields just as she had as a child. She thought about better times, when she used to eat in restaurants in Phnom Penh.

Sithy didn't bother with daydreams; she lived in reality, attuned to every opportunity that might make their lives just a little better. The girls were assigned to separate work groups. When they weren't working, they used pieces of mosquito net to catch small fish in the river for the family to eat. The fishing was allowed because the area did not harvest rice, and they were given no rice to eat. Still, a diet of only small fish left them hungry.

When a chicken wandered into their compound one day, Sithy quickly snapped its neck. Knowing the chicken's owner would come looking for it, Sithy stuffed the carcass in a bag in which they kept rice husks. When they saw the chicken's owner approach, Sithy sat on the bag. What Sithy had done was incredibly risky, as the chicken's owner was a member of the Khmer Rouge who oversaw the land on which they worked. Stealing from him could get you killed. But then the family was in equal danger of starving to death.

Sithy got away with it, and later that night, when everyone else was sleeping, they used the rice husks to start a fire and cook the chicken. After they finished eating, they carefully hid the chicken bones so they would not be found out.

Not long afterward, the chicken man began to question San about her background. He wanted to know what she had brought with her from Phnom Penh. When she told him she hadn't brought anything, he insisted that she must have. He told her that he suspected she had worked for the government. She told him she had worked in a bookstore. The lie seemed to work. He left her alone. She was safe there, for now.

Then the Khmer Rouge moved her again.

7

THE WIFE WITHOUT A HUSBAND

Sambath Nhep and Chea Bou would probably be referred to as high school sweethearts if Sambath had ever made it to high school. But she was fourteen years old when they got married. Chea was sixteen. Sambath dropped out of school in seventh grade after becoming pregnant with their first child. Chea finished high school and got a job. More jobs and more children followed. They raised their family where they spent their formative years, in East Oakland, California. And this is still their home; at least Sambath still lives there.

The first thing you notice when you enter their home is a small Buddhist shrine accompanied by framed photographs of dead relatives. There is also a large family portrait taken when Sambath's daughter, Julina, was just a baby and her two youngest sons were still smooth-cheeked boys with short hair. In the corner of the front room is a yoga mat; to the side of the table is a dog bed. Snowflake, a small white Pomeranian, is under the table attacking my feet.

Aside from Snowflake, Sambath is the only one who lives here anymore. None of her five children are here. Even nine-year-old Julina, the youngest and sole girl, no longer lives at home. Sambath has to be at work before Julina starts school, so Julina stays with an uncle who takes her to school along with his own daughter. After Sambath finishes work, she picks Julina up from school and tries to spend time with her. But more and more now, Julina asks to be taken straight to her uncle's house so she can play with her cousin. Only on the weekends do the mother and daughter live together. Julina hasn't lived at home during the week since her father was locked up and subsequently deported. It was Chea's job to take her to school each morning.

During the summer of 2015 there were rallies, petitions, and media stories on Chea's deportation case. The coverage was sympathetic and often included the story of Daniel Maher, another man who was facing deportation to China. In August there was a support rally for both Chea and Daniel in the San Francisco Bay Area. The next day Daniel was granted an extension, according to Katrina Dizon Mariategue, the immigration policy manager at the Southeast Asia Resource Action Center (SEARAC), one of the organizations helping to promote Chea's cause. Chea was not granted an extension. His deportation order stood. But there was no move to issue him travel documents; that meant he wouldn't be deported right away. When I spoke to Katrina in early September 2015, she said more than two thousand people had signed a petition to stop Chea's deportation to Cambodia. The petition was sent to Immigration and Customs Enforcement. Emails were sent to the Department of Homeland Security (DHS). The case for granting Chea a stay of removal seemed strong, as he was a nonviolent offender who had only been sentenced to a year and a day for drug-related crimes.

I thought I had enough time to interview Chea, but I waited too long. In October 2015 Chea was deported to Cambodia. Sambath arrived there a day later. It was the first time either of them had been back to their homeland since their families had fled when they were children. Sambath was eleven years old when she moved to the United States after spending years in refugee camps in Thailand. She is forty-three now and has long, thick, dark hair that she wears pulled back in a tight, low ponytail. Her eyebrows look as if they have been painted on. Sambath doesn't remember much about Cambodia; she was so young when she left. What she does recall is vague, such as running at night with her parents.

Chea remembers more. He was slightly older when he left Cambodia, around nine years old. In newspaper accounts he talks about carrying a knife to protect himself from the soldiers as he and his family made their way to Thailand. He recounts walking barefoot, carrying a younger brother on his back, and being separated from his parents for several days. He mentions eating insects and losing two siblings.

When Sambath returned to Cambodia in 2015, she found Phnom Penh hot and polluted. She was unable to recognize an older sister whom she hadn't seen since she fled the country as a child. No family resemblance, no feature sparked a memory. The only things she noted were that her sister had lighter skin than she did and that she was poor. Sambath's relatives live in the countryside near the country's second-largest city of Battambang in the northwest. They don't have running water, and their toilets are the squatting kind.

Originally Sambath and Chea thought Chea would live in Battambang Province as well. It is where quite a few deportees end up because, like Chea and Sambath, they have family members there. Battambang is an agricultural hub, where many were sent to work under the Khmer Rouge. It is also close to the Thai border; thus, it is one of the last places refugees who ended up in Thailand and then in the United States were likely to have lived before leaving the country. Consequently, it is probably the place they are most likely to still have family.

But Battambang was too removed for Chea—too far from the airport, too far from the capital with its Westernized restaurants and shops and, more important, air-conditioning. Cambodia is hot, and Sambath isn't accustomed to its stifling heat after years spent living in coastal California. She stayed inside as much as she could, venturing out only if it was to go to an air-conditioned mall. When Sambath did go out, she found the streets were crowded with motos (motorbikes), taxis, and cars fitting in any space they could. The only thing the couple enjoyed, besides each other, was the fresh fruit. At the end of every day, they cried.

"I'm thinking, how could my husband end up over here?" says Sambath.

It is a long way from their home in Fruitvale, an East Oakland neighborhood that has its own shortcomings. Most recently Fruitvale was the setting for the film *Fruitvale Station*. Based on real events, the movie follows a young man in the hours before an officer with the local Bay Area Rapid Transit subway system kills him at the Fruitvale Station. Just a few blocks from Sambath's house is International Boulevard, known for its streetwalkers. The homes there have barred windows and metal security gates. It is the ghetto. It is where Sambath and her family were resettled after leaving war-torn Southeast Asia in the 1980s.

Chea and Sambath's families both ended up living in the same apartment building on Twenty-Sixth Avenue in East Oakland. It was a big building, and many of its residents were Cambodian. Oakland in the 1980s was similar to many American cities at the height of the crack epidemic—extremely violent. In 1986, the year Sambath and Chea married, there were 146 homicides in the city, the highest number on record at the time. In years to come, Oakland would continually find itself on the list of America's deadliest cities.

Chea and Sambath went to the same middle school. Chea was a nice, honest guy who always wanted to help other people, says Sambath. He was her first and only boyfriend. They dated about six months before getting married. It wasn't their choice so much as their parents', a preventative measure to make sure Sambath had a husband before she had a chance to "get in trouble." Sambath continued school at first, but once she had her first child, Kevin, she dropped out. Three more boys followed and, finally, her daughter, Julina. Chea got work as a janitor, as a security guard, and as a card dealer. Sambath took care of the kids and her parents. Her mother died in 2000. Her father developed Alzheimer's disease and required more attention. When she could, she would work part time putting together medical devices, a job she still holds.

In 2001 after having watched her parents and friends become citizens, Sambath became a U.S. citizen. It wasn't too expensive then. She isn't sure why Chea didn't apply at the time. Maybe it was because as a legal permanent resident he didn't see a reason to do so or because of an earlier conviction, a 1993 criminal conviction for possessing a firearm. Whatever the reason, it no longer matters. Unlike his wife, he did not become a U.S. citizen.

Early one morning in March 2011, she says, the police kicked in the family's door. They searched the house and then took Chea in for questioning.

"The kids and my father, we was so scared," says Sambath. "We don't know what's wrong, why the police coming to our house."

Chea's arrest was part of a bigger law enforcement operation involving loan sharking and drug dealing at the Oaks Card Club in Emeryville, where Chea worked, and at Artichoke Joe's Casino in San Bruno. Federal authorities indicted more than a dozen people, including Chea, on racketeering and narcotics offenses in 2011. The indictment accused workers of mixing money from loan sharking and drug dealing with legitimate club funds. According to court documents cited by *East Bay Express*, Chea said his supervisor asked him for help buying ecstasy pills. In 2010 Chea unknowingly sold an undercover agent almost two thousand ecstasy pills and at a different time to another agent almost two thousand BZP (benzylpiperazine) pills.

He was the middleman, says Sambath, "their fish bait." She continues, "He's not like a drug dealer."

Chea was released ten days after the raid and remained free until 2014, says Sambath. During this time their roles were reversed, as Sambath went to work and Chea cared for the kids and his father-in-law. He cooked and cleaned and chauffeured. Because his crime was nonviolent, at first Sambath didn't think he would face deportation.

She found out otherwise. In 2014 Chea began serving his sentence of twelve months and a day. According to Sambath, the judge said Chea should be allowed to serve his time close to his family. Instead, he was sent to Texas, where Sambath and the children were unable to visit him. He served ten months and then went directly to immigration detention. At around this time Sambath's father died.

That story explains where her husband and daughter are but not her four sons. Aside from photos there is little evidence of their presence in Sambath's life. When asked about her boys, there is a long silence. Sambath's English is limited, but that isn't why she hesitates. Her youngest son, Anthony, is seventeen years old. She explains that he got into trouble after his father was arrested. She is vague on the details. It isn't clear if she simply doesn't understand the charges or if she just doesn't want to share them. There was a robbery. Anthony went to court. He was released home on an ankle monitor, which he cut, violating his probation. After that he was sent to a group home in Redding, California. Not long ago he came home for a visit via a bus the group home put him on. After a few days Sambath left him at the same place where she had picked him up, and another bus took him back to his group home. Sambath has a brochure for the place, but she has never visited. Anthony never finished high school, but he told her he is getting his high school equivalency certificate at the group home. They haven't talked about what he wants to do once he is out.

Kerry is away for much longer. He is twenty-seven and in prison for murder. He has been behind bars since his sister was just a few days old. The other two boys—her eldest, Kevin, and second youngest, Johnny—are dead. Kevin was killed in 2006 while visiting a cousin in Stockton. He was at a liquor store with a friend, an argument occurred, and he was shot. He was only nineteen years old.

"Wrong time, wrong place," says Sambath.

The man who shot him was Khmer. They knew each other. Maybe the man who murdered her first born was drunk, she says. Later she explains that the murderer felt sorry. Kerry felt mad. He wanted revenge. He struggled, says Sambath.

"I'm not sure what he did," she says. That is how she explains the murder he committed.

And that leaves Johnny, the recipient of the numerous sports trophies that decorate the fireplace mantle. He was diagnosed with leukemia two days before his father was arrested. When he was offered an experience by an organization that grants terminally ill children wishes, he didn't ask to meet a celebrity, to travel to Disneyland, or to go on a shopping spree. He asked that his father not be deported.

"They say that one they can't do," says Sambath.

He chose a shopping spree instead. Johnny died in 2012, before his father served his time. He was seventeen. His photo is now by the altar in the front of the house alongside that of Kevin and the children's grandparents. There are no photos from Sambath and Chea's traditional wedding; it was too small an affair. There is one from their twentieth wedding anniversary when Sambath dressed up again and they went to a nice restaurant.

Chea's lawyer, Linda Tam, applied for a stay of removal for Chea three times. Three times it was denied. Sambath didn't get a chance to see Chea before he was flown to Cambodia, so she made plans to meet him there instead. She used all her vacation time and brought along Julina. Together they found Chea a studio. Then Sambath and Julina returned to California. Chea cried, says Sambath. Now she cries at the memory.

"He remember all the time we were together, and then when I left, he said he look all the room is empty," she says.

She doesn't expect him to get a job. The jobs he is qualified for would pay so little it wouldn't be worth it. Instead, she pays his $140 monthly rent and for his food and his utilities. She saves what she can so she can visit him again next year. They talk every day on video calling. They talk in the evening and at night. Sometimes he calls to wake Sambath up in the morning. The only time they don't talk is when Sambath is at work and asleep. When she gets together with friends, Chea is there on the video call.

"We try to keep each other company because I know he's alone," she says. "So anything we share."

When Anthony was home on a recent visit, he got on the video call and told his father to take care. Chea, in turn, told his son to take care of himself, to stay out of trouble, and to take care of Sambath and Julina. When Chea was home, Anthony would listen to him, says Sambath. He doesn't talk to her or Julina. When he is home, he usually stays in his room. He was closer to Johnny. After Johnny died, Anthony was angry. He complained of chest pain. Doctors diagnosed anxiety. As far as Sambath knows, he wasn't given any medication, and he never saw a counselor or therapist. Chea was diagnosed with post-traumatic stress disorder in 2014, but he also does not seem to have received any treatment.

Sambath says sometimes Anthony goes in a corner and cries. When Sambath asks him what is wrong, he says he misses his family. Now he has his own family, a girlfriend with a baby on the way. He tells his mom he wants to change; he wants to make sure he is there for his baby. Soon he will be eighteen years old and out of the group home.

Julina still thinks her father will come back. When he was locked up in Texas, her parents told her he went there to work. Now they tell her he is in Cambodia just for a little while. So far she believes them. It could still happen; he could still come home. Chea's lawyer is working one more angle to try to get him home. In 1992 Chea was beaten and robbed in his apartment stairwell. Because he cooperated with the police, he was considered a witness in a criminal case and could qualify for a U nonimmigrant visa (U visa), which is meant for victims of violent crime who aid law enforcement. Sambath doesn't put much faith in the legal system.

Both she and Chea were raised as Mormons, but over the years they stopped practicing. Recently Sambath started going to church again. Her reasoning is simple: "I'm just thinking only God could help us."

In the end it was not God but the U.S. government that had the final say regarding Chea's status. Chea's U visa application was denied because of his criminal history. Linda Tam is appealing the decision but does not hold out much hope that her appeal will succeed. She has told Sambath this and that there isn't anything else she can do for Chea. She isn't sure Sambath understands.

"I think she just doesn't want to give up hope at all," says Linda. "It's really hard for Sambath to accept that this deportation—it's for life."

Sambath hears about other deportees who are barred from the United States for ten years and figures her husband must be barred for a decade as well. Linda has explained to her that because Chea's drug trafficking conviction is an aggravated felony, he is barred for life, forever. It just isn't sinking in. In Linda's experience, it is much harder for someone who has had a green card or something similar to give up hope than it is for someone who has never had anything, such as a migrant without papers, to accept they won't be getting help, like a green card.

Linda understands that it is especially difficult for Sambath and Chea, who have been together since they were teenagers. She appreciates Sambath's confusion. She notes that it's not as if the government tells you when it gives you a green card that it can be taken away.

Their status is "called lawful permanent resident," says Linda. "But people don't realize it's not permanent."

Unfortunately there is nothing Linda can do about any of this. The East Bay Community Law Center where she works as an attorney has done what it can by providing Chea with free representation. The center cannot change reality. Still, in her appeal, Linda included information about how Sambath and Chea raised money to buy rice and other needed items for some of the poorer families Chea knows in Cambodia.

Before pursuing the U-visa, Linda applied for a stay of removal that would have allowed Chea to stay in the United States for a time. The initial application and the appeal were both denied.

"I'm not surprised," she says. Drug trafficking "is like the worst possible kind of crime in the eyes of immigration, other than killing someone."

In recent years, tough drug sentencing laws have come under fire, but when it comes to immigration, a 2015 Human Rights Watch report found that drug crime enforcement is as strict as ever. Between 2007 and 2012, deportations of noncitizens whose most serious conviction was for a drug offense increased by 22 percent, accounting for one out of every four removals of noncitizens with a criminal conviction. Out of the 266,000 deported this way, 34,000 had marijuana possession as their most serious conviction.

This helps answer the question about Chea's one-year-and-one-day sentence. When the sentence is fewer than 365 days, defendants of certain crimes are not necessarily deported, but because his conviction was for drug trafficking, he was deportable even if his sentence had been shorter than a year. Linda believes ICE might also have been less sympathetic to Chea because his crime was recent. The system tends to have more sympathy for someone who is being punished for something they did long ago, she explains. She thinks that is why the man who participated in the joint anti-deportation rally with Chea in the summer of 2015 was granted a stay of removal; his crime happened years ago.

Linda wasn't given a reason for the denial of Chea's stay of removal, but she had plenty of reasons for asking for one. She began by arguing that Chea wasn't a security or safety threat and that his family had already been through enough hardship. She cited a probation report that basically said Chea wasn't a danger to society and wasn't a flight risk, mentioning his lack of criminal history. The report also cited Chea's lack of criminal sophistication; he did not financially gain from his actions. She found further proof that the government did not view Chea as a threat or a flight risk in the delay in the serving of his sentence. Chea was given a year to spend at home with his terminally ill son before having to fulfill his prison sentence. If the government had considered him as dangerous or a flight risk, it is highly unlikely it would have allowed him to remain free in the community so long before locking him up.

After ICE headquarters in Washington DC denied the second stay, Linda tried to find out what had gone wrong. She was told that headquarters found the case very compelling, but it does not like to overturn decisions made by a local office. Because the local office denied the stay, headquarters also denied it. Had the local office been in San Francisco, things might have turned out differently; instead, the local office making the decision was in Texas, where Chea was serving his sentence for a reason unknown to either his family or his lawyer. Linda tried to get it moved to the San Francisco office, but ICE would not transfer it. She believes this decision was unfortunate.

"That being said, though," she says, "ICE has complete discretion. They could have granted a stay of removal."

But it didn't.

8

STEALING FROM THE DEAD

Cheur Khmao, Cambodia, January 1976.

The Khmer Rouge wanted to transform Cambodia into a modern country by 1990 without outside help. The group went about doing this on the backs of the people, building everything from canals to dams by hand and from scratch. Those who might have helped, the ones who had been in charge, had been killed. In their place were young loyal soldiers, who were sometimes barely literate. Agriculture was the building block on which everything was based. People were grouped by sections and zones. Each zone was responsible for meeting certain agriculture quotas. People were moved at the whim of the authorities, brought from one area to another depending on what labor was needed. The first movement was the evacuation of Phnom Penh and other cities.

In September 1975 the government started moving people once again. San and the other new people in Cheur Khmao were moved in January 1976. They were told they would be returning to the capital. San was ecstatic. She gave away the few belongings she had accumulated since settling in Cheur Khmao the previous spring. Back in the capital, in her own home, she wouldn't need kerosene lamps or kerosene. At home there would be electricity. There would be food. There would be clothes.

They began the journey on foot, walking for hours, and then crossed the Mekong River in paddleboats. Then they boarded military trucks. Instead of heading toward the capital, the trucks headed away from it. That is when San realized she wouldn't be returning home. Instead, the trucks left them by a set of railway tracks, where they waited for a week. A freight train then took them not to Phnom Penh but to a spot in the jungle in the north of the country from which they walked to Prey Roneam. There they learned they were needed to help harvest the rice.

Instead of returning to her home, San had to construct a new home. Deposited in a jungle bordering rice fields, San and the others were given small knives to cut trees with which to build their own shelters. With Sithy and Phan's help, San made a small six-by-six-foot structure with sticks. She covered it with rice hay to shade them from the sun. Then she returned the knife, as required.

Again they woke at 3:00 a.m. to work. They were no longer allowed to fish or eat together. Instead, they were forced to eat in a group cafeteria, where they were fed watery rice. Cooking pots and kettles were no longer allowed, but Sithy managed to hide theirs. They never had a chance to use either of them again.

After a month, they were moved to another rice field in Boeng Chrang. It was there that Sithea first became seriously ill and that Sithy was beaten for the first time. Sithy had been trying to bring her family extra food. Soon after they arrived she, like the other children, was given the task of collecting wild plants for the communal kitchen. When she went out each day to collect plants, she also secretly fished and worked out a way to hide the forbidden fish from authorities. Before heading back at the end of the day, she would conceal the fish in her basket, right under the plants, and deliver them to San before turning in the rest of her haul to the Khmer Rouge.

One day she was late returning from the jungle. A group of young Khmer Rouge officials stopped her before she could deliver the fish to her family. They looked in her basket. Then they beat her.

San waited for Sithy for hours. She had no idea what had happened to her eldest daughter, only that she had not come back. Finally around midnight, Sithy returned, covered in bruises. The next time she was caught, they told her, she would be killed.

Sithea was already dying. For some time she had been suffering from severe diarrhea. She had grown so thin that Jennifer, scared by the skeleton that had replaced her sister, would no longer sleep with her. San didn't know what to do. There were no doctors. The Khmer Rouge had killed them. In their place, they trained "people's doctors" in herbal medicine. In *When the War Was Over*, author Elizabeth Becker explains that these so-called doctors generally did more harm than good and, for the most part, lacked both medicine and training.

Local villagers told San that Sithea was possessed by an evil spirit and urged her to take Sithea to a traditional healer who could remove it. Only after the spirit was removed, they said, would Sithea improve. Lacking any better alternative, San took Sithea to a medicine man. He proceeded to hit Sithea with a bamboo stick. Sithea, racked with pain from the abuse, cried out: "I'm going out! I'm going out!"

Sithea was so weak afterward that her mother and older sister had to carry her. Using what little strength she had left, she explained that she had called out as if she was the evil spirit so the healer would stop hitting her.

"There is no evil spirit inside of me," she said. "If I don't say that, they will keep hitting me, and I might die."

San didn't know what to say. She didn't believe in the medicine man either, but she needed to do something. She couldn't just watch her middle daughter die.

"Please, don't take me back there," Sithea begged. "Please, don't let him hit me again. I won't be able to take it."

San swallowed hard before answering. "I won't take you back there," she said.

That night she heated a piece of rock and placed it by Sithea's side. Even with the added warmth, her daughter felt cold. Sithea's body was too thin and weak to keep her warm. The next day Sithea was no better; instead, she continued to get worse. She was wasting away in front of San. She was so thin, San had trouble looking at her. When she could bear it no longer, she told Sithea she was taking her to another medicine man. "We have to try again," she told Sithea.

Sithea was too weak to protest, too tired and cold to fight. They found a different medicine man, and he inflicted a new form of torture. San watched as the man used hot burned cotton to burn the pain out of Sithea's stomach. Sithea didn't complain, not even when the burns became infected. She was too weak now to offer any protest. She would have died if another "new" person hadn't come forward. He approached San cautiously.

"Your daughter is very sick," he said. "She is going to die. You have to get her an antibiotic."

San looked at him suspiciously. "I have taken her to two traditional healers and nothing has helped. How do I know what you are telling me will work?"

"All I can tell you is that it will," he said.

Then he left. He was an actual doctor who had hidden his former occupation from the Khmer Rouge. He was also the first person to tell her something that sounded educated, as though it was what she would have done in her old world. In that world getting an antibiotic might have been easy, but in her new world antibiotic pills were not readily available. The only way to get them was from the Khmer Rouge, and for that you needed to be able to pay. San took a 24-karat ring she had hidden and approached a woman who she knew was friendly with the Khmer Rouge.

"I need antibiotic pills for Sithea," she said, pressing the ring into the woman's hand.

The woman nodded and walked off. When San saw her next, she had two pills. Sithea was barely able to swallow the pills, her mouth was so dry. The next day she was able to hold down a little food; the day after, a little more. Slowly she put on weight and began to move about a bit. Extremely weak she walked with a cane at first. She was never able to work during the year they spent in Boeng Chrang. Because she didn't work, she received less food. When they could, San, Sithy, and Jennifer tried to sneak Sithea more food, adding forbidden fish to her diet when possible. The rest of the time, they survived on rice soup with wild plants. If they spotted a lizard, they were lucky. It was too risky to cook it, so they would simply kill it, peel it, and eat it.

Years later, when San told this to her grandchildren, they screwed up their faces and said, "Gross." She explained to them that in Long Beach it was easy for them to say that, but if they had to go through what she had been through, which she hoped they never would, they would think differently. "Back then," she said, "you eat whatever doesn't kill or poison you—rat, everything . . . I don't know how to explain this."

Around the time Sithea got the antibiotics, her friend Phan began to waste away. Struck with the same severe diarrhea, Phan decided to check herself into the "hospital." There were no doctors, nurses, or medicine at the hospital; it was merely a place one went to wait to die. If you could work, you worked; if you were sick, you went to the hospital and died. It was simple, really, and Phan didn't fight it. She tried to explain it to Jennifer when San and the girls went to visit her at the hospital. Sithea was still too sick to visit, but Jennifer and Sithy were there. Phan had sores all over her body that had become infected and oozed a white puss. She passed in and out of consciousness. She spoke to Jennifer first.

"When two people are sick, one has to die," Phan said. "I am going to die so your sister Sithea can live."

"I don't want you to die," said Jennifer.

Phan smiled weakly. "I have something I want you to give to Sithea."

She took a white cloth with a footprint on it and handed it to Jennifer. She shut her eyes and faded from them. As they were about to leave, her eyes opened briefly.

"Rice," she said. "Could you bring me rice?"

There was no rice, but San could not tell this to her dying friend. She simply said, "Yes." She found a pair of earrings and traded them for rice for Phan. When she brought Phan the rice, her friend asked for one more favor.

"After I die, please place my hands in prayer."

San didn't try to reassure her that she wouldn't die, that she needed to keep fighting. They were long past that. "I will," she said.

Phan died soon afterward, and San placed her hands in the prayer position on her chest. Then the body began to stiffen, and Phan's hands fell to her side. San struggled to put them back into a position of peaceful repose, but they wouldn't budge, hanging stiffly at her friend's sides. San gave up and went in search of someone to help her move Phan's body outside for burial. Phan was little more than bones, but San was too weak to carry her. Some men hefted Phan outside.

"After you are done, be sure to step on her grave," they said. And before San could ask them what they meant, they were gone.

She was left alone with an ugly corpse that once had been her beautiful friend and a stick with which to dig her friend's grave. She managed to dig a grave about a foot deep and roll Phan into it. Then she pushed the dirt back on top of her friend. She stood up and stepped on her dead friend's makeshift grave. A horrible sound came from the ground—the sound of air escaping the body, a sound that still haunts San to this day.

That was Boeng Chrang. The next place they were moved to was Phumi Chak Toch. The rumor was that the authorities at Boeng Chrang had been too easy on them. The authorities at Phumi Chak Toch were never accused of a similar shortcoming. It was said that the people who had lived at Phumi Chak Toch before them had all been killed.

The Khmer Rouge purged both party authorities and regular people in certain zones. According to Elizabeth Becker, reports in the east were that "whole villages of people were moved to nearby fields and clubbed to death."

San's new location was merely a base camp from which she and her daughters were sent to work at various work sites. Her first assignment was carrying dirt to reinforce irrigation ditches. She slept at her work site, coming back to the base only for holidays. The girls had their own work groups. San returned whenever she could to check on her girls. Walking for hours after a long day's physical labor, she arrived in the middle of the night, spent a few hours with them, and then left to walk back later the next day.

Months would pass between visits. Once San returned to the base camp at midnight to find both Sithy and Sithea but not her youngest, Jennifer. Asking around, San discovered that Jennifer had been sent to a camp about eight hours away, where she was being trained as a Khmer Rouge. San set off on foot at 3:00 a.m. and arrived at 11:00 a.m., soaked from the steady rain that fell on her the whole way. She found her youngest daughter naked, aside from a mosquito net, shivering in front of a fire pit where the communal food was cooked.

The little girl had washed her one set of clothes. While the garments were drying, they had blown into the lake, and Jennifer had been unable to retrieve them. All she could find to cover herself was the mosquito net. Luckily San had brought with her a pair of pants she had fixed for Jennifer and an extra shirt she herself was wearing. The mother and daughter had only a half hour together before San had to begin the trek back to the base camp and from there continue on to her work site.

Jennifer was not the only one in danger of being found naked. Clothing was not easy to come by, and the few items of clothing San and the girls had with them when they left Phnom Penh were falling apart from their constant use and exposure to sun, rain, and dirt. The only available regular supply of material with which to repair them came from the dead. People died working in the fields. Other people were killed in the fields. Every day San stepped on their bodies. At night wolves moved them here and there. In time they decomposed, so only the skeletons and clothes were left.

When the bodies were no longer recognizable, San would take their clothes. She would wash the clothes in the river as best she could and then use them to repair her family's shirts and pants. It wasn't hard to do. She says, "The body and the bone of the people, that doesn't mean anything to us anymore."

Death had become mundane. Violence was the price of survival. Sithy's indoctrination was more extreme than that of her sisters. She was older, she was capable, and she was willing. One time when San returned to the base camp, Sithy stopped by only briefly, explaining she was with the Khmer Rouge now, and they were teaching her things. She told San she was learning to get along with them to survive. They forced her to accompany them when they killed people, making her watch as they banged the people's heads together. That is what she told her mother. They showed her dead bodies and body parts, warning her that if she did not obey she would become one of the bodies.

The first time she was forced to watch them murder someone she had a seizure. The scene—and the seizures—would stay with her the rest of her life. She survived, but the cost was great. In the killing fields, she and her family stopped fearing death.

San had been raised to fear ghosts. When she was a child, her parents had warned her to stay away from certain places because they were haunted by the dead, by ghosts. Back then she had feared death, feared ghosts, feared what would happen when she died. In the killing fields that changed.

"During that time I said, 'I hope ghosts come and help me to get out of here,'" she remembers thinking. "I'm not afraid of ghosts anymore."

PART 2

LIMBO

9

THE FATHER

Solomon Ros is seated on his father's lap. He is four years old now, an official preschool student. At first, he liked school. Then he didn't. David doesn't care much either way. Solomon has to go to school, "no ifs, ands or buts" about it. If he stays home, he has a time out. David can be tough on his son. Maybe it is because he already sees a hint of the troublemaker in Solomon. The kid is not shy. He has been telling jokes pretty much since he could talk. Now bored by his father's adult conversation, he slides off David's lap and runs to his half-sister, Alaysia. They briefly sit quietly on the porch swing. Then Solomon starts kicking his sister's boots. She doesn't stop him. An honor roll student, Alaysia, who is eleven and Debbie's daughter from a previous relationship, has a tendency to melt into the background when her little brother is around. Solomon is flashier, dressed today in a tank top, large athletic shorts, and a gold cross necklace.

The necklace is a gift from David's mother. All of David's siblings are devout Christians. His younger brother, Nathan, is a pastor at a Southern Baptist church, the same type of conservative church that their original American sponsors attended. David attends his brother's church occasionally. He was raised a Christian and studied all about it when he was in prison, but he is more politically and socially liberal than the rest of his family. His oldest sister, though, is like him. She lives in the bungalow in his mother's backyard. At present she is sitting outside, knitting. His twin little grandnieces are in oversized T-shirts, their curls bouncing as they toddle about the backyard. David likes to take his son to his mother's house so

Solomon can learn Khmer. Debbie speaks Khmu, a Laotian language that sounds like Russian to David, so at home they speak English.

It is mid-October and humid. Heavy rains from the day before have left one major regional highway closed due to mudslides. Another freeway is backed up because a man on the pedestrian bridge above is threatening to jump. At David's mother's Long Beach home, this all seems far away. The big news here is David plans to take Solomon and Alaysia to a pumpkin patch in a few hours. Even before he had his own children, David liked spending time with kids. He was always grabbing a niece, a nephew, a little cousin, or a neighbor and taking the child to the fair, the park, any place he went. His friends would comment on it and joke that whenever they saw him, David would have a kid or two in tow.

It's always been like that. Or at least always since he's been out of prison, or about five years. In Seattle before Solomon was born, he would take Alaysia and Debbie's nieces and nephews camping. In Long Beach David takes whatever young relatives he can with him when he takes his children places like Knott's Berry Farm.

"If I can fit five kids in my car, I'm taking five," he says.

His car, a gift from his mother, has a Baby on Board safety sticker on it. David comes from a large family and used to dream about having as many as ten kids, a Little League team. He laughs, then grows serious. He really would like to have more kids. "I just don't think I should have more while I'm under this situation."

The "situation" means his impending deportation.

He plays with a screw absently as he talks. It is Friday afternoon, and he is still dressed in the dark-blue medical scrubs he wore to work. Solomon has taken a syringe from his father's pocket and turned it into a water gun. The preschooler likes to follow his father everywhere, do everything with him. His is more than just the usual childhood attachment. He is scared David is going to leave.

It has happened before. Not the permanent absence that deportation would mean—Solomon doesn't know about that—but the temporary time when his father is gone for a few days that feels as if it's forever for a young child. When Solomon was a baby, the absences were even longer. Recently they have been shorter, with David spending a few days away at his mother's house after fighting with Debbie. Once when David returned, Solomon backed away from his father and looked as if he was going to cry. When David approached him, Solomon backed up farther.

"Go back to Grandma's house," Solomon said. "Go back to Grandma's house."

He kept repeating it over and over again, not letting his father near him. David remembers the scene clearly; it is why he tries not to disappear after fighting with Debbie. Solomon remembers it too, and every time David puts on his shoes he asks his father the same thing: "Daddy, are you going to come back? You coming back? Can I come with you?"

It breaks David's heart. He'll be going to take out the trash or get something from his car, and Solomon will be by his side, worried he is going to leave him. David hates how his fights with Debbie affect the kids. The kids, especially Solomon, are the main reason they are together, he says. He hadn't necessarily planned on being with Debbie long term. Then she got pregnant. After Solomon was born, David and Debbie weren't always together. But when they were apart, David always made sure Solomon still saw him on video calls. When his probation was up, David moved back to Long Beach. It was what he had always planned on doing. Debbie and the kids followed.

The move was hard on Debbie, who is not as outgoing as David is. He describes her as lacking self-confidence and emotionally burdened. He says her insecurity and jealousy are what come between them. They get along maybe half the time. The other half they are fighting. David turns to his family during the difficult times, but Debbie's family is back in Seattle. David's sisters and his brother extend invitations; his mother grows papayas in her backyard because she knows how much Debbie likes them. In the end, though, they are David's family, and when David and Debbie fight, they only hear his side of the story.

David worries about what will happen to Debbie and the kids when he is gone. Despite the fighting, they are his family, and he feels responsible for them. Without him he knows it will be difficult for them. It isn't just male pride talking; David is the family's main financial support. Debbie works at a day-care center part time. The real money comes from David's job. He would like to use it to buy a house, but a down payment would take all his money, which he needs to pay the monthly bills. Financially his deportation will dramatically affect his immediate family's welfare. What upsets him the most is that his family will suffer from his deportation. He can handle it. But Debbie? The kids? He worries about them. He may not be a U.S. citizen, but Solomon is. By deporting David, the United States is punishing one of its own, Solomon. The country isn't just taking away Solomon's father but also taking away the family breadwinner and forever altering the boy's social, emotional, and economic future.

"And there's a ripple effect to that," says David. "What is the family going to do? They're going to go on the state [welfare]."

Instead of the state receiving taxes from David's earnings, the state will be providing support to Debbie and the children, a move from "positive to negative." David is proud of how he has been able to support his family, especially considering how difficult obtaining work is when you are an ex-felon facing deportation. In prison he took a course on job hunting that taught him how to answer the tricky questions. Once you have been out of prison as long as he has, the question about whether you have had a conviction in the last three years is easy; the answer is no. But if they ask if you have ever had a conviction, he hesitates. One time he simply left it blank. When he was asked about it, he replied that it was easier to explain in person than to put down on paper. Up until then things had been going well in the interview process. After he mentioned his conviction, the vibe of the interview changed. He tried following up with a letter, as they had taught him in prison, but he knew he had already lost the job. That is due to the ex-felon part. Then there is the deportation part. Because his green card is no longer valid, he has to pay $380 each year for a work permit. He finds it ironic that he has to pay to get paid.

His current job came through family connections. It began with his working for his sister's driving business, transporting patients to dialysis appointments. In time he got to know the woman who owned the dialysis center where he delivered passengers. When the woman told him she needed someone who spoke Khmer to deal with her Cambodian patients, he told her he was interested in the job. Then he told her his situation.

She decided to give him a chance anyway. When she saw he was a fast learner, she sent him to school so he could learn how to care for the dialysis machines. He spent six or seven months studying to become a biomedical technician. With the new skills came more money. Still David believes if it weren't for the limitations of his background, he would be paid more and treated better. A while back his wrist became inflamed, making it painful to work, but he couldn't afford to take time off, so he worked through it.

He has no idea what kind of work he will be able to find in Cambodia. If he is deported while his mom is still alive, he thinks he will be okay. His mother has enough connections and relatives to smooth things over for him. From what he has heard and seen, some of his family members are doing pretty well. His cousin on his father's side and another relative visited Long Beach not too long ago and took David and his mother out to eat. The relatives ordered crab that cost close to $1,000 from a fancy restaurant the likes of which David had never seen before. What they do for a living in Cambodia, David isn't exactly sure. Gold shops? Real estate? Whatever it is, they seem to do it well.

Their exact occupation isn't all that David is unsure about. He doesn't know if the cousin he met is the son of his father's twin brother or of another sibling. The brother who fled with his father was his twin. Whether they were fraternal or identical twins is one of the many things David never asked about his father. He knows more about his mother's side of the family. One of her cousins was a judge. He has since died, so there goes that connection. David's fear is that by the time he is deported, all the people his mother knows who could help him will be dead. His mother is in her late sixties and in bad health. According to David, she has been dying since they moved to the United States.

First it was cancer of the female reproductive organs. The doctors gave her three years to live. That was thirty years ago. Then there was breast cancer. Now her kidney is giving her trouble. She has diabetes and hypertension. Recent research focused on the long-term health of Cambodian refugees has found rates of diabetes, hypertension, and hyperlipidemia in Cambodian refugees to be far higher than in the general U.S. population.

Diabetes and hypertension, or high blood pressure, are the first and second leading causes of kidney failure in the United States. David has seen this firsthand, as most of the patients he treats at the dialysis clinic have very high blood pressure. If his mother's remaining kidney gives out and she passes away before he is deported, he doesn't know what will happen to him in Cambodia. He also doesn't know what will happen to Debbie and the kids in the United States.

Debbie has talked about following him to Cambodia. He doesn't see that working out too well. It has been hard enough for him to figure out how to support Debbie and the kids in the States. In Cambodia it would be worse, because Debbie and the children neither speak Khmer nor hold Cambodian citizenship. David himself initially may rely on distant relatives to help him out. Asking relatives he barely knows to support his girlfriend and two children seems too much. He imagines instead that Debbie and the kids will go back to Seattle. He doesn't think it's a good idea, but he thinks that is what will happen.

They were just in Seattle for a long vacation—and a funeral. They had been planning to vacation there anyway; it is where Alaysia spends the summer with her biological father. They decided to spend some time in Seattle and then bring Alaysia home. David secured several weeks off work and a place for them to stay. They knew Debbie's father wasn't doing well, but they thought they would arrive before he died.

They didn't make it in time, and David feels bad about that. Debbie held her father in high esteem, as did much of the community. He had been a general in the Laotian army and used his U.S. connections to bring many Laotian refugees to the States. Debbie spent years looking out for him after he developed dementia. She did all she could to keep him at home with her and care for him. It was hard because he tended to wander. According to David, he was also an alcoholic who had many wives, leaving Debbie with half-siblings all over the world. A couple of Debbie's siblings are in the United States. David is none too fond of them.

"There's a lot of stuff that's illegal," he says. He doesn't offer specifics. He only says that out of all Debbie's siblings he knows in the States, Debbie and one other sister are the only ones not involved in something "detrimental to their lives."

Just then David's cell phone rings. It is Debbie. She cancels on the pumpkin patch. It was a long day at work, and she is tired. David doesn't seem surprised. He will take the kids without her. The other night, when he was half awake, he remembers Debbie talking to him. Because he has to get up before 2:00 a.m., he tries to go to bed before 10:00 p.m. Debbie joins him later. He must have been stirring on this particular night, because he remembers having a conversation with her almost as if it were a dream.

"I don't know what I'm going to do if you get deported," she said.

David told her to start saving as much money as she can. Debbie isn't a saver. When David suggested she let him hold onto some of her money so he could save it for her, she refused. He thinks she was worried he had an ulterior motive for offering to keep her money. He thinks she thought that he was going to take the money and run away to Cambodia.

"That's her thing," he says. She accuses him of planning to take the money and go to Cambodia to marry a girl. "Because that's what they all do," he adds. "They all marry young girls down there."

David openly talks about how his mother has offered to find him a wife in Cambodia. And yet he faults Debbie for not trusting him, something he blames on her background. She also has a short fuse, he says, a temper. He blames the relationship for costing him friends, for taking him away from his activism. When they were separated and he was living with his mother, he used to devote his free time to fighting the deportation of Southeast Asians. In all the years he has worked on the issue, he knows of only one or two people who successfully fought their deportation orders. There might be more, but he doesn't know about any.

Then there is Many Uch, the activist who helped Touch Hak. Back when he was big in the movement, David was close with Many, one of the early players in the fight profiled in the 2006 documentary *Sentenced Home*. Many traveled the country to draw attention to the case of potential deportees and helped found the group Khmer Girls in Action. In 2007 Many asked the governor of Washington State to pardon his 1994 crime. He was eventually granted a pardon for his assault with a deadly weapon charge, but he still has to check in with Immigration and Customs Enforcement. And he is still deportable.

When David reaches Many on the phone, Many explains the situation. Even though he was pardoned, immigration law says because he has a weapons charge, the charge can't be waived. Essentially he was pardoned for the robbery he took part in, he says, but not for carrying a weapon at the robbery.

"If it were rape, it could be waived," he says. "But because it's a weapon charge, it can't be waived."

Each deportation case is different, and the outcome can vary greatly depending on the charge. Drug charges are another difficult one to get around. Still, there are some who have been luckier. Many explains that some people have gone back to court to have their cases reopened. They then are resentenced to less than 365 days; thus, as long as their charges don't restrict them from the relief, they are not subject to mandatory deportation. Many remembers a guy who had an assault charge with a butcher knife who was able to escape deportation in this way.

It wouldn't have worked for Many. But he does have a pardon in his immigration file, so he shouldn't be top on the list for deportation. ICE is supposed to deport those who are a threat to public safety. If your crime has been pardoned, Many figures, then you can't be considered much of a public safety threat anymore—at least that is what he tells himself every time he goes for his annual immigration check-in. He is still trying to get himself off the deportation list. He is looking at possibly reopening his case so he won't have to worry every time a group is sent back to Cambodia, something that he said happened just this month.

David's record has a lot worse than a weapons charge: he killed a man. There aren't many loopholes he can slip through; still he used to be active in the fight against the deportation of Southeast Asians. Initially he says both those facing deportation and those in the larger community in general were reluctant to show support for the movement. Some didn't out of fear. Some didn't out of apathy. Some didn't want anything to do with the "criminal elements." Then as time passed, they saw how the deportation of those criminal elements affected another generation, how the children were suffering because of the loss of a parent. Slowly, he says, some stepped forward and joined the fight. Younger siblings started fighting for older siblings. Respectable conservative people such as David's younger brother supported him in his efforts. The movement grew.

In Cambodia artists and activists told the story from the other side. The deportees who got involved in the arts community there, the poets and dancers, attracted media attention with story after story. People outside the community started to learn about the deportations. Still not much changed. Now a new campaign is about to be launched, a campaign aimed at tackling the issue from a different angle, a campaign that will once again draw David back into the fight. The campaign is being organized by the Southeast Asian Freedom Network, a national collective of Southeast Asian groups. The 1 Love Movement is one of the groups in the network playing a large role in the efforts. The Southeast Asia Resource Action Center is also lending support.

One of the first groups to advocate for the Southeast Asian community in the United States was SEARAC, although back then it had a different name. The organization helped establish the Refugee Act of 1980 and the Office of Refugee Resettlement, basically establishing the country's first formal refugee resettlement program. Over the years SEARAC continued to keep an eye on the government's treatment of refugees and helped community organizations do the same. When deportations became an issue, SEARAC helped lead the fight against them. It continues to train community leaders, something David took advantage of in 2012. Since then a number of other organizations have gotten involved in the fight. Then the movement seemed to grow quiet.

In 2015 the movement picked up again, big time, using the news peg of forty years since the first Southeast Asians were resettled in the United States to continue the fight against the deportations. Since 1998 more than fifteen thousand Cambodian, Laotian, and Vietnamese Americans have been ordered deported. As always the movement draws attention to the 1996 Illegal Immigration Reform and Immigrant Responsibility Act and the Antiterrorism and Effective Death Penalty Act, which expanded the definition of "aggravated felony" under immigration law to crimes that are not considered aggravated or felony under state criminal laws. But this time instead of focusing on changing the U.S. laws, the activists decided to focus on the 2002 repatriation agreement between Cambodia and the United States. By putting pressure on Cambodia to change the agreement, they hope to force the United States to revisit it. Their ultimate goal is to have Cambodia's agreement resemble the one the United States has with Vietnam that says only deportees who came to the States after 1995, when the countries established formal diplomatic relations, will be accepted. The Laotians do not have an agreement with the United States, but Laotians have received deportation orders.

The new campaign features a series of timed video releases. David will hold a launch party for the first kickoff video on Saturday, October 24, 2015. It will be one of the first big things he has done for the movement in quite a while. He is excited about it. But he is equally excited about Halloween. He has a picture of Solomon in a Samurai Ninja outfit on his phone. The costume was cute but a bit small, so David got him a bigger Batman costume. Now he looks over at his son playing in the dirt.

"Solomon," David calls.

Solomon looks up. "Huh?"

"Nothing, I just want to look at you," says David.

Solomon goes back to digging. Not long afterward, David joins him.

A few days later David texts about the upcoming campaign launch party and a later series of town hall meetings, including one in Long Beach. He also mentions he has to check in with ICE on December 15.

10

AN EDUCATION IN SILENCE

The SUV pulls up at 7:00 a.m. Sithy and another woman hop out. KC keeps the gray SUV idling while Sithy rolls back the security gate surrounding S & S Fashions Inc. She had planned to get to work at six-thirty this morning so her boyfriend KC could get to work by seven, but they had both overslept. KC is already late for his job driving a frozen food delivery truck. But he still waits for Sithy as she disappears inside the sewing factory.

A few minutes later Sithy returns, holding a floral comforter and several matching pillows. Yesterday her boss asked her to get rid of the salvaged bedding. Sithy forgot to take it home last night and now hurriedly stuffs it in the SUV. She regularly takes discarded fabric, clothes, and other items home from the factory and adjacent businesses, sharing them with friends and family. It is one of the perks of working at a sewing factory in Signal Hill, a tiny hilltop city entirely surrounded by Long Beach.

With the comforter and pillows safely out of the sewing factory, Sithy heads back inside. Her boots thud loudly as she crosses the bare cement floor. They are not work boots but trendy short boots with wedged heels. Sithy is dressed in tight jeans paired with a sexy black vest and a white blouse. Her long, layered hair falls loosely down her back. Sparkly purple nail polish and eyeliner complete the look. She is outfitted more for a nightclub than a sweatshop. Her surroundings tell a different story: the sign—"No one under the age of 18 allowed beyond this point"—the sewing machines arranged in tight rows, the lack of windows. Bare light bulbs hang from the high ceiling. In winter, especially on chilly December mornings like this one, the cold seeps inside your bones. In summer the air is heavy with heat. At a little after seven o'clock the machines are eerily silent. The seamstresses don't arrive until eight, giving Sithy time to tell her story.

She talks fast and jumps from subject to subject. She is animated, re-creating past conversations by changing the tone of her voice, acting out scenes with her arms and body. Sithy's energy can be intense, absorbing, exhausting. She possesses the kind of hyperactivity that leads people to think she is on drugs. She tells them she isn't, not now. In the past, yes; now, no. This energy, she says, is natural.

When they were leaving Phnom Penh in April 1975, Sithy didn't cry; none of them did. She and her sisters were just little girls back then. Sithy was nine; Sithea, eight; and Jennifer, five. For them it was fun, an adventure. The people on the side of the road were sleeping. It was their mother's friend Phan who told Sithy the truth: the people were dead. Then Sithy heard the land mines go "puff and explode and kill a lot of people." In the days, weeks, months, and years that followed, Sithy grew tired, longing for sleep. Before the Khmer Rouge took power, Sithy's mother, San, had to cajole and threaten her to get her to go to bed at night. After the Khmer Rouge took over, sleep became a luxury. Work began at three o'clock in the morning and didn't end until evening. All Sithy wanted was to sleep, to rest, to lie down. All these years later she is still bothered by sleep. During the day, if she is still, she tends to fall asleep. At night she has trouble going to bed and is often up, playing games on her phone.

Right now she is perched on a stool, playing online slots on her phone. She isn't paid by the hour but by the work she does, and today there isn't much to do. She gets $300 a month to clean the floor once a week, a job her friend is now doing and for which she will give her friend a cut of her paycheck. Sithy is generous, but then she is often in need as well. In addition to the $300, Sithy makes $0.12 for each item she folds and packages. She works at a large raised counter separated from the sewing area by a few steps and surrounded by racks of hanging clothes and bins and boxes full of cloth. When it is busy, she folds and packages six hundred or seven hundred shirts a day, but often it is just two hundred or three hundred. Today, it will be even less; they just finished a large load, so there really isn't anything much to fold.

Sithy could do other things. She has done other things at the factory. She used to stamp the clothes with a tag via heat transfer. That paid better, $800 a month, but she got tired and confused, started stamping the information upside down, and messed up too many shirts. She was even worse as an inspector. She sabotaged that job by messing up when the seamstresses asked her to fix their stitching. She had trouble sitting and working at the table; sitting still tends to put her to sleep. It doesn't help that she needs glasses. She wears a pair, but they aren't prescription glasses and make her dizzy. She says she doesn't have the money to get her eyes checked. If she told her mother, her mother would pay for the eye exam and glasses, but she would also ask why Sithy doesn't have money when she works. So Sithy doesn't tell her. Not being able to see further limits her employment options. The jobs she can do, she says, are "anything do not use glasses, anything do not use English. And do not let me sit down too long one place."

Oh, and anything that doesn't look too hard at her immigration status, because she is on the list to be deported. Add the fact that she suffers from seizures and does not have a driver's license or a high school diploma, and her job options are pretty slim. At the sewing factory, she stands when she works, so she doesn't fall asleep. Her heavily accented English is far better than that of the rest of the employees, most of whom have recently arrived from Cambodia.

Sithy is candid about all of this. She doesn't hide her shortcomings or her situation, even when it might be wise to do so. She comes across as exceptionally honest; like a child, she is unaware of why the truth is sometimes better kept hidden. And yet, also like a child, her truth is slippery. She lies, but then she tells you about her lies. Her real age is fifty-four or fifty-three—she isn't sure which—but she prefers to say forty-eight. She is supposed to take medication for her seizures. When doctors and family members ask if she is taking the medicine, she tells them she is even though she admits that she has been cutting back on the medicine for years. Her lies are natural and, in her mind, necessary. There is nothing wrong with what she is doing. How to lie is a lesson she learned early. She learned it from the best, the Khmer Rouge.

At her mother's house a few weeks before, Sithy and San talked about the lies the Khmer Rouge elicited from them. San told the first one. She didn't start out lying. Originally when the Khmer Rouge asked her who she was and what she did for work, she told them the truth. She told them her name and that she had worked for the government. The next day a woman was nice enough to warn San that her truthful answer would get her killed and that she had better run. San and her family ran, and from then on San lied. When people asked where she had worked previously, she told them she worked in a bookstore. She never told them her real name again.

The Khmer Rouge lied right back. They told San and others like her from Phnom Penh that they would take them back to the capital. The first time, when San revealed she worked for the government and was grouped with others like her, the Khmer Rouge told them they were going to take them to meet the king.

"That's how they lie to them," says San. "A lot of people fall for the trick."

And they were the ones who died. Only those such as San, the liars, survived. That was the first lesson Sithy learned: telling the truth could be dangerous, could be deadly. Lying was necessary, needed. Other times Sithy didn't so much lie as hide the truth. She didn't like the Khmer Rouge, but she acted as they did so they would trust her. She worked with them so she could live with them and eat their food, which was better than the food given to everyone else. She discovered this after a brief stint in a hospital. At first Sithy was made to pick up cow dung all day and dig irrigation ditches by hand. She was given just two bowls of watery rice a day. Then she got sick and was sent to the hospital, where she noticed that the young Khmer Rouge nurses would rather flirt among themselves than spend time collecting the plants they used to make their "medicine." Sithy figured out what they needed to make the potions and ran around the jungle gathering it. While she was out, she would deliver some of her food to her mother and sisters. Gathering plants was easier than the farming work she would have been assigned otherwise, and the rations were better.

Knowing that as soon as she was no longer useful to the Khmer Rouge she would be sent back to the fields, she tried to find other things she could do for them. She started repairing their uniforms, sewing the red trim on their black shirts. She watched to see what was needed and how to fill the need, and then she did it, making herself indispensable. She was beaten, but they never tried to kill her.

"Because they need me," she says. "Because I do all the jobs. I do what they need."

She survived by being useful. She credits her mother with providing her with the skills she needed to be useful. Before the Khmer Rouge, her mother had enough money to hire a maid. Instead of just having the maid do everything, her mother instructed the maid to teach Sithy and her sisters how to clean, cook, and sew. Later, after the Khmer Rouge took everything away, Sithy noticed how other privileged children who had been raised by maids were helpless. Sithy, in contrast, had the skills to make herself useful: she could cook, she could sew, and she knew how to watch, learn, and copy—all of which she credits to her mother.

"My mom, she kind of like different everybody. She get a good education. That's why I so happy to get her," says Sithy. "Without her at that time I think we all die. We not that strong you know."

Sithy also remembers the boat headed to Vietnam, the chance that they could have all escaped. Her version is slightly different from her mother's. Instead of missing the boat because she and her sisters couldn't swim, they missed the boat because she and her sisters couldn't speak Vietnamese. Either way, the girls were the ones who prevented the escape. Neither she nor her mother tell the story with judgment. There is no blame or guilt, only the facts. It is as simple as that. The girls couldn't swim, or the girls couldn't speak Vietnamese, so they couldn't escape.

Sithy tears at a Kleenex. She holds up a few of the confetti-size pieces. The Khmer Rouge used to use little pieces of cotton like that to burn her stomach. They would hold the cotton to the fire and then place it on her stomach. She pulls up her shirt to show off the scars. They aren't obviously visible anymore. Sometimes they used grains of sand. Other times they kicked and hit her—in the head, stomach, back, all over. The punishments were for stealing. It was the only time she didn't listen to the Khmer Rouge. No matter how often they warned her, no matter how many times they beat her and threatened to kill her the next time they caught her, she continued to steal. Mostly she stole food—for herself and for her mother and sisters.

The worst punishment was not when they hurt her but when they made her watch them hurt other people. It was both a warning to keep her from crossing them and a training to make her tough. Before she went to work each morning, they would make her stand and watch while they killed a group of people. The victims were blindfolded; their hands, tied. The Khmer Rouge used a short knife to stab them in the back. It was said they didn't like to waste bullets. Afterward their victims were still alive, still talking, screaming.

"Mother, please help me!"

"Please, God, help me!"

Then the Khmer Rouge stabbed them again.

"Go like this," Sithy says, motioning her arm erratically in the air. "And stick the hand in, take the liver, take the heart, they take."

Some of those who were forced to watch the ordeal had a heart attack and died. Sithy fell down. That was the first time she had a seizure. After that, she learned to stay upright and watch, but the seizures returned at other times. This was how they trained her to be like them. She watched because she wanted to survive. She understood that either she had to stand with them or she would be slaughtered by them. There were no other options. Other survivors' accounts talk of the Khmer Rouge eating livers, backing up Sithy's account of their removing their victims' livers.

Out of her family, Sithy had the strength the others lacked. In impossible situations she learned how to work the system best, to get the best food, to find the best housing. She helped them survive under the Khmer Rouge, and she helped them make it to Thailand after the Vietnamese invasion.

At first there were just a few Vietnamese soldiers after the Vietnamese invaded Cambodia and ousted the Khmer Rouge in 1979. Then more and more arrived until the Khmer Rouge seemed scared and started fleeing toward Thailand, forcing the people along with them. Sithy and her family walked for weeks, noting how the Khmer Rouge were losing power and control as they went. The rules eased. They started seeing people engaged in trade, people going to Thailand to buy goods and coming back to sell them in Cambodia. They heard about a camp near the Thai border and decided to head there. Near the border, they could find goods and engage in trade and buy themselves food. First though, they had to get there.

San's stomach had ballooned so severely from malnutrition that she had trouble finding pants that would fit. Her toenails had fallen off after taking an advance solo walk to check out the situation by the border. Sithea had never been well under the Khmer Rouge, and Jennifer had a swollen leg. Sithy was the strong one. Sithy was the one who found a bicycle once again. Even though the bike had no tires, Sithy pushed her family in turns toward the border. She would push her mother first, taking her until she could barely see her sisters anymore. After she dropped her mother off, she would turn around and retrieve her sisters. Sometimes Jennifer helped push. Other times she couldn't. Sithy never had a choice. She always had to push.

In this way they made their way slowly toward the border. They left the bike as they drew near. In the region by the border between Cambodia and Thailand, they had to run. The war was supposedly over, but the Vietnamese and Khmer Rouge patrolled the jungle area between Thailand and Cambodia. They needed to get past some of the patrols to reach Nong Samet, or "007," a border camp on land considered to be on the Cambodian side. There were rumors the Cambodians were being killed in the refugee camps on the Thai side. The border camps on the Cambodian side were brutal places as well and run by different military groups. Safety was relative.

Sithy said there were things in the ground that cut their feet. People had crossed the area before them, so they could see where to go.

"But sometimes, the shooting, you just run, you can't, you don't know where, you just follow the people running. Some people get hurt," says Sithy.

Near the camp there was food. Sithy saw eggs. She wanted them, but she had no money with which to pay for them. She noticed that people needed drinking water and decided to sell it. San received 120 Thai baht ($16 in today's money) for the broken pieces of an 18-karat gold necklace. The Khmer Rouge wanted only 24-karat gold, so the necklace had been useless previously, according to San. They used 90 baht ($12) to buy a bucket for carrying water and the rest to buy a cooking pot and rice. They went far into the jungle to get clear water, which they could sell for more than the murky water found closer to the border. They took turns fetching and selling the water until they had enough money to buy another bucket. Then they had enough to buy eggs. Then they had enough to buy the ingredients to make a bean dessert. Sithy sold it all.

"Little money, you can buy something bigger. So I start little by little."

From the dessert she moved on to tobacco. She would buy a large bag of tobacco for $20 and then repackage it into smaller bags and sell them for a total of $40. Another scheme she came up with was candles. In the camp everyone needed candles at night because there was no electricity. One day Sithy decided to buy all the candles from all the merchants before night fell. No one suspected what she was up to; no one else thought of doing the same. When it became dark, Sithy sold the candles for double the normal price. People complained. She had no patience for them.

"You don't want it, fine. You can't go get it," she told them. She had bought all the candles so there was nowhere else for them to go; they had to buy them from her. "Because everybody need a candle. That's how I start make money. I double [the price], they still take it."

She gambled and won. Other times, the gambles cost her. At first she merely traveled close to the border to buy goods. Then one day she decided to cross to Thailand to buy pants and sarongs. There was a shooting and robbery. She became confused and ran the wrong way. It was dangerous for a young Cambodian girl to be in Thailand alone. She was warned she would be taken to Bangkok to work in the sex trade. She was a teenager by then, but being so malnourished, she was tiny and looked much younger than her age. All of them did. Sithy hoped that would protect her. But the Thai soldiers were also looking for her. She hid in a home until it was safe. Then she ran to another and another, and eventually, after nine days, after her mother had given her up for dead, she made her way back. She lost money when she tried to offload the goods. The next time she figured out how to do it better, keeping her family alive until they found safety. Eventually they crossed into refugee camps in Thailand and then later still on to the United States.

Sithy's life for the years she lived under the Khmer Rouge and then in refugee camps in Thailand was dreadful, yet, in some ways, she thrived. Sithy was good at survival mode. It was harder for her to do ordinary life.

It started in Thailand. She would have nightmares, waking up screaming because people were trying to kill her; the nightmares turned into seizures.

Later, in the States, it was as if she was still in survival mode. Her body and mind remained in shock. She did not have her menstrual period until she was twenty or twenty-one. The seizures continued. The doctor who treated her seizures taught her the little English she picked up. Her formal education ended almost as soon as it began. As noted earlier, a series of abusive boyfriends followed, one after the other. She gave birth to a number of children as well, none of whom she raised. Her employment choices were colorful: working as a cocktail waitress at a gambling house, serving beer at a bikini bar, pushing drinks and massages at home gambling games.

Had Sithy been able to continue her education or improve her English, her options would have been different. But the trauma she suffered under the Khmer Rouge stayed with her in the form of post-traumatic stress disorder, which a therapist who specializes in torture survivors later diagnosed. Short-term memory loss is a common consequence of PTSD, making it hard to learn anything new, said Thang D. Nguyen. His organization, Boat People SOS, spent decades working on the consequences of torture among Vietnamese refugees.

Of Sithy's abusive boyfriends, most are from the same background as Sithy and had been subjected to the same torture and trauma. According to Thang, it shouldn't come as a surprise that family violence is a huge issue in the Laotian, Cambodian, and Vietnamese refugee communities. "Because many of the abusers are themselves victims of torture," said Thang, "they are traumatized, and they are passing the trauma around to other members of the family."

Unfortunately, the abuse goes largely unaddressed. Thang believes mental health issues also go mostly untreated.

S. Megan Berthold, an assistant professor of social work at the University of Connecticut, agreed that due to the stigma the community associates with mental health, many in the Cambodian refugee community do not get help until they are struggling to function in their daily lives. As a result, she said, "I think a lot of people just never got services who probably could benefit from it."

Their symptoms, including nightmares and lack of sleep, are often triggered and exacerbated by environmental stressors. During the 1992 Los Angeles civil unrest, Megan said a number of her Cambodian clients at the Los Angeles clinic where she was working experienced a worsening of their PTSD symptoms. The looting, fires, armed militia, and general violence and chaos reminded Megan's clients of the Khmer Rouge's evacuation of Phnom Penh. Because PTSD can follow a chronic fluctuating course with symptoms growing worse when there are stressors and diminishing when they are absent, sufferers may need treatment for several years. To complicate matters, treatment may not be fully effective if they suffer from undiagnosed head trauma, said Megan, and it is believed many in the community do.

Adaptive behaviors, necessary for survival under the Khmer Rouge, can hold refugees back in their present lives. Under the Khmer Rouge it was dangerous to show emotion, said Megan. "So what was adaptive and life-saving then might not be conducive to creating friendships, support networks and good working relationships with people in their current context." Yet those who were resettled in violent U.S. neighborhoods, where they continued to feel unsafe, might have felt it necessary to rely on these coping mechanisms.

Sithy has remained in the inner city of Long Beach, surrounding herself with people who survive in whatever way they can, similar to how she lived in Cambodia. Despite the environment and all the kids and drugs, she still looks good. She is used to being told she is beautiful, but she knows she is no longer young. She isn't new anymore; and once you stop being new, if you don't have an education, she says, Asian men don't respect you. With an education, they kiss your ass; without one, it's hard. When she was young, she didn't care. She would break up with one boyfriend and find another one. Back then, she didn't cry about love. Now she obsesses over her boyfriend's text messages to an old girlfriend. She worries he will cheat on her. She gets up early to cook for him, to take care of him. She makes sure she looks good, because "when you older, it hard to broke up."

She doesn't worry about KC's criminal record or the fact he is on probation for decades after spending twenty years in prison for murder. He works, he doesn't do drugs, and he is good to her. She held off telling her mother about his criminal record at first. Waited until after he came to help when her mother was sick, carrying her mother when San couldn't walk. They have been together more than two years now. Her life is almost stable or closer to it than it had been before. She is spending time with the kids of her eldest daughter, Lauren, in a way she never did with her own.

Still, there are holes. She hasn't seen her youngest son in more than a decade. She can't even picture what he looks like. She still lies, telling little, calculated ones. She stopped taking seizure medication so she can get work, so she can drive. She gives a younger age because her looks have worked for her, and aging is hard. She figured out how to manipulate the system, stretch the truth, and make reality work for her. She knows how to please people when she needs them. She knows what to do to survive. What to do to live a normal life is what she doesn't understand. She knows how to break rules, but she doesn't understand how to follow them. In her world, laws are arbitrary, and you ignore them if they don't work for you. That is what got her in trouble.

She has a few more months before she is due in court on February 1, 2016. She doesn't focus on the date. She leaves that to her stepfather, Tom. All she knows is that Tom and the lawyer have figured out an argument, a reason she shouldn't be deported to Cambodia. It hinges on her health and an abusive ex-boyfriend who is now in a position of authority in Cambodia. If she is sent back, she will be in danger from the boyfriend and receive improper medical care. That is how she understands it. When she was in Thailand after the Khmer Rouge, they didn't know how to treat her seizures and simply gave her heavy medicine to knock her out. She believes the medicine messed up her memory.

"But whatever in the Khmer Rouge, I don't forget it," she says. "Like in my mind until now, I remember, but not exactly what day, what month. But I remember what they did to us. It's too hard to forget it."

And with Sithy, that is the problem. She has never been able to leave it behind.

11

A SECOND CHANCE

There is a cross above the front door and a Buddhist altar in a corner display case. The Christmas lights decorate the outside of Chanphirun Meanowuth Min's Bellflower home only in winter, but the lights surrounding the living room altar stay on all year round. The shrine is for Chanphirun's parents and his son—the son he had before Max, a son whose existence Chanphirun mentions now for the first time.

It is December 2015, and a small Christmas tree is in the living room and a red-and-green paper chain is hanging down from a kitchen wall. Max is huddled on the couch, still dressed in his school uniform of navy shorts and a crisp, white button-down shirt. He isn't feeling well, and he speaks barely above a whisper when he asks his father to help him go to the bathroom. Afterward he returns to the couch, his pale face with fine features and his mop of dark hair peeking out from a pile of pillows and blankets. His mom is still at work, his fourteen-year-old half-sister is in her room, and his grandmother is in yet another room. His other grandparents, Chanphirun's mother and father, exist only in images. So does Chanphirun's first son, Matthew, who was five years old when he died, the same age Max is now.

More family photos are on the living room wall. There is a picture of Chanphirun as a boy with his three sisters. Another shows Chanphirun's father and a few other military men standing by an unexploded bomb they are about to examine.

"It's not a good idea," Chanphirun admits. "But it's there, so they have to investigate it."

The photo of Matthew was taken at a swimming pool a few years before he died. In photos, Max looks eerily like Matthew, a pale boy with soft features and dark hair. Max and Matthew don't just look alike; they act alike as well, says Chanphirun.

"I believe Max is a reincarnation for Matthew," he says. It is something he senses. It is also something he wants—needs—to be true.

This evening Chanphirun is dressed in jeans, tennis shoes, and a purple V-neck sweater. His hair is longer and lighter than it was earlier in the year, and there is slight stubble on his chin. He wears glasses and a gold chain, a combination of urban sophisticate and ghetto fabulous.

After Matthew died in a car accident, Chanphirun prayed daily for God to give him another chance. When Max was born more than a decade later, Chanphirun's faith in God was reaffirmed. All you have to do is pray, and your prayers will be answered. He believes all of this because he has to; it is how he lives with himself because, you see, Matthew didn't exactly die in a car accident.

"When Matthew was alive, I was not a proper dad. I was a horrible dad," says Chanphirun. "I didn't give him a chance."

The "car accident" took place in front of their house. There was a car, but Matthew wasn't in it. He was playing outside, near the street, while Chanphirun worked on his car in their driveway. There was a line in the pavement that Chanphirun told Matthew not to cross.

Chanphirun was working under the car. There was a boom. Chanphirun knew right away it was Matthew. He raced into the street and found his son's head underneath the front wheel of a car. There was blood everywhere.

"I pulled him out," says Chanphirun. "He died in my hands. A horrible death."

It was more than a month before Chanphirun could talk again. It took him years to get over Matthew's death, just as it took him years to get over his parents' deaths. During those years he did stupid things, self-destructive things, criminal things. He did things for which he did time behind bars and faced deportation proceedings. He was given a second chance to stay in the United States and a second chance at fatherhood. He is either extremely lucky—or extremely unlucky.

Next to the photos is a framed poem Chanphirun discovered while in prison. It is about God. The author of the poem uses footprints in the sand to symbolize her walk through life. Looking behind her, the author notices two sets of footprints for most of her life, except at the end, during the lowest and saddest part of her life. At that point, the author sees only one set of footprints and asks the Lord why she did not see the Lord's footprints beside her own when she needed him most. The Lord replies that during that time there was only one set of footprints because the Lord was carrying her. The words are both saccharine and comforting, a summation of modern popular Christianity.

Chanphirun was and still is a Buddhist. His wife Terry Min is a Buddhist. But Chanphirun is also a Christian. He likes to joke that "two parts are better than one—so far." Squaring a religion that believes in a single God with one that does not believe in God might seem confusing, but for Chanphirun there is no contradiction. The unusual pairing makes sense when looked at through the numerous phases of his life, phases that lack links or transitions but instead simply appear and disappear.

Terry arrives home after Chanphirun has begun chopping onions and lemons for chicken soup. She takes over, completing what Chanphirun refers to as the "half husband/half wife" dinner. These days Terry does most of her cooking with her mother, who is only now learning the skill. In Cambodia, before the Khmer Rouge, Terry's family had maids. Back then her mother didn't have to cook. In the United States, after the Khmer Rouge, her mother was too busy working as a cashier in a doughnut shop and as a house cleaner to have time for cooking anything more than the basics. Terry works but only one job, servicing printers. Unlike her mother, she speaks English, so she is not limited to low-wage service jobs. She is forty-three and has spent the majority of her life in the States.

Terry was three when Pol Pot came to power. Her father was away from home when the Khmer Rouge took over the country. Half Chinese and a member of the previous government's army, her father had two major strikes against him in the eyes of the Khmer Rouge. Terry is pale like her father, a physical characteristic that worked against her during the Khmer Rouge years, when the dark skin of those who worked outside was valued above all else. Her grandmother told her the other children used to beat

Terry and her brother up because of their light skin. Terry's own memories of life under the Khmer Rouge are limited.

A few things stick out: crying for her father, her mother hitting her hand, and an older cousin pulling her aside, stroking her hair, wiping her face, and telling her not to ask her mother too many questions. Being told not to call for her "papa" or her "dad." The Khmer Rouge did away with most familial terms. Her cries would give her away. They could lead to questions about who her father was, where he was, and why. The terms identified her as a new person, or one of the wealthy from the city whom the Khmer Rouge despised. Terry was just a toddler, though, so she kept crying for her father. Then one day her mother explained that the Khmer Rouge were killing whole families, pointing out those who had met their demise as they walked past their homes.

"She said, 'If we don't do what they say, they going to do that to us,'" says Terry.

Terry stopped calling for her father. Her mother was taken to a camp. Too young to work, Terry and her baby brother stayed with their grandparents. She remembers being hungry, always hungry. She remembers walking for months, sleeping in the forest during a rainstorm, hearing the sound of gunfire in a camp in Thailand. Then she remembers settling in Downey, not far from Long Beach, when she was eight. She remembers not knowing how to answer when she entered third grade and was asked her name in English, a language she didn't understand.

Her father arrived in the States first, but he already had a new family. She calls him a bad boy. Her husband calls him a player. Her father and husband knew each other before she met Chanphirun. She found pictures of them together on Facebook after she first met Chanphirun on the site in 2000. They didn't get together until some years later. Having a child wasn't something they planned. Terry already had a daughter. She named the girl Pearl after a character in two books—one, a classic; the other, a trashy novel. Chanphirun chose Max's name, a name partly inspired by Maximus in the movie *Gladiator*.

Matthew hadn't been planned, either. Chanphirun's marriage to Matthew's mother lasted until Matthew was two years old. Chanphirun admits he wasn't much of a father back then. He did drugs in front of his son. He served time behind bars.

After Matthew died, Chanphirun went to Hawaii. He sold men's suits, worked in a frame shop, and attempted suicide. It was a continuation of the life he had been trashing ever since discovering the Khmer Rouge had killed his parents. He doesn't tell Terry much about his family, and she doesn't ask much.

Unlike her, he didn't witness the killing fields. The Cambodia he pictures is the one that existed before, the one his family helped run. The photos of his family, the photos from his childhood, are now mostly gone. Those he has left are from his teenage years, taken not long before he left the country. There he is by a jeep with official government license plates, a vehicle his uncle gave him so the police wouldn't stop him. In another he and a friend pose beside a motorcycle, a popular and expensive mode of travel at the time. It was a privileged life. The war remained largely absent from his world. Chanphirun's youth and his family's position sheltered him from the reality faced by the refugees of the conflict who had poured into the capital. His Cambodia was advanced and sophisticated, a world of high dives in exclusive swimming pools. His home was one of the only homes on the block to have a television. At night they would position it near the compound gate so the neighbors could watch.

Other photos show him and a group of three or four friends posing around the capital. It is the mid-1970s, and their hair is long, their jeans flared, and their shirts tight and patterned. They have just graduated from high school, and they are cocky young bucks ready to take on their promising futures. Privilege has made them self-assured. They will study in college what their families studied and fill the same elite positions in society that their families now hold. For Chanphirun that meant politics. He was being groomed to be a politician like his uncle, the leader of the country. In the pictures, they seem blissfully unaware of the fighting going on in the rest of the country. Thin, confident, straight-backed Chanphirun and his friends Vang, Lo, Ty, and Leap met the camera head-on. Their faces are slightly out of focus, but their futures were assured. They had no idea what was coming.

"All of us about to go to university right here, but I left the country," says Chanphirun. "I left them behind."

They are all gone now; like his family, they were killed after the communists came to power. Across the world, Chanphirun remained safe, but he was no longer Chanphirun. He was not going to be a politician. He was not even going to college. He started calling himself Kokma, or "orphan." He was a man without a family or a country. And yet in 2003, the United States wanted to return him to Cambodia, a place he no longer acknowledged. He fought his deportation to Cambodia and won. The U.S. government agreed it would be unsafe for him to return to Cambodia, where those in power had ties to the regime that had murdered his family. The same man who ruled the country in 2003 is still in power today, but much has changed in Cambodia since then.

Has it changed enough that Chanphirun might one day visit? His answer comes back without warning, offered in the same matter-of-fact way he shared information about Matthew earlier in the evening: "I just got back a month ago."

From Cambodia, the country he fought so hard to never return to. He has been going back almost every year for the last half decade. He spends a couple of weeks visiting the capital, wandering around the provinces, relaxing in tourist-friendly Siem Reap. The first time he returned was in 2007. Back then he was scared, unsure of what he would find. His home was still there just as he had left it. It looked the same. And yet it wasn't. When he left, his house was the biggest on the block; now it was the smallest. The spot where he used to practice kung fu had been walled, and where the garage was there was now another house. Then there was the roof. When he had lived in the house, the roof had been flat; now it was slanted. The changes were not altogether unexpected, at least not the roof. Before his journey he had a dream in which his mother visited him and took him to their old house. In the dream the roof was slanted. His mother was trying to show him where she had hidden some valuables, but he was distracted by the slanted roof.

In 2007 he saw the slanted roof in reality. He didn't look for the treasure, but he was looking for something, a feeling, a memory. He knocked on the door. The residents answered warily. They didn't believe his claims.

"Describe what the house looked like before," they demanded.

He did, in detail. They let him inside. Then they disappeared upstairs. They did not want to talk. They did not want to hear his story. Maybe they were scared he would want his house back. Maybe they had suffered terribly under his uncle. Or maybe they were just tired of listening to tragedies.

Chanphirun left as empty as he had entered. "I was looking for something I could feel [that] I should stay there," he says.

He didn't feel anything. Maybe whatever connection he had to the house was gone. His connection to the country is stronger. It is safe for him to visit now. The rulers may be the same, but the populace has moved on; the country's youths never even knew the genocide. The Americans are the ones he has to worry about. If they know he visits Cambodia, that it is safe for him there, he is scared they might make him stay there. It doesn't worry him enough to change his habits and to stop his yearly visits. He leaves all that up to fate, to God.

"Wherever I am, I'm supposed to be exactly where I supposed to be," he says.

Right now that is here in a corner house down the street from a liquor store. The interior walls of the house are a cheerful bright yellow, at Terry's request, and the door is red. Here in the evenings, Chanphirun enjoys a cigarette and a shot of something strong. On the refrigerator are photos of his stepdaughter, Pearl, but no one in the family calls her Pearl. They all call her by her Cambodian nickname. They live in Bellflower, not far from where Terry grew up in Downey. Long Beach is only a dozen miles away, but until Terry met Chanphirun, she knew little about the Cambodian community there. Her father kept the family removed from the Cambodians in Long Beach, taking them there only on special occasions when they had out-of-town guests as if they also were tourists visiting from far away. Maybe it was for the best.

In his Long Beach apartment, Song is in a philosophical mode. He suffered another stroke while visiting Cambodia over the summer, and it has left him contemplating religion, the afterlife, and, of course, politics.

"Most Cambodians are walking around with ghosts," says Song. "Not me. Because I not see Pol Pot."

He is dressed in medical scrubs on top and loose cotton pants below. The little plastic basket in which he stores his prescription medicine bottles is overflowing. He is having trouble standing, but his mind is sharp—and his tongue even more so.

"The Cambodians active in U.S. now uneducated, know only Pol Pot. They misunderstand current government Cambodia and call me puppet."

Song is less a puppet than an opportunist, a natural politician if there ever was one. The current leader of Cambodia, Hun Sen, may have belonged to the Khmer Rouge, but he also helped push the group from power. He may have done so with the support of the Vietnamese, but he did so nevertheless. Whatever you think of Hun Sen's past—his allies, his personality—he is the one in power at present, the one who has pretty much ruled Cambodia in one form or another since forcing the Khmer Rouge from power. That is how Song sees things. In his view, there is no point in protesting the current Cambodian government. Song would rather compromise and work with Hun Sen's people than stand on some principal, protest, and remain apart and isolated from those who hold power.

Maybe he can make the choice because he was not tortured under Pol Pot. Or maybe he just likes to stir up a bit of controversy, a bit of gossip. If you take his word for it, that is something he enjoyed even as a child.

In the little village in Cambodia where he grew up, Song says he used to carve the village gossip—who was doing what, who was sleeping with whom—on the bark of a banana tree. Then he would post it somewhere where everyone could see it. Later he wrote official press releases as a government spokesman. Now he lectures whoever will listen on Cambodia, politics, and journalism. Mostly he does this through Facebook.

He doesn't hold back in his criticisms. And others don't hold back on criticizing him. Long Beach's Cambodian community is famous for that. Even among those who support the current regime in Cambodia, there are slights and grudges. The sides are not always clear, with some survivors supporting Hun Sen. There is lots of anger, hurt, and resentment. In Song's opinion, Long Beach Cambodians are a community of damaged survivors who never successfully adapted to American life. Others see it as an example of a thriving cultural enclave that has played a role in maintaining

Cambodian art, culture, and religious traditions in the United States. Either way it is hard to ignore the community, which plays a role in politics in the States and in Cambodia.

In the beginning, when resettlement was getting under way in large numbers, Song sponsored Cambodian families, as did other Cambodians who had previously settled in the United States. At the time there had been little previous migration from Cambodia and no real substantial Cambodian community in America. Song watched the newcomers struggle to communicate, not just when they tried to express themselves linguistically, but also when trying to understand cultural norms. The Cambodians bore the legacy of French rule. They were used to French elitist attitudes.

"You know how the French are—snob, elitist, condescending and arrogant," says Song. They looked down on Cambodians, so the Cambodians were expecting Americans to do the same.

Song tried to explain that Americans weren't like that, that they tried to treat everyone the same. But the refugees struggled to understand the American people and the system they followed. In Cambodia the police and government employees are authoritarian. They don't serve the people; they serve themselves, says Song. The Cambodian refugees couldn't comprehend that government employees in the United States were there to serve them and that they could be trusted.

Of course, they had reasons not to trust the Americans. Most of them were resettled in depressed areas. In the 1980s there had been talk of spreading the Cambodian refugees out, so they would be forced to integrate more into American society. The Office of Refugee Resettlement looked for places with service agencies that could sponsor refugees, places where the refugees had friends and families, and places where there were cheap housing and entry-level jobs. The refugees themselves were drawn to areas with warmer weather that matched the climate they were accustomed to and to places where their countrymen were beginning to congregate, like Long Beach. The downside of this was that they were less likely to learn English, less likely to integrate into the larger community, and more likely to maintain the mentality of their past. Because of this, many see Cambodia with the same eyes they saw it when they left, says Song. There is only black and white for them, no gray. And when it comes to the current Cambodian government, it is all black.

According to Song, they see the bad—the trees being cut, not the trees that are still there. To be fair, there is a lot of bad to see. According to Human Rights Watch, Prime Minister Hun Sen, president of the Cambodian People's Party (CPP), is the sixth longest-serving political leader in the world, right behind Zimbabwe's Robert Mugabe. His detractors argue that Hun Sen has used violence, repression, and corruption to hold onto power for more than three decades. Among the often-cited criticisms are his role as a Khmer Rouge commander in areas where crimes against humanity were committed; his execution and imprisonment of dissidents, journalists, and political and social activists; and his participation in a bloody coup in 1997. There are more specifics: a forced labor program in the 1980s, death squads in the early 1990s, and a grenade attack on an opposition leader in 1997 in which Hun Sen's personal bodyguard was involved. He is also criticized for his obstruction of efforts to hold the Khmer Rouge responsible for international crimes.

Song is willing to overlook all of this and focus on the country's advancements: rapid economic progress in the 2000s, increased tourism and trade, and a significant reduction in the poverty rate. He sees the corruption. He knows people involved in it and others who have been harmed by it, but he excuses it, saying, "Everybody is corrupt." The government may not be good, but it is better than the other options. "Honestly, I don't think you could have a better government in these circumstances," he says.

On his last visit to Cambodia, Song talked with Hun Sen's eldest son, Hun Manet. They talk often, he says. Song advised Hun Manet to work with America. He wants the younger generation to move forward and not get stuck in the past. The past is for the old, says Song.

"That's me," he says. "That's my role. I get stuck in the past."

He believes there are bad things that the young should know, but once they learn them, he wants them to move forward and be excited about the future instead of dwelling in the past. Judge the son by his current actions, not by his father's past. It is a perspective that no doubt helped Song when he worked for Lon Nol's government. He could justify it because he felt it was the best option at the time. It was better than the Khmer Rouge. And that excused the corruption, the repression, the mismanagement, the utter incompetence. The Americans did the same and continue to do the same in so many countries they support, propping up one political party simply to keep another they deem worse at bay. Maybe there was, or is, no better option. Song has no regrets.

The next morning the girlfriend Song calls his wife serves him instant coffee, toast, cookies, and bacon. As he piles bacon on top of his peanut butter toast, Song boasts about having friends who were in the Khmer Rouge. On his cell phone is a picture of another friend, an American man who has spent decades trying to help Cambodian deportees. They worked together for a time. Now they are both white haired. Bill Herod lives in the jungle with a monkey, or he did until the monkey recently died. Song lives in an urban city surrounded by people, by an audience he is eager to capture. When the conversation lulls he throws out another enticing tidbit, hoping his guest will snatch it and stay seated at the table. The founders of Long Beach's Cambodia Town are embroiled in a financial scandal. He knows one of them; they are friends or were friends. He is cagey about his current alliances. Careful about passing full judgment, he is always leaving his options open, especially when it comes to powerful people.

The young are easier to impress. He refers to the young ones who grew up in Cambodia and know how to respect their elders, not the American-raised middle generation, those Khmer Rouge survivors who have returned to Cambodia to rule. They drive fancy cars and forget to offer to show Song around, even though he has no driver, no vehicle, no way of moving around. Then in talking about some of the founders of Cambodia Town again, their alleged financial indiscretions seem less important to him than their social slight. He is old and sick and in danger of being forgotten, something he was reminded of once again when he had his stroke in Cambodia.

It was after his girlfriend had returned to California. He was on his own. Family and friends visited while he was in the hospital. Friends posted about his status on Facebook, asking for people to pray for him. He slipped in and out of consciousness. He had strange conversations with people he hadn't seen in years. When he was awake, he marveled at how the system had collapsed, at how the French would be disgusted at the state of Cambodia's hospitals. There was no nearby bathroom he could access. In the United States he might have been scared by his condition, but in Cambodia there was little he could do, so he accepted it. He listened half awake as relatives spoke about the process of dying. It was as if his death had been decided. He understood their thinking, because in Buddhism how you die is important. Like Chanphirun, Song was once a Buddhist and remains one partially while also professing to be a Christian. He believes in the moral guidelines of Buddhism but not the religion itself, not the spiritual component. Still when he was sick, he prayed in both religions, covering his bases as he always does.

Then when he was better, he attacked the Buddhist teachings on attachment. He wrote a column about the Buddhist goal of eliminating attachment, because attachment causes suffering. In this way Buddhists are supposed to be free. And yet, when you are dying, there are no attachments to worry about, says Song. When you are dying, you don't have any energy for attachment. In that moment, you are just kind of floating around, and you have nothing to cling to, to attach yourself to, to anchor yourself.

"You just sort of float around and then fade into emptiness. That's what death is," says Song.

From this experience, he decided attachment gives life, not suffering. Attachment is what Christians call love. He defines attachment his own way. And in his version, attachment is life.

12

THE MEDICINE MAN

Phumi Chak Toch, Cambodia, 1979.

Sithea was dying, again. Her hair had fallen out, her stomach was swollen, and her lips were no longer able to cover her mouth as her flesh had become so wasted. Bed bugs crawled over her half-naked body. She was in the hospital, lying on a bamboo strip bed. Her pants had been removed so her diarrhea could pass directly onto the floor.

When San had last visited her middle daughter the week before, Sithea had been frightened. She cried, convinced the ghosts of the dead were coming to take her away. She said she heard them at night in the hoots of the owls. Now the eleven-year-old girl asked her mother to be sure to bury her after she died. She had seen the wolves eat the bodies left in the rice fields, and she didn't want that to happen to her body after she died.

San sat and looked at her daughter. Sithea was wasting away, barely more than a skeleton, and there was nothing she could do for her: no food she could give her, no medicine she could offer her, no help she could promise her. They had been living under the Khmer Rouge more than three years now, and San knew better than to hope. She put Sithea's bald, bug-covered head in her lap and prayed. She talked to her daughter. She cried with her daughter. Her presence was all she could offer the girl, and even that was limited by her work duties.

Then she remembered that there might be one thing she could do. The village medicine man was in love with her. As an old person who had been a peasant even before the Khmer Rouge made everyone peasants, the medicine man was treated relatively well by the Khmer Rouge and his fellow villagers. They called him Ta Meng. He was around sixty-five years old and ugly. Months ago when San had arrived in the village, he had asked her to marry him. She had turned him down. San did not know where the girls' father was, and she did not find Ta Meng the least bit attractive.

Now she thought of him again. If Ta Meng could save Sithea, San decided she would marry him.

Southern California, December 2015–January 2016.

The first text arrived early in the afternoon on Thursday, December 31: "his katya center this is sithy yi I have a bad news my stepfather Tom courcher he at the life support right now he don't have that much time."

The next text came three days later, on January 3, 2016. It was just as breathless and grammatically challenged: "Tom gone from us already we never see him again I'm not his kids but the way he take care me and my children like his own kids what eve I do right or rong he alway Sport me and tall me do the right way he's passed away on New Year at afternoon and my mom see will make a funeral on December [January] 14th on Thursday I miss him."

There were no more texts after that. It was several months before I spoke with San. It was as if no time had passed at all.

"After Tom pass I feel like bird with broken wings," she said. "I don't know what to do anymore."

Despite all the death she had experienced in her life, Tom's death hit San hard. Death, she said, doesn't come the way we expect it. She knew Tom was old and that he was sick, but she didn't think he would die now. He had been bleeding in his rectum. The doctors discovered something in his colon and decided they needed to remove it. Before the surgery, Tom told her they would take a trip to Australia once he recovered. San knew Australia was too difficult a journey for someone in Tom's fragile health, but she wanted him to believe it, so she played along.

The first day after the surgery, Tom was fine. The second day, he was still okay. The third day, everything failed at the same time: his kidneys, his liver, his heart. San kept expecting him to get up, but he didn't.

When she returns from grocery shopping now, she still anticipates seeing him leaning on his walker, waiting for her by the door, telling her how much he missed her while she was gone. The spacious home echoes with silence. The never-ending kitchen is all but useless. San no longer cooks, as the person she cooked for is gone and she has no taste. She can't eat at the table; all she sees when she sits there is Tom's empty chair. So she eats in front of the TV or at her granddaughter Lauren's home. The television and the great-grandchildren distract her from the hole she can't seem to fill. Even the cockatoo seems depressed. During the day, San powers through, but at night she can't seem to stop crying.

Then there are the practical matters. Tom took care of all the details involved in living in modern-day America. He handled the taxes, he hired the lawyer to take care of Sithy's deportation case, and he took charge of the stacks of files in the garage. Now San has to sort through all the papers and figure out how to survive on her own when she can't even write an email. Taxes are beyond her. The boxes and file cabinets of papers are too immense for her to even contemplate. She has no idea where to start and no one to tell her what to do. Lauren promised to help sort the files, but San doesn't even know where to begin. It is all from Tom's business, and she doesn't know what needs to be kept and what can be thrown away, what needs to be shredded, and what can be recycled.

"People tell me I am strong, but right now I am not," she says.

She has handled life without a husband before—under the Khmer Rouge, in America. Tom was not her only partner; there were two before him. He wasn't a young love she has never lived without. They were only married a little longer than two decades; yet, in that time, she learned to let someone else take care of her, to trust someone with her life in a way she had never been able to do in her previous relationships. Tom and San were from different cultures. Their backgrounds didn't match up, but Tom made an effort to learn about San's world and help her negotiate his. With Tom's passing, San lost all sense of security.

Toward the end, when he was on life support and in pain, the doctor told San that Tom wasn't going to make it. San knew she should take him off life support, but she couldn't sign the paper. She remembers thinking that she didn't know how to survive by herself. She held his hand as he died.

Even though she had lost plenty of family members and friends, this was different. Tom was dying in a real hospital, a hospital where people were saved. It wasn't like the Khmer Rouge hospitals, where people went to die. American hospitals healed people, and Tom had just been going in for surgery. He wasn't supposed to die. Tom had always been there when she needed him. The same couldn't be said for the men who came before him.

While she and her daughters suffered under the Khmer Rouge, the girls' father was outside the country. Later she learned that he had married another woman. Her marriage to the medicine man was not one she had ever desired. But she had kept her promise. After the medicine man saved Sithea, San had married him.

Cambodia, 1978–79.

The marriage marked an improvement in San's life under the Khmer Rouge. Before she married Ta Meng, she was starving. She was sent to and from various locations in the rice fields to work: building dikes, planting seedlings, and harvesting the fields. She spent days, weeks—there was no real point in keeping track of time—harvesting rice during the rainy season. They slept under the open sky and labored in flooded fields, leeches locking onto their legs. While working, they were not allowed to remove the leeches. It was only at night, after they had finished harvesting and had climbed out of the flooded fields, that they could pull the bloodsucking animals from their legs. It was painful and left marks, scars she still has to this day. Sithy was the one who told her about putting saliva on the back of the leeches before removing them. The saliva caused the leeches to back out, making it easier to pull them off.

Sometimes the degree to which her daughters had adapted frightened San. Little Jennifer, the baby of the family who had been in private school before the Khmer Rouge, lit up when she caught a frog and broke its legs. San could only partially cook it before they ate it, but the girl was still over-joyed, proud of having found food for herself and her mother. That was what hunger did to you. That is what the Khmer Rouge had done to them. They were more animal than human.

They spent all their time harvesting rice, but they never got enough for themselves. The harvest was sent elsewhere, and they remained hungry, receiving only two small bowls of rice mixed with wild plants a day. At night, under the cover of darkness, people started picking the wild snow peas that grew near the rice fields. It was forbidden to take the wild vegetables for their personal use. The punishment for defying the order was death.

The girls decided to go one night anyway. They were starving, and the snow peas meant food. The night they went local guards raided the area. San waited for the girls in their shelter, hoping the guards would not come by and ask where her daughters were. She knew if her daughters noticed the guards before the guards noticed them, then they had a chance of escaping. All she could do was hope and wait, even though hope was something she knew better than to believe in. She waited alone, in silence. After many hours, Sithy and Sithea came home. Jennifer was not with them.

Her youngest daughter could not see at night, probably caused by malnutrition, and was dependent on her older sisters to lead her around. Sithy and Sithea explained that while they were hiding from the guards, they had become separated. After the guards left, they called for their little sister. She didn't answer. They looked all around. Jennifer wasn't anywhere. They reasoned that either Jennifer had made it home on her own or she had been captured. Either way standing among the snow peas was not going to bring their sister back, so they went back to the shelter, hoping they would find Jennifer there. She wasn't there. They waited for her the rest of the night. She never came.

They assumed she had been caught. Then, in the morning, when there was light, Jennifer returned. The little girl explained what had happened. When she heard the commotion caused by the guards, she hid. Once the guards were gone, she realized she was lost and had no way of finding her way in the dark. She didn't hear her sisters calling her. So she waited in her hiding space all night. Only when it was morning and there was enough light for her to see once again was she able to walk back to the shelter. It had been a long night for all of them, but they were safe now. They had escaped capture once again. They knew the next time they might not be as lucky.

San was not as good at evading capture as her daughters. Her current job was to carry rice from the fields to the camp in a basket on her head. She had heard that some people had successfully hid some of the rice for themselves and gotten away with it. So she learned how they did it and followed suit, making a little packet in which she could place a small amount of rice and hide it in her hat, which hung down her back while she carried the rice bucket on her head. She made it successfully back to camp. She was placing her rice basket down for inspection when the secret rice packet fell out of her hat. The response was immediate. She was whisked off to the camp commander and interrogated.

"How many times did you do this?" he asked.

San answered him truthfully: "This is my first time."

"You know you will be punished for this," he said. "So why did you do it?"

"Because I am hungry," she replied. "I will never do it again."

He headed out, telling her on his way, "I will pronounce your sentence when I return."

Several hours passed. San knew that the punishment for her crime was death. She had seen it happen to others. There was a military base a few miles away with a network of spies, or "recons." People like her—new people, or April Seventeenth people—were disappearing. Bodies and body parts were found in the rice fields, on the walking paths. There were rumors that before being killed, you were asked to dig your own grave. When people went missing their families never mentioned it, fearful of what would happen to them. San had seen all of this. She knew how people such as herself were treated.

The camp commander returned. "Was this really your first time doing this?" he asked again.

"Yes, it was."

"Will you do it again?"

"No," San said. And she meant it. She would not risk her life like this again.

"I am going to release you. But next time you will be killed."

There would be no next time for San. Sithy was different. No matter how many times she was caught, she continued to steal. She was beaten and abused but never killed, so she kept gambling, believing she had made herself too valuable to the Khmer Rouge for them to kill her. San had not gotten as close to the Khmer Rouge, so she played it safe. At least she did until Sithea got sick the second time. Then she gambled her life in a different way.

When Sithea was sick the first time, San used her last piece of jewelry to buy Sithea two antibiotic pills. Sithea had gotten better but never fully regained her strength. Now Sithea had diarrhea again. She was losing what little weight she had. Her body was weak and wasted, unable to perform the manual labor the Khmer Rouge required. Because she couldn't work, again she got less food. With less food, she grew even weaker. Sithea was staying in the shelter while the rest of her family had been sent to various locations to work. When she could, San walked three hours from her work site to the shelter and gave Sithea some of her own food. Sithy gave some of her food as well.

One evening when she visited, San found Sithea cold, weak, and alone. Sithea had placed a cloth on her bald head in a desperate attempt to keep warm. She could barely walk and told her mother she wasn't sure if she could survive. San fed her, hugged her, and urged her to visit the medicine man in the morning. Then she made the three-hour hike back to her work location so she would be there in the morning when they counted everybody.

It was another week before San could get away again. This time she found Sithea in the hospital, even worse off than before. That is when San sent word to the medicine man that she would marry him if he could save Sithea. He came as soon as he heard. He brought Sithea two antibiotic pills and a small amount of food.

As they had before, the pills stopped Sithea's diarrhea, and she was able to keep down food. A week later Sithea was well enough to work, and San married the medicine man. He may not have been good looking, but he was kind and life was easier as his wife. San and her daughters' social standing was elevated now that they were associated with an old person. Life was still difficult—Sithy and Jennifer were sent away to work—but San and Sithea were allowed to live in the medicine man's home.

Not long after her marriage, San began to see soldiers. The soldiers were from a different area. They stayed only long enough for their wounds and injuries to be treated. The medicine man cared for the wounded, and in return the soldiers treated the family well. It was 1979. Time passed and the number of soldiers increased. They could hear gunfire in the village. It grew closer.

Something was going on, but what? There was no way to know. There were rumors that the Vietnamese had invaded. Before they could be confirmed, the village was evacuated, and San and the others were told to move to a nearby mountain. San told the medicine man to go ahead without her. She would find him once Sithy and Jennifer returned from their work locations. She didn't want to leave without them. She planned to meet the medicine man again later once she had all her daughters with her, but they never found each other again.

Once Sithy and Jennifer returned, they started walking. San and her daughters walked for a month, sleeping in fields at night. The Khmer Rouge were less strict now. The girls could gather plants and whatever small animals they could find to eat and not worry about guards punishing them for it. Rumors that the Khmer Rouge were fleeing from the Vietnamese became more common. Finally San figured out that the rumors were true. She backtracked toward the Vietnamese. The Khmer Rouge were mostly gone by this time, having fled toward the Thai border, and San thought maybe the Vietnamese would be able to help her with work and food. Reaching them posed its own problems. They had to cross a bridge near Battambang, the agricultural hub in the northwest. Before fleeing, the Khmer Rouge were said to have mined the bridge. San and the others had to be careful to walk only in the middle of the bridge, lest they set off an explosion. They arrived safely, but the Vietnamese had nothing to offer San—no jobs and no food.

Sithy climbed mango trees and picked fruit for them. To avoid the painful red ants that bit her when she climbed the trees, she covered herself in ash. They walked for hours to dig up cassavas, which they exchanged for rice. When the cassavas ran out, they did the same with sugar cane. Then the sugar cane ran out. They had been there about three months, sleeping in the fields, walking for hours and days to harvest whatever they could, and then returning to exchange it for rice. During this time they had noticed people bringing back items from Thailand to trade. It was a two- to three-week walk to Thailand, too far to bring things back and forth without a bike. San had heard about a camp near the Thai border and decided to go, check it out, and see if it would be safe for her and her daughters to live there and possibly engage in trade closer to the border.

The route to Camp 007, or Nong Samet, passed through the jungle. San had to avoid both Vietnamese and Khmer Rouge patrols. She walked for days in the mud, barefoot. She walked in the exact footsteps of those who had made the trip before her so she wouldn't step on a land mine. Along the way she lost all of her toenails. After she decided it was safe for her daughters, she returned to them and made the trek once again. Again Sithy found a bicycle on which to help transport her mother and sisters.

Close to the border they had to step over two bodies. A guide took them and several dozen others through the jungle past two Vietnamese patrol lines. They hid in the bush, watched the first patrol line pass, and then ran quietly past. Then there was a river. Jennifer crossed on Sithy's shoulders.

They stayed in Nong Samet about four months. It was here that Sithy proved her business savvy, selling first little items like water and candles, then moving up to tobacco, and finally clothes. In this way she made enough for them to buy food and survive. But they knew they couldn't live there forever. They were considering moving to the camps in Thailand when another camp launched rockets on Nong Samet. Running from the rocket attack, they ran into another camp, one controlled by a rogue group of fighters who would not let them leave. The camp was fenced off, and the men who guarded the perimeter were armed. When they tried to exit, the guards shot at their feet. To get out, they would need to trick the guards. Sithy was the one who decided this—and was the one who came up with the lie that would allow them to leave.

Sithy went first, approaching a guard and telling him she had become separated from her mother and needed to find her. The guard let her go, warning her not to go far and to come back quickly after finding her mother. Sithea and Jennifer were next, they each approached a different guard. Then it was San's turn. She used the same story only in reverse; she had lost her children and needed to go look for them. Again she was told it was okay to go but not too far.

As soon as she was out, San went to the prearranged hiding place where her daughters were waiting. Then together they ran quietly for the Thai border. They arrived at a pagoda in Thailand on the afternoon of January 5, 1980.

Red Cross trucks took them to Khao I Dang refugee camp in Thailand. The refugee camp operated from 1979 to 1993, housing nearly 140,000 refugees in bamboo and thatched house shelters at its peak. At Khao I Dang, San and her daughters were given mosquito nets, material to build a simple shelter, blankets, and food. At the camp, life was peaceful in the way a jail is peaceful, for the camp was surrounded by barbed wire, and they were not allowed to leave. They stayed about a year. The girls began to put on weight and took up traditional Cambodian dancing. They were basically healthy and happy. San was now the sick one. She had always suffered from asthma, but now it became worse, with nightly attacks that made it difficult for her to sleep. Breathing was torturous.

During the day, San wrote letters. For the first time in years she had to think about their future, about more than just surviving. They needed a place to stay permanently. They also needed a sponsor who would vouch for them so they could leave the camp. The girls' father was the logical person, but she had no idea where he was. He had been working as a merchant marine, had spent time in Germany and Paris, and during the Khmer Rouge takeover had been working on a ship in Singapore. She thought maybe she could find him through his friend in Paris, but all she had was a name. Then she ran into a man she used to work with who told her their old boss was in Paris. She wrote to him, telling him about the girls' father and his friend. A month later two letters arrived.

The first was from the girls' father. He promised to have his friend send them $100. He told San that her brother, James, was in the United States and that her parents were both still alive. He promised to find her father's address and write him. The second letter was also from the girls' father. Again he promised $100. Then he told San he could not sponsor her or their daughters because he had assumed they were dead and had married another woman.

Her best hope now was her brother, James. Her father had already contacted James, and several weeks later James wrote to San and asked for all their information so he could sponsor them. He also asked about his wife and children. San told him she didn't know what had happened to them.

They then went to another camp, Kamput Holding Center in Thailand, a processing center for immigration to the United States. The center was run by the Thai military, whose rules were harsh: lights out at 6:00 p.m.; no radios or any other noise after lights out. A friend of the girls was beaten for accidently leaving on his radio. Accusations against the Thai military controlling the centers included indiscriminate violence, abuse of the refugees, and rape. They stayed three months, or until about May 1981.

San's asthma grew even worse, and she became so desperate she tried a local remedy—rice liquor and burned toad. It worked. Sithy was not so lucky. At the center, Sithy's seizures began in earnest. Under the Khmer Rouge, Sithy first started experiencing blackouts but not like this. Now she would be doing something ordinary, such as walking with friends, and the next thing she knew she was in the hospital. The seizures started to occur every few days. Sometimes they came at night, after a bad dream. Sithy would wake up shaking and then go into a frenzy, falling on the floor, unable to breath, her hands and head flapping around violently. Her neck would expand, her face would go red, and her strength would become so great it took three people to hold her down and prevent her from hurting herself. The only way the doctors were able to stop the seizures was by drugging her, knocking her out for hours with medicine. There was no explanation for the seizures. San didn't need one; she believed they were a result of the beatings Sithy received under the Khmer Rouge.

Their next stop was another camp in the Philippines. Sithy's seizures came almost daily now and were even more severe. In August 1981 they arrived in California, where James was living with his new wife. San wasn't surprised to see that he had remarried. No one, including her, believed his first wife could have survived. A young woman on her own with a newborn baby and two very young children had almost no chance to endure the hardships of the Khmer Rouge years. James had worked in intelligence in Lon Nol's army and had been out of the country when the Khmer Rouge took power. But his journey was not without difficulty. He had made it to California but ended up in a camp, not a home. He had to be sponsored out of Camp Pendleton, and the group that did so was the Mormon Church, for whom he had translated the Bible into Khmer years before while in Bangkok. It was through a Mormon contact that James sent letters looking for his wife. Then he got in a bad car accident in California that left him unable to work. He lost his job at a grocery store and got kicked out of the place where he was living. A Cambodian woman took pity on him and took him in. He later married the woman's daughter. That is the abbreviated version San tells.

The version they continued to tell themselves involved the death of James's first wife and three children. In the late 1980s, when Cambodians began returning to Cambodia to search for relatives and look for business opportunities, San still clung to this version. A friend who had traveled to Cambodia told her he had a friend at a radio station that broadcast information for missing family members. He told San she should look for James's wife. San told him she was dead.

"Don't assume that," he said. "Give me her name and a letter for her, and I will give it to my friend working at the radio station."

San wrote the name. James wrote the letter. The radio announcer located James's first family. They were living in a province near Thailand, a province that Thailand and Cambodia continually fought over, making it hard to know to which country it belonged and hard to know how to find people who lived there. They had all survived: James's wife, his two daughters, and the son he had never met. His wife had not remarried. In 1990 San went to visit them. James was working during the day and going to school at night, his second wife was working as a nurse, and they were raising several children of their own. James couldn't go to Cambodia, but he gave San $3,000 to give to his first family. It was a lot of money at the time, and San had no idea how he had managed to save it. When she gave it to James's wife, her sister-in-law didn't even smile. When San tried to hug her, she didn't hug her back.

"She wanted her husband. Got me instead," says San.

James's second wife back in California became equally distant toward San. Both women blamed San for the awkward situation. San didn't blame anyone.

"It's so hard. . . . I don't blame her, and I don't blame James," she says. "Because during the time the situation different, people try to survive one way or another."

After San's visit, James sponsored his first family so they could come to California. One of his daughters had already married and did not want to come, but the other daughter and his son did. Now both live in Long Beach. His first wife came to visit, but she didn't want to stay. Whenever she saw James, she would say something to hurt him, to make him feel guilty, says San. Still when his second wife died young, leaving James with five young children, James thought about returning to his first wife. San warned him against it. She could see that her former sister-in-law would never be able to forgive her brother and would just make his life miserable. So she advised him, "Let the past life go."

San's former sister-in-law never told them what had happened to her and the children under the Khmer Rouge after she became separated from San and San's sister Rinh. Later, when San spoke with Rinh, she pieced some of the story together. After San was separated from them, Rinh and James's wife remained together. They were assigned to work at a location not very far from where San was at the time, but because no one was allowed to leave either location, they never saw each other. One day when Rinh went to work in the fields, James's wife was allowed to stay behind and watch the baby and do easier work. When Rinh returned from the fields, she was gone. Rinh had no idea where she went. Had the Khmer Rouge come and killed her and her children? Had she been sent to another location to work? Had she died of exhaustion or heartache? Today they still don't know how she got to the province near the Thai border or what she endured along the way.

Rinh remained alone from then until now. She is older than ninety years of age and lives in the family home in Vietnam. She became a Buddhist nun years ago. None of her children survived the Khmer Rouge years. She learned the fate of three of them but not of the fourth. They were young adults and sent to different work locations. Her younger son was sent out of his village on an errand one day. Ron—San believes that was his name, but she can no longer remember for sure—came across his older brother while on his errand. The older brother was in a field with several Khmer Rouge soldiers. As Ron passed, his brother called out to him.

"Ron, can you tell mom I go?" he said. "Just say that—'I'm going.'"

Nothing else needed to be said. They both knew the soldiers were about to kill him.

The next child, a girl whose real name San cannot recall, became sick with bloody diarrhea and died. But the youngest one died first. She had always had a temper and was the kind of kid who talked back when you told her to do something. "That's why they kill [her] early," says San.

The Khmer Rouge dumped her body in the Mekong River. The body got stuck in branches by the shore. Someone who knew Rinh recognized the girl and told Rinh what had happened to her.

"The last one, we don't know, we don't know. He just missing," says San.

She has had announcements made on the radio in Cambodia many times for him. If he was alive, she believes he would have answered. So she assumes he is dead. Rinh is the only one left. She came to visit when Tom was alive. Tom enjoyed telling stories about how the cockatoo liked to sit on Rinh's shoulder. Now it's 2016, and Tom is gone.

Accommodations have been made, cards sent, the funeral planned. Sithy's court date was postponed until May 31. With all of that out of the way, San has had the time to dwell on Tom's absence in a way she was never able to dwell on death before. It made her think about her sister Rinh. She has James in California. He is on his third wife now; they live nearby and stop by often. But James doesn't always understand San when she talks about the Khmer Rouge because "he wasn't there." Rinh was. They weren't together, but they were both there.

Now San wants to go back to Southeast Asia for the last time. She wants to see Rinh before she dies.

13

EXPIRED

Sweat began to pour down Puthy Hak's face. In an instant he was soaking wet, as if he had just stepped out of a shower. He wanted to talk, but he couldn't form words. His body was frozen, unable to move. He could hear his dialysis machine beeping loudly. He knew what the warning sound meant: his blood pressure had dropped dangerously low, with his systolic reading down to 56. Puthy watched a biomedical technician adjust the machine and noticed his blood pressure began to creep back up. The whole time he was aware of what was going on, but he was unable to do anything about it, as if his body no longer belonged to him.

It had happened before. And it would probably happen again. At the center where Puthy usually goes for dialysis, he often hears the biomedical technicians calling "wake up, wake up" when someone blacks out as a result of low blood pressure. A sudden drop in blood pressure is not uncommon among dialysis patients, and over time these incidents can contribute to strokes, seizures, heart damage, and death. Once Puthy's blood pressure went the other way, soaring past 200. That time he had to be taken to the hospital.

The other week when he went in for his regular Friday dialysis treatment, he noticed that one of the other regulars, a man Puthy considered stronger than himself, was missing. "What happened to him?" Puthy asked.

"Oh, he's gone," replied a technician.

Puthy knew that happened, that patients died. He had experienced the loss once before. But it still came as a surprise to him that a man who had looked fine on Wednesday could be gone by Friday. It was less of a surprise to Michael Chua, the living donor nurse-coordinator at the University of California (UC)-San Diego Health who works with Puthy and Touch. "The longer you are on dialysis, the higher your chance of dying from being on dialysis a long time," said Michael.

Dialysis can only do about 10 percent of the work that a kidney can do, according to Beth Israel Deaconess Medical Center of Boston. In addition, it can often cause other serious health problems, such as infection, anemia, bone disease, heart disease, and nerve damage. Life expectancy for dialysis patients is not good—five years and as long as ten years for the lucky. During that time one out of every four dialysis patients dies of a heart attack. Puthy has been on dialysis almost four years.

Santa Ana, California, mid-December 2015.

Touch is still here. His expiration date has been extended. That is what he calls it, his "expiration," meaning the day last August when his one-year stay of deportation ended. August 5—that is the date he remembers, although there have been so many important dates in the last year that he has trouble keeping them straight. He thinks it was August 8 when Immigration and Customs Enforcement denied his request for a second one-year stay of deportation. He knows it was in September when they approved it. He also knows that now he won't be deported to Cambodia until September 2016.

It was not an easy road to get here. According to his lawyer, Jacqueline Dan, most people don't make it at all. People submit stays of removal or deportation, they pay the filing fee, and they're denied. "In general, stays of removal, ICE just doesn't grant them," she said.

Someone with a criminal history such as Touch, who is "an enforcement priority"—top of the list to be deported because of his drug charges—is even less likely to get a stay of removal. It just doesn't ever happen, said Jacqueline.

And yet, it has, twice. But for Touch, the extension still isn't enough. Touch needs to stay in the United States so he can help his older brother, Puthy, who has kidney failure. They aren't a match, but they could participate in a paired exchange. However, the transplant team at UC-San Diego Health won't accept Touch into the program unless it is assured he won't be deported for at least two years. And ICE won't grant Touch more than a year's stay unless he is accepted into the transplant program. So Touch waits, once again, while his future is tied up in bureaucracy. It is stressful, but the one-year stay of deportation has given him a little breathing room. Before that, "it was a rough ride," he says.

We are sitting in Puthy's Santa Ana living room, with a Los Angeles Laker's basketball game playing on the expansive flat screen television. Touch is wearing his usual pageboy hat. On his left wrist is one of those trendy rubber bracelets. Touch spent the last few months constantly wondering, "They gonna take me or what?"

The question was for ICE, but it could have been for the transplant team at UC–San Diego Health as well. The answer he wanted from each was very different.

At first everything seemed to be going against Touch after his initial one-year stay of deportation was granted in 2014. He had to jump through so many hoops that he didn't find out until shortly before his stay was up that he wasn't a donor match for his brother. On the medical side, he had two options—paired exchange and incompatible blood match. If the donor and recipient have matching or compatible blood types, there is less risk of organ rejection. If they are not a match, like Puthy and Touch, the donor can still donate. There is a way to remove some of the harmful antibodies before the organ is transplanted, but the procedure is still rare and more complicated for the recipient. Touch pretty much eliminated that option. That left paired kidney exchange, which would match Touch and Puthy with another incompatible donor-patient pair. The idea is to match Touch with a patient paired with a donor who is a match for Puthy.

"What they do is just find the connection, just like a dating site," says Touch.

When he first heard the analogy, he laughed. He still smiles as he explains how the whole thing works similar to dating websites. A caseworker with the transplant center explained the advantages to Touch. The wait time for Puthy for a deceased donor's kidney through the National Kidney Registry could be longer than seven years. The wait time for a living donor's kidney through a paired exchange is around one to two years. The exchange takes place when a donor is not able to donate to the intended patient because the donor is not a match due to blood type or antibody incompatibility. The pair is then matched with another pair in an exchange that allows the donor from one pair to donate to the recipient from the other pair and vice versa. As a pair, Puthy and Touch would also be eligible to be considered for a chain, which is made possible when one altruistic person donates a kidney without a particular recipient in mind, setting off a chain of donations involving paired exchanges.

In addition to the shorter wait time, the living donor option has other advantages. Because there is more warning prior to the operation, the recipient is better prepared physically to receive the kidney. Kidneys from a live donor also tend to last longer, said Michael Chua, or around fourteen to twenty years instead of the ten to twelve years for a deceased donor's kidney. For Puthy that means taking immunosuppressant drugs for the life of the kidney.

Touch's postsurgical prognosis would be less complicated. Many people live completely normal lives with just one kidney, said Michael. Recovery time is minimal, with most donors spending only two days in the hospital after the operation. The biggest complaint donors have is often the postoperative gas pain from when they were inflated for the operation and not the procedure itself, said Michael. The surgery is minimally invasive; four small incisions are made so instruments can be inserted to perform the surgery underneath the skin.

Of course, with any surgery, there is always the chance of complications. Issues can also develop afterward, so the transplant team follows the donor for two years after the operation. This is a problem because Touch is nearing the end of his year's pass to stay in the United States. When Touch told the case worker this, she explained that just conducting all the medical tests to clear him for the procedure would take six to eight months. Then she told him she would need to notify her supervisor about Touch's immigration status. She promised to get back to him.

"It didn't take long," says Touch.

A day or two later they declined him. Unless he had documentation from ICE saying he wouldn't be deported during the process, they couldn't do it. He had already asked ICE for one stay of deportation; asking for another seemed out of the question. In the back of his mind he thought, "It's over. It's done." Part of him wanted to take off, to just leave it all. Then he thought of Puthy and knew he had to stick with it. He listened to Jacqueline and the others who had taken up his case, including those at the Southeast Asia Resource Action Center. He visited politicians and asked them to write letters of support to ICE. SEARAC started a petition, circulating it on Facebook and generating hundreds of signatures. Eventually he received another one-year stay.

That is when the kidney program denied him a second time.

"You know; one year is not enough time," they told him.

"So, like, what else?" Touch hits his hands together, emphasizing the finality. "What else can I do?"

As an individual, maybe not much. But with the backing of SEARAC and Jacqueline, who is with the national legal and civil rights organization Asian Americans Advancing Justice in Los Angeles, quite a bit. The exact sequence of events is murky because everything seemed to happen at once for Touch. It definitely happened quickly. SEARAC flew Touch to Washington DC for a whirlwind three-day visit during which he met with numerous politicians, members of Congress, California representatives. In one day he went into half a dozen different offices, each time telling his story as briefly as he could. Katrina Dizon Mariategue, SEARAC's immigration policy manager, tried to coach him through it. She advised him to rehearse his speech ahead of time. He couldn't do it; he just told his story the only way he knew how, the way it came out.

Some of the people working in the offices had already heard of him. "How is Puthy doing?" they asked.

Touch wondered how they knew. The media and advocacy campaigns carried out on his behalf had clearly left a mark. Politicians agreed to write letters of support for him. In November Touch found out ICE would offer him an additional two-year stay if the kidney program accepted him. It was good news, but Touch still didn't know how the transplant center would respond. The more he learned about the program, the less likely he thought it was that they would be able to complete everything in even three years. There were no dates set for any operation, as nothing was for sure. It could be five years, or it could be five months, or it could be much longer. Touch didn't have much hope of being accepted into the program. Still he waited to see how the center would respond.

Three days later the center called back to say it would conditionally accept him. Once he has passed some basic physical tests and his brother's health insurance has confirmed that it will cover him, the program would officially accept Touch. After that happens, ICE could officially extend his stay of removal. The process is convoluted and confusing, and like most lay people, Touch doesn't totally understand what exactly happened.

"He was trying to explain it to people in the office yesterday," said Jacqueline. "He was very cute. He was like, 'I mean, I'm very thankful, but there's still a lot I don't know.'"

Even Jacqueline doesn't know everything. Touch was originally released from immigration detention, she said, because his flight to Cambodia had been canceled, and he had already been detained for around five months. She isn't exactly sure how the flight was canceled, but she believes it was the result of advocacy done on the ground in Cambodia on Touch's behalf. SEARAC and a number of community organizations had been working hard to spread Touch's story to the media, and quite a few publications had picked it up. Advocacy groups in the United States also reached out to advocacy groups in Cambodia. Who exactly pulled the strings, Jacqueline doesn't know.

"Probably some backdoor advocacy based on some relationships they have, which they want to protect, which I respect," she said. "Obviously it's working and it's helping people, so I'm not going to pry."

Touch filed his first application for a stay of removal on his own. It is a relatively simple process. Using a form on a website, you present information on why you think your deportation should be delayed. Depending on what you say and what the agency feels, ICE can grant or deny it. There's really no legal standard, said Jacqueline; it's really up to ICE. Touch's original application, the one he did on his own, was not very good. The explanation was a single sentence.

He was denied.

Jacqueline filed another for him shortly after his flight was canceled, and he was released from detention. That is when he was granted his first one-year stay. Jacqueline also helped with his second, more recent stay. In the letter, when the agency finally granted his stay, ICE mentions a liver transplant, not a kidney, which had Jacqueline wondering how much attention it was spending on the case if it couldn't even identify the right organ.

Like Touch, Jacqueline said at first it was looking as if Touch would be denied. Then they went to the office of U.S. congresswoman Loretta Sanchez of California's Garden Grove District. After their visit they were told her office had sent a letter to ICE. Not long after that, Touch's second one-year stay was granted. Around the same time, Touch took off for Washington DC. While Touch was advocating for himself in the country's capital, Jacqueline was following up with politicians, explaining the language the hospital would need from ICE to allow Touch into the program. She believes these politicians then forwarded that information to ICE so ICE could include it in a revised letter, which it submitted, a result that she again noted was far from typical. Even with the extraordinary facts of the case—with Touch allowed to stay, he would essentially save the life of a U.S. citizen—the first stay of deportation and both applications had been initially denied, said Jacqueline.

"In general, it's extremely difficult to win a favorable [ruling], especially because his drug conviction makes it what's called an enforcement priority," she said. "And a three-year stay of removal has never happened."

The longest previous one, she believes, was two years, and even that is rare. The usual period is one year. The problem is, even with the extra time, Puthy may still not get his transplant in time. If that happens, they will request another stay. It is a long-term, ongoing case, said Jacqueline, but for right now she has done all she can do.

"The rest is dependent on his insurance and his own personal health. Assuming those two things check out, he and Puthy will be enrolled in the program," she said, "which means his brother has a shot at getting a living donor."

And Touch will be given his official additional two-year extension. What needs to happen now is that he must get cleared by the insurance company so he can begin the battery of tests that will determine if he is healthy enough to donate. Touch is doing what he can to make sure he passes, going to the gym five days a week to lift weights and do a little running. In prison he did calisthenics—push-ups, body weight exercises—but not free weights. The free weights are what get Touch pumped, help him relieve stress. They are something he can control.

When he started a year ago, he could bench press less than 200 pounds, maybe 165. Now he is up in the mid-200 range. His goal is 300. He works out in the morning, biking to the gym before his afternoon shift as a machine operator in a small factory. He makes minimum wage, $9 an hour, which does not help him save much for when he goes to Cambodia. That is when he thinks he will need the money more. People tell him Cambodia is good now; it's okay. He knows that means it is good if you have money. "But if you going over there with no money and no family out there, how you going to survive?"

He doesn't want to have to depend on his family over there. He is a man; he needs to take care of himself. It is a refrain he frequently utters but has not always lived up to. Looking for a better-paying job is made difficult by the fact that he doesn't have a driver's license. He lost it following a drunk driving violation years ago. He was living in Florida at the time and had come back to California to attend a wedding. Although he says he paid restitution and performed community service, he didn't attend a special drunk driving program. He stayed in state to attend his court case, but he wanted to get back to Florida and his job, so he left without completing the program. To get his license back now, he has to pay around $160 to the Department of Motor Vehicles and several hundred more to complete the drunk driving program. He estimates that in all it will probably cost him around $600 to $700 to get his license back. That's why he still doesn't have a license, even though he has been living in Santa Ana more than a year. Without a car or a license, his job options are limited. So he stays at the factory where his cousin-in-law also works second shift and can transport him to and from work.

He has been at the factory almost a year and has already taken at least ten days off. He hasn't built up any vacation yet, so all of his days off have been unpaid. Many of them have been to help his immigration case. He used several to go to Washington DC, and he is using another today for an event on deportation that is being held in Long Beach to which a cousin is driving him.

Puthy won't be there; it is Friday and he has dialysis. He goes every Monday, Wednesday, and Friday, leaving work early to prepare for the sessions, which last about three and a half hours. Today he comes home at a little before 3:00 p.m.

"Oh, you right on time," Touch calls from the living room.

Just inside the front door, Puthy smiles but doesn't answer. He removes his shoes and then heads off to take a shower. He has been on dialysis for years now. He calls it his part-time job, a description Touch has since adopted. He has never accompanied Puthy to a session, so he doesn't know what his brother does during the treatment.

"He don't like nobody to go with him," says Touch.

Puthy is weak more than he is healthy now. In the last year he has lost a lot of weight, says Touch. As if on cue, Puthy coughs from the bathroom. Touch considers it his role to lift heavy things, to do everything around the house his brother can no longer do. He is still mad at himself for not being there to help Puthy move the washing machine two weeks ago. He told Puthy he would be there, and then he forgot and wasn't. Puthy moved it by himself and ended up sore for days.

Touch also tries to do fun things with his brother. They go to the movies, work on cars. Aside from family, Touch doesn't know many people in Santa Ana. He doesn't have friends.

"My friend is my brother. That's it," he says.

He knows more people in Stockton. They drove there recently to spend Thanksgiving with their parents. While they were there, Touch also got to see his daughter, Priscilla. He took her on a shopping spree. Touch's ex-wife still lives in Florida, but in August she sent Priscilla to live with her own mother in Stockton. Priscilla is fifteen years old, in tenth grade, and getting into trouble by cutting class and spending time alone in the house with boys.

Sometimes Touch acknowledges the role he might have had in this. "I don't blame her a lot because she was fatherless for so many years, and it take a toll on her too," he says.

Other times he blames his ex-wife, claiming she left Priscilla at home unattended too much. He says he wants his daughter to come stay with him in Santa Ana. Then he provides all the reasons why it wouldn't work, why it hasn't happened yet, and why it won't happen in the near future. At first it was because he only had a one-year stay. Then it was the distractions—the job, taking care of Puthy. Trying to be a father on top of that would have been too much.

"I had to eliminate a lot of stuff and one of [the] stuff was her, and I feel bad," he says.

And even if he gets his license, he doesn't have a car and probably won't because he is broke. So he has no transportation, no way to get her to school. Saving for a car will be hard, as his credit is horrible. Plus he still needs to settle in.

His cell phone rings. His cousin is already here to take him to Long Beach. It is early. He doesn't have to be at the event until 4:30 p.m., but his cousin is worried about traffic. He tells her to come in and wait a little bit. A minute or two later a little girl of about six years old wanders in, followed by a toddler and then their mother, Touch's cousin. Touch asks the little girl where her older sister is and smiles patiently as she wanders off while offering her answer.

Priscilla was about the same age, seven, when Touch was locked up. He remembers how at first she used to cry on the phone. "Daddy, I need you!" she would wail. "I want you. Please come home now, now!"

They don't talk on the phone now; they just text. He has to be the first one to text. In nine years behind bars he saw her once, in 2013, when she came to visit him in prison. Last Christmas was the first time they had really spent time together in almost a decade. Priscilla stayed with him in Santa Ana for two weeks. It was awkward. Neither of them knew how to act. All Touch knew was to love her as he did when she was a little girl, to hug her. She wouldn't hug him back. "Get off me," she would say when he tried to hug her.

He saw her again when he was in Stockton at Thanksgiving. He isn't sure when he will see her next.

He is still living his life in limbo, not really planning too far ahead or settling down. He keeps a few baseball caps in the room where he stays at Puthy's house. He has a Cambodian flag, a backpack, a bed, and a small coffee table. It resembles the temporary room of someone in his twenties who is still trying to figure out his next step, his next location, and what he is going to do with the rest of his life. It isn't the room you'd expect of a father, of a middle-aged man. At first he didn't do much with his room because it was only temporary; he was only going to be here a year.

"Now since I know I have three years, I just going to get some kind of drawers or something. Make it like a real nice home," he says. He stops, corrects himself, "I mean, room."

On his bed is a small stack of papers with writing printed in a very large font. He made it big so he can understand it more clearly. The people who helped Touch asked him to speak at the event tonight. He decided he would; he owed it to them.

"I have to be there because they showed me a lot of love and support. So if I don't go, what kind of man I am?"

David Ros will be there, so will Katrina from SEARAC and the local community group Khmer Girls in Action. Touch is becoming a bit of a pro at public speaking after his trip to DC and an event in LA at which he was asked to speak. He likes educating people about deportation, not just because it affects him, but because he believes it is wrong in general. He doesn't believe that taking families apart will have positive results for anyone. He doesn't think people understand the separation isn't temporary; it is forever. That is what he wants others to understand. He himself also wants to understand more about the procedure. As far he knows the Cambodian government has no identification documents for him or any of the other deportees. Some weren't even born in the country, while others had their papers destroyed by the Khmer Rouge. Between 1970 and 1975 the recording of civil status decreased by 10 percent in Cambodia and was suspended altogether under the Khmer Rouge, according to the United Nations Children's Fund. What Touch doesn't understand is how the U.S. government can say he is Cambodian if there are no documents in Cambodia to back up the claim.

"If there's proof that I am Cambodian citizen, then yes, okay, go ahead and deport me," he says. "But you have no documentation of who we are over there."

Touch is confident about the lack of proof because he knows something most people don't. He went through the interview that happens just before deportation. He says the Cambodian consulate conducts the interview behind closed doors and does not record what has transpired. An ICE official is present, but because the documents are written in Khmer, the official has no idea what is going on. Touch says he asked for a copy of the document on which the consulate officials filled in answers to several questions, but they wouldn't give him one. He believes they send that document to Cambodia and then create a birth certificate to prepare travel documents that allow the deportees to return to Cambodia as Cambodian citizens. It may just be a theory, but he believes it. With limited information, theories and rumors are what most of the interviewees go on. Lawyers and advocates seem to know little more. What the officials know, they aren't revealing.

After getting much of a runaround, Ouk Bonim, second secretary in charge of the Consular Office at the Cambodian Embassy, told me that the embassy did not work on deportation cases. According to Bonim, Cambodian government officials from Phnom Penh fly to the United States to interview deportees and issue travel documents. Bonim insisted he had no contact information for the Cambodian officials who deal with deportation, and only ICE could provide that. An ICE representative explained in an email that the agency could not provide that information, but the Cambodian Embassy "represents the Cambodian government in the U.S. and should be able to provide that information."

This lack of transparency is exactly what Touch has a problem with and wants others to know about. And he is one of the few who can tell them about what happens during the interview. Most of the others who went through the interviews were deported.

"That's it," he says. "Gone." Sent to Cambodia.

Touch talks to his deported friends all the time. He knows a lot of them don't have family in Cambodia. They may have family in the United States, but he wonders how their families are supposed to help them in Cambodia when they are on assistance in the States. Some of the deportees are struggling with worse alcohol and drug addictions than they had in the States. Others cry daily for their families. They are lost; they don't know what to do. He sees their posts on Facebook.

"I miss my family."

"I want to go home."

"This is not the place for me."

He keeps pinching himself to remind himself he has been spared; he is not going through this. But one day he knows he will. He has three years to try to change things, if not for himself, then for those who will come after him.

"I have to do something while I'm still here," he says. "Because when I go out overseas, I don't think I can do anything. So I have to try. I have to try."

1. Sisters Sithy Yi (*left*), Jennifer Diep (*middle*), and Sithea San (*right*) with the family maid, Than, in Phnom Penh, Cambodia, around 1972. Photo courtesy of San Croucher.

2. San Croucher and her daughters, Sithy Yi, Sithea San, and Jennifer Diep, in the Kamput Refugee Camp, Thailand, in 1980. Photo courtesy of San Croucher.

3. San Croucher (*left*) with her daughter Sithy Yi in San's yard in Eastvale, California, in November 2016. Photo by Katya Cengel.

4. Brothers Puthy Hak (*left*) and Touch Hak in front of a Cambodian painting in Puthy's home in Santa Ana, California, in November 2016. Photo by Katya Cengel.

5. David Ros at New Year's parade in Long Beach's Cambodia Town in April 2016. Photo by Katya Cengel.

6. Spectators at New Year's parade in Long Beach's Cambodia Town in April 2016. Photo by Katya Cengel.

7. Cambodian American deportee Nheb Thai washes his hands in the pond in front of his home outside of Battambang, Cambodia, in January 2017. Photo by Katya Cengel for *Pacific Standard*.

8. Cambodian American deportee Khe Khouen and the boy she says she takes care of outside her home in Battambang Province in January 2017. Photo by Katya Cengel.

14

"NOT HOME FOR THE HOLIDAYS"

David Ros hands me his wallet. Then he gives me his Dallas Cowboys key lanyard. He warned me he would be doing this. Whoever accompanies him on his biannual Immigration and Customs Enforcement check-in gets his keys and wallet before he is called in—"just in case." In case he is detained. In case he doesn't come back out once he goes in to speak with a deportation officer. In case he isn't released from custody until he is in Cambodia. There is always that chance. And he doesn't trust ICE with his wallet and keys, both of which he must hand over if he is detained. Besides, if he is sent back to Cambodia, he won't need the keys to his Long Beach home.

I know that is what could happen. He could go in that door a free man and become a prisoner. And yet, until those keys are hanging around my neck, I don't really realize what that means. He has a lot of keys. I imagine one must be for work, one for his house, one for his car, one for his mother's house, one for his girlfriend Debbie's car. There are more. I am not sure what they are for; I just know that they are connected to more things that tie him to the United States, to California, to Long Beach—the tangible weight of objects that open the structures that keep him here.

That is what I am thinking as we wait inside room 2204 of the downtown federal building in ICE's Los Angeles field office. I am not sure what David is thinking. I know he is nervous. Immediately after entering the room and slipping his file through a reception slot, he headed straight for the bathroom. He was there a while. When he came out, he handed me his wallet and keys. I put the wallet in my backpack and the keys around my neck.

I silently wonder what I will do if he doesn't come out. Should I drive his car back to Long Beach? Can I remember how to get there? How will I tell Debbie? I don't even have her phone number. And Solomon, what will I say when I see David's son next time? How do you explain to a four-year-old that his father has been sent to a far-off land from which he will never return?

David likes to take Solomon with him when he checks in, but Solomon started school this year so David decided not to bring him along. There are other young children in the waiting room. The place is packed, with the twenty or so seats inside all occupied. David and I lean against the wall and wait. That is what you do after you sign in and drop your file: you wait for your name to be called so you can go into another room and meet with an officer. The whole setup is not unlike a doctor's office.

David whispers in my ear. There is no rule against talking, but somehow whispering seems right. He tells me about the time he went to check in with Debbie and a friend and decided to play a trick on Debbie. After he was done with the check-in, he sent his friend downstairs to where Debbie was waiting to tell her he had been detained. Then he went outside and waited for both of them. When Debbie saw him, she was more relieved than mad. She gets nervous every time he has to check in.

"She always calls and asks me, 'Call as soon as you out,'" says David.

A few weeks before, David texted that things weren't going well between them. The relationship might not last, he wrote. I wonder how she does it, living with the uncertainty that any day her boyfriend—the father of her son, the man who brought her to Long Beach—could be whisked away. The waiting room is filled with couples and kids. I wonder how any of them do it. Someone they love and depend on could be taken from them in a few minutes' time, and yet they seem relaxed, distracted by day-to-day life. A young man uses his phone to send a text. A couple fusses over their baby. An older man and a younger one, maybe a father and son, talk quietly. They all seem calm, too calm.

I am in the bathroom when the first announcement is made for those not checking in to wait downstairs. I manage to wait with David another few minutes before a woman behind a glass screen asks if I am there to check in. I am easy to spot. I am tall and white, one of only three white people in the room. I shake my head no. Most of the people there are Latino; a few are Asian. As I leave David whispers, "Wait for me by the elevators."

I walk to the elevators and wait. A few other family members or friends of other future deportees are already there. We wait together in silent companionship. A guard walks by and tells us we have to wait downstairs. I ride an elevator down to the first floor. I position myself in the lobby where the elevators let out. Each time one of the elevator doors opens, I scan those exiting, hoping one of them will be David.

A half hour passes. I see people who checked in before David come down. Another half hour passes. It is almost lunchtime now. I see a man who checked in after David come down. I start to worry.

Then I get the text.

Two hours earlier, David's doorstep, Long Beach.

I knock and Alaysia opens the door. David is in the bathroom washing his face. He has on black dress pants but is still wearing flip-flops and a tank top. It is a little after eight o'clock in the morning on a cold weekday in December 2015. A blanket is pushed against the base of the front door, and several space heaters heat the single-story townhouse, as a remedy to keep the heating bill down. It has been a cold few months in Southern California.

Two weeks earlier fourteen people were killed and twenty-two seriously injured in a mass shooting in nearby San Bernardino. Yesterday Los Angeles County schools were closed because of a bomb threat. Long Beach schools were not affected, so David will drop Alaysia off at her school before heading to downtown Los Angeles for his biannual check-in with ICE.

Debbie has already left with Solomon, whose preschool is right next to her workplace. David puts on dress shoes and a long-sleeve top. He fixes himself some tea. It is Wednesday. He usually tries to check in with ICE on a Wednesday or Thursday, figuring the middle of the week will be less busy. His last check-in was in June. That time he didn't even see an officer; someone just marked his file and told him to come back in another six months. When he sees an officer, he or she asks him general stuff: Where are you working? Where are you living? The officers are constantly changing; that makes David a little apprehensive about his current situation. He has no idea who he will see and how the agency will react when they learn he is late to check in.

He was supposed to check in last Wednesday, not this Wednesday. He isn't terribly concerned. Because it is his first time ever being late, he thinks the officers will go easy on him. They usually allow you to check in a few days on either side of the actual check-in day so you can arrange it around your work schedule. But a week is not "a few days." David was supposed to be there on December 9; now it is December 16.

He isn't quite sure how he made the mistake. Maybe it was the "15" in 2015 that he saw when he was glancing over his paperwork. More likely it is because he misplaced the paper on which his check-in date is written during the redecorating following their move a few months ago. They left a cramped one-bedroom for the current more spacious townhouse where they now live. The front room is filled with pictures. In one shot David is shirtless, sporting huge biceps and a heavily tattooed chest and neck. "That was when I was inside," he says.

In another shot he is in prison blues, two little girls by his side. Then there is the picture of him and his mother that a fellow inmate painted. Those are the prison reminders. Otherwise, the home is like any other, with a laptop left on a bookcase, a children's book—*How Do Dinosaurs Say Goodnight?*—on the coffee table. Under the Christmas tree is a package of racecars; above it, a plaque inscribed with the word "hope."

David grabs a slim folder in which he keeps his ICE information and heads for the door. Alaysia follows. She is dressed in short shorts, knee-high socks, and a letterman's jacket. In the car she asks if they are going to stop somewhere to pick up a quick breakfast. David has a handful of coupons he planned on using, but they are running late, so he tells Alaysia they don't have time for breakfast. She says something else in a voice so quiet it is impossible to hear.

"You said you have what, Alaysia?"

She repeats herself, louder this time: "Free dress and my honor roll thing tomorrow."

Debbie will go to the honor roll ceremony. Alaysia almost always makes honor roll. Academically she has adapted well to Long Beach; socially she has struggled since moving from Washington. She has had trouble making friends. Despite Long Beach's heavy Cambodian influence, there aren't many Asian students at her school. She is silent the rest of the short drive. David is not. He is animated, excited about tonight's big event, a community forum on the impact of deportation in the Southeast Asian community, the same event where Touch will be speaking.

Recently it seems there has been a new push in the activist community regarding the issue. Tonight's event is playing off the fact that it has been forty years since the first Southeast Asian refugees arrived in the United States. The event is part of a larger campaign by the Southeast Asian Freedom Network and the 1 Love Movement that is supported by a number of other groups and includes a series of launch videos, community forums, and trips to Cambodia. All the activity has energized David to get involved again. He feels compelled to capitalize on the action, increase his own efforts, and keep the momentum going. He tries to get others in his situation to do the same. It isn't easy. David has been trying to convince one man in particular, one who has a lot of pull in the community. But the man is AWOL, not checking in with ICE—"just totally skipped that part"—which gives David pause. He wants the influence of future deportees who have sway with others who have deportation orders. But, he admits, "if they're still running the street anyway, there's not much positive that can come out of getting them involved."

Then he contradicts himself. He is clearly disappointed that others in his situation are not taking this as seriously as he is, that they are not doing their part to try to change things. David is in the same spot they are in; he also has a family and concerns about what will happen. Like them he fears speaking out will draw attention to his case and result in his immediate deportation Yet he feels strongly that they need to speak out. He has a speech he gives to try to motivate them.

"There's 2,500 people still on the list [to be deported], and I guarantee you, you are one of them and I'm one of them," he says. "One of these days we will be on that list, and we will be on that plane if we do not address this issue now."

Some of them believe by not checking in with ICE, they are safe from deportation. And they may be, for now. But David believes that after they get the others, the easy ones who check in, they'll come after the hard ones. If they come across you, he says, they are going to send you back, period. When that happens, he tells them, you will look back in regret that when you had the opportunity to fight the issue you stayed silent. He tells them to think about that. He also tells them there won't be any ICE officials at that night's event.

He is hoping there will be a good number of people from the Cambodian American community who are not directly affected by deportation. Getting them to show up is sometimes almost as hard as getting the potential deportees involved. They don't like the politics, says David, the wrangling. David splits them into two groups—those who understand and support the movement and those who don't want to get involved because of their beliefs. The latter group sees it as karma, he says, "that you reap in life the stuff that you take in life."

What he wants them to see instead is how deportation affects families. Maybe the deportees get what they deserve, but what about the sons or daughters they leave behind? Is it fair that a child has to grow up without a father or mother because the parent did something wrong and has already served a punishment? When David explains it to them in that way, they are more sympathetic, more understanding.

We have arrived at Lindbergh Middle School. He pulls to the curb, and Alaysia hops out, voicing a quiet "bye" as she slams the car door behind her. David idles for a minute while he enters the address for the ICE field office in his phone's GPS system.

"I should know my way there by now," he says. "But I don't for some reason."

He laughs. Then he heads onto the I-710 freeway. The address for the field office is written on the front of a manila folder. Inside the folder are three sheets of paper. David's thumb and index finger prints are on the first page. The next two pages are a long list of check-in dates. The last remain-in-place notation was on June 30, 2015, six months ago. Once David's check-in schedule was extended to a year, but immediately after his first annual check-in, he was moved back to a biannual schedule. He didn't question it at the time; he thought he was lucky to have had an annual schedule, even if only briefly. Then he found out that a lot of other guys were on annual check-in schedules. A friend of his who was released after serving twenty-two years is on an annual schedule. When David first got out of prison, he had to check in monthly, then every two months, until he gradually increased to a year, and after that they bumped him back down to six months. He isn't sure of the reasoning. He works consistently, checks in regularly, and complies with everything. He plans to ask the deportation officer today if he can check in annually.

"In 2.4 miles take exit 7B to merge onto I-110 North toward Los Angeles." The phone's GPS system calls out directions. Traffic is heavy. David is restless. He has taken the day off work and is eager to get his check-in over with and head home to prepare for tonight's event. The video launch party he held at his house on October 24, marking the campaign's kickoff, went well. His place was overflowing with people, many of them potential deportees who were attending their first anti-deportation activism event. Still David would have liked to have seen more people. He wanted to make an announcement about it at his brother's church, but his brother turned him down, saying he didn't allow any announcements. David's family spread the word in other ways, watching the video and sharing it with their friends.

Tonight David's mother will be one of the people speaking. David thought it was important to have the voice of a family member there, and she agreed to do it. David isn't hosting the event—Khmer Girls in Action is—but he agreed to help spread the word. A large turnout will show the invited politicians that the community stands behind the issue. That is what he is working for. But he also has both a full-time job that recently has had him working seven days a week and a family that includes a son who was up late last night with a fever and an eye infection. David had to go out in the middle of the night to buy eyewash for Solomon. He administered it conservatively, keeping in mind what the pediatrician told him about not giving young children too much medicine. When he felt Solomon's forehead this morning, the fever was gone.

His phone rings. It's Debbie. He puts the call on speaker so he can keep driving. "Hello. Hey, I'm on the freeway. We are almost there. Actually, I'm in traffic."

She asks him why he didn't go somewhere, accuses him of forgetting. He says he didn't forget; he just didn't know. "We're almost there, just in traffic right now. But I'll let you know once I come out of the place."

"Okay."

He asks how Solomon is doing. She tells him she'll be picking Solomon up soon and getting him ready for a Christmas party. They hang up.

Traffic on the freeway is almost at a standstill. David took a wrong exit a while back while distracted about the event tonight and now is on an unfamiliar route. He doesn't come to downtown Los Angeles often. The GPS on his phone calls out additional directions. He ignores it and takes a different route. This is his home, so he should know his way around—the shortcuts, the back roads. But the Los Angeles area is always expanding, always growing, and because traffic is so bad, people tend to stick to their own neighborhoods. It is a bit like New York that way, with the insular neighborhoods.

David isn't sure what Phnom Penh will be like as a city. He continues to contact deportees on Facebook and try to find out more and prepare himself for his inevitable relocation. He follows Song Chhang's friend Bill Herod, the American who has helped deportees since they first began arriving. Bill is the man with the monkey, a man who lost vision in his right eye while struggling to prevent a deportee from killing himself. When a female deportee posted on Facebook a request for donations to help buy a plane ticket so her son could visit her, David helped draw attention to the post. Keeping up with the deportees in Cambodia while still living in Long Beach is a bit trying at times, sort of like living in limbo, stuck between two lives. That is how David defines his status. Officially, he says, he has no status. That is what the deportation officer said when David asked what his status was as someone who no longer had a green card but was still living in the United States and had not been deported yet.

"He said, 'Right now, you have no status. You are considered no status; you're just waiting to be deported.' That's it," says David.

He laughs and repeats the words, as if they will become clearer if he says them again: "No status. You're just waiting to be deported."

He is downtown now, looking for his usual parking place. He likes to use the meters, where he can pay for two hours' parking instead of half a day. It never takes longer than two hours. Outside the federal building is a line of people waiting to pass through security. Despite the risk, David isn't that nervous today, not as he is sometimes.

The most common time to be detained is during check-in, he says. They don't warn you about when they will detain you. If they warned you, David admits, he would think twice about turning himself in. But then he isn't sure where he would go or how he would be able to continue working. He lists his mother's address, not his new address, on his paperwork. That might buy him a little time but not much.

He jumps to another topic. It isn't nerves; it's just how he is—high energy, always thinking about something. He mentions how his mother used to have nightmares. When he was a kid, he remembers waking up to her screams. She still has them, he says, but not as often.

After passing through security, he heads upstairs to the check-in room. I am waiting for him downstairs when he texts: "I got detained. They let me make one call."

The next minute I see him step off the elevator. It was a joke, a bad one. We walk back to the car, trying to talk over the noise of blaring sirens and jackhammers. Being late had almost gotten him on the "bad boy list," which means ICE has to go out and get you. The officer who saw him warned him not to be late again or he will make the list. He apologized, explained about the move. She asked for his updated contact information. Then she asked whether he had made any efforts to contact the Cambodian consulate or embassy about his travel documents. He told her he had, and that was the truth; his activism had resulted in a meeting with the consulate. Then he asked if he could check in on an annual instead of a biannual basis. To do that, she said, he would have to write a letter to the Cambodian consulate requesting travel documents, make an effort to get the deportation process rolling, and provide proof he had done so.

"Meaning, helping myself get out of here," says David. "Why would I do that?"

He says officially part of the agreement they make when they are released from detention is to help secure travel documents for themselves. Now, he says, ICE is pushing people to uphold it. One of his good friends was asked to request travel documents from the Cambodian side and provide proof he had done so to ICE. When he asked David what he should do, David didn't know what to tell him. David was lucky; his officer gave him a choice: he only had to ask for the documents if he wanted to extend to an annual check-in. He decides he'll stick with checking in every six months. The officer did extend him a little, and his next check is in August, eight months from now. He tried to feel her out on other issues, asking what happens if a person doesn't check in. She told him if someone doesn't check in, the agency puts a notice out to officers in the field.

"I don't think she's telling me everything," he says.

It is hard to get the full story from anyone, but David tries to piece it together as best as he can. Last month he met with a number of Cambodian government representatives, including some stationed in the United States—such as the Honorary Consulate of Cambodia in California and the Cambodian ambassador in Washington DC—and some from Cambodia. David was encouraged to do so by his contacts at the 1 Love Movement who have connections with some politicians. He also met with members of the Cambodian People's Party, the current leading party under Hun Sen, and an organization in Long Beach that is trying to recruit people to the party. David believes the CPP is trying to establish support overseas through youth organizations. He doesn't think it is working. He says party members tried to recruit him and some of his fellow activists. He turned them down, telling them he was fighting for the community and couldn't align himself with any one party. He didn't tell them that his mother would have killed him if he did. She is very outspoken about her hatred for the CPP and can rattle off examples of its corruption, abuse, and violence against the opposition. From what David has witnessed, he feels the party is all about influence and power, not about helping the people.

We are back at his car. David texts Debbie to let her know he is out. Then he gets in the car and heads back to Long Beach. He has a lot to do before this evening's event. He wants to make sure it is a success, as his

previous activities have been. He tries to make use of every opportunity
he is given. During his meeting with the Cambodian government figures,
he tried to figure out who decides who gets deported. He has determined
it is not the Cambodian government representative with whom he met.
Who it is, he doesn't know, and whoever does know, isn't sharing. He also
doesn't know who verifies that a deportee is a Cambodian. He believes it
is someone who comes over from Cambodia, but he has no proof of this.
He believes he did manage to win the government representatives over.
They treated him with respect, he says. Toward the end of their meeting,
one of them suggested stopping deportations for people with minor crimes.
David agreed that would be helpful. Then he reminded them that those
with both minor and serious offenses had served their time. Then he told
them he was a violent offender; he had shot somebody and the person had
died. He wanted that to sink in.

They assured him that he would be fine in Cambodia, that English
speakers were needed, that there would be job opportunities for him in
tourism. They told him that people with skills such as the deportees possess
are needed in Cambodia. David told them personally he wasn't worried.

"I'm okay. I can go over there. I can die," he told them, speaking about
whatever happens to himself. "But what about my family left behind? Who
is going to take care of them?"

David wanted them to understand how deportation affects the families, its
ripple effect. Again and again he tried to bring it back to the family. Toward
the end, he says he could see in their eyes that they understood. They told
him if his name came up, they wouldn't have him deported—ever. But it
was a verbal promise, and he isn't just fighting for himself. He is fighting
for the whole community.

David is lost again. He got distracted while driving. He needs a road that
connects to I-710, which goes right through Long Beach. It should have taken
him ten minutes to get home. Now twenty minutes after leaving downtown
LA, he is still another twenty-two minutes from home. It is lunchtime. Usually
he picks Solomon up from preschool and spends his lunch hour with him,
but today he is focused on getting ready for tonight's event.

Several hours later, he sees teenagers are hanging red-and-green paper chains outside the community center at Ernest McBride Park in Long Beach. Inside cheesy Christmas tunes are blasting. Young adults help serve spring rolls, and teenage girls make paper lotus flowers. It is 5:00 p.m., and the room is packed with around 150 people. Many of those sitting in the seats and leaning against the wall are teenagers and young adults, but there is a small contingent of elderly, middle-aged, and very young people as well. Seated on stage is a panel of activists and community members. Touch, outfitted in a sport coat, button-down shirt, and his trademark hat, is situated toward the center. On his right is David's mother, Chanthaveth Ros; on his left, Katrina Dizon Mariategue from SEARAC.

Toward the front of the audience, next to the local dignitaries, is Song Chhang. People approach his wheelchair reverently, almost bowing as they address him. Mary Blatz, a woman who has taken on the deportee fight, has brought him and his girlfriend. Song is eager to see what it is all about but is skeptical as to whether the energy and talk can be transformed into action. Everyone seems so young, he says, even though most of the organizers are in their thirties and forties. He laughs: "I should be young."

Sophya Chhiv, a founding member of Khmer Girls in Action, is the first to officially speak. She is in her thirties, smartly dressed. She talks about her older sister, one of the first women from the Cambodian American community to face deportation. That was years ago. Support letters kept her sister here, but her case is still pending, says Sophya. Her sister could still be deported. The first slipup could send her away. Her green card has been revoked, and she has to check in with ICE monthly. As with the others on the list, she is "just hanging around," says Sophya. "Questioning, what's the purpose of life? Should I have a partner? Should I start having a family?"

Sophya shakes her head. She can't imagine living with the uncertainty. She knows better what the families face. She wanted to hold this event during the holiday season to acknowledge the issue's devastating effect on the families.

Most of the invited local elected officials discreetly leave soon after the speeches begin; only an African American representative remains. A monitor plays prerecorded messages from several deportees, and a panelist quotes a text they received from a deportee that day. Touch tells his story first. As incredible as it is, in a formal setting and while reading a script, he comes across as wooden. David's mother follows; she is vague. The real impact comes when Stephanie Sim talks.

Stephanie is still in high school and brimming with raw emotion. She is almost breathless as she races through her speech. She is the youngest of nine children; only the last three were born in the United States. The brother she is talking about, the one who was deported in 2012, was born in a refugee camp in Thailand. He was three years old when the family arrived in the States in 1989. In California her parents found low-paying work in the garment industry. Her brother graduated from high school and worked on cars. He spent time in jail for stealing car parts. After his last stint in jail, he got a job, moved in with his girlfriend, and was about to become a father when he was detained and told he was going to be deported.

It is an all-too-familiar story, according to Katrina with SEARAC. In California, she says, Southeast Asian Americans in particular are impacted by some of the highest rates of arrest and incarceration. They are also subject to some of the highest, strictest, and harshest sentencing punishments, which also result in their facing deportation later in life.

As do so many others, she cites the 1996 laws as the beginning of the criminalization of immigration. The antiterrorism and illegal immigration laws, she explains, essentially expanded the number of offenses for which individuals—specifically those in immigrant communities who grow up in poverty and are subject to all of these barriers—can be deported. The laws also made it difficult for judges to look at cases on an individual basis, to really assess a person's circumstances.

"So if you are a refugee, if you came here, if you live in an impoverished community, if there was a lack of support systems for you to fully integrate into society—they don't take any of these things into consideration," says Katrina.

The government created a system where enforcement is the priority. A majority of the thousands of Southeast Asian Americans who have been issued deportation orders since the passage of the 1996 laws have received the orders due to old criminal convictions, she explains. Then she outlines the familiar path to deportation for Southeast Asian Americans: barriers in the school system that lead to bullying, victimization, and low high school graduation rates; ensuing gang membership for survival and support; and the resulting entry into the criminal justice system.

Chhaya Chhoum, another speaker, is familiar with the pattern. She arrived in the Bronx with her family in 1985 when she was seven years old. At the time the crack epidemic was in full swing. The Bronx was literally burning, as landlords were torching apartment buildings for insurance money. The apartments that were still standing often lacked hot water and heat. The family went from refugee camps to poverty. "How can you survive?" she asks.

She lists some of the ways the U.S. government failed Southeast Asian refugees: dismantling the English as a Second Language programs for the older generation, isolating refugees in the ghettos and in the projects, and instituting welfare reform. Deportation is the ultimate failure of the American refugee resettlement program, she says. "The ultimate failure."

One effort they have used in her area to fight deportation has been to push for sentences of 364 days instead of 365. In this case one day can mean the difference between someone being deportable and someone being allowed to stay. But it doesn't work for all crimes; some crimes are deportable regardless. The current push, being led mainly by Southeast Asian Freedom Network and 1 Love Movement, is focused on memorandum of understanding (MOU) agreements between the United States and the countries of Laos, Cambodia, and Vietnam. In the MOU with the United States, Vietnam said it would not take anyone who arrived prior to when the two countries established relations in 1995, making most refugees safe from deportation. The campaign is focused on changing the Cambodian agreement to mirror Vietnam's but using the date of 1993. They also want it to be retroactive, enabling most of those who were already deported to return to the States. They want Laos to have an agreement with the date of 1992 and Vietnam to keep its current agreement. Next month they will take the campaign to Cambodia. Tonight in Long Beach the audience responds with applause.

But the response that matters most is that of Kathy Ko Chin with the President's Advisory Commission on Asian American and Pacific Islanders.

As the eyes and ears of the community for President Obama, Kathy's words of support inspire hope—until she gets to the end of her statement. The commission purview, she says, "is only on domestic policy," and since these recommendations have foreign policy implications, the commission's role will be limited.

"However," she adds, "we are very committed to making sure we can get you the access to the State Department as well as to the Department of Homeland Security."

Her response, both of understanding and limited support, is similar to that of David Ros's sister Harene Chau, forty-three, who is attending with her husband and kids. She can see how fleeing from another country and having to acclimate to the culture here might have affected David in a way that he got into trouble. She also points out that when he committed crimes, he was a juvenile and their mother was already a citizen; so she thinks that information should have been taken into consideration. "If you are younger than eighteen years of age and a green card holder when your parent becomes a citizen, you usually then become a U.S. citizen." (She is correct, except the law she is referencing, the Child Citizenship Act, did not take effect until 2001. An earlier law required both parents to be citizens, yet David only had one parent.) Still, she is careful about placing too much blame on the system.

"I don't know," she says. "I don't want to blame that situation, whereas personal responsibility . . ."

David is not her only sibling facing deportation; her older sister is as well. The threat hangs over them all. David returned home safely from ICE today, but the story Stephanie Sim tells about her own brother reminds them all how precarious check-ins can be. Stephanie was at middle school when she got the call from her brother's girlfriend. The couple was at her brother's routine ICE check-in, only this time it wasn't so routine.

"She sounded very panicked. She told me that my brother was being taken to jail, that he was going to get deported," says Stephanie.

At this part in the story, Stephanie breaks down. She stops reading and starts crying. It takes her a few minutes to compose herself. It is hard to imagine the pressure she must have felt as a middle school student, having to call and tell her mother what was happening to her brother. She could barely understand it herself. Over the next few months, she had trouble keeping up as her brother was transferred to different places in the United States in advance of his deportation. Around the holidays, her family traveled to Seattle and saw her brother right before he was deported.

"That was the last time I saw my brother, and that was the first time he saw his one-month old son," she says.

The deportation took a huge financial and emotional toll on the family. Already struggling, they now had to try to support Stephanie's brother in Cambodia as he was having trouble finding work. Her mom, she says, continually worries she will lose another child and has not been able to move forward since her son's deportation. Stephanie doesn't think about her brother all of the time, and for that she feels guilty, selfish.

It is important to end deportation, she says. "Because it would be the end of our stress, unhappiness, and the end of our trauma."

15

NEVER-ENDING NIGHTMARE

Battambang, Cambodia, September 1979.

They walked for five days and four nights. The Vietnamese had invaded. The Khmer Rouge had fled. In Battambang, where Nheth Hak and his extended family had been when the Khmer Rouge were ousted, there was a severe drought. The entire country of Cambodia had suffered widespread drought that year. There were rumors that there was food in Thailand at the refugee camps. Getting there meant passing through territory near the Thai border that was still being fought over by the Vietnamese and Khmer Rouge. If the Khmer Rouge caught you, they would kill you. The Vietnamese were dangerous as well, especially when they were engaged in a firefight. Nheth Hak could be leading his family to their deaths.

It didn't matter. There was no food. If they stayed in Battambang, then they would die anyway. So they started walking.

On the third day they encountered Vietnamese soldiers who advised them against crossing into Thailand. The next part of the journey was the most dangerous; without the soldiers' support and guidance, they risked walking into firefights and stepping on land mines. They couldn't go forward. But they couldn't go back either. If they returned to Battambang, then they would starve. They were in a forest filled with soldiers. They couldn't stay where they were.

Nheth and his family decided to stop and rest while they figured out what to do. They collected wood for a fire. A Vietnamese soldier helped them. Afterward the soldier sat with them by the fire. He kept staring at Nheth's niece, Onna Oum. She was just five or six years old, but Onna was tall and light skinned. People noticed her.

The soldier, far from his home in Vietnam, had his own reasons for staring. "She looks like my daughter," he said.

They cooked the little rice they had. The soldier left. When he returned a little while later, he brought food with him and gave them some. He sat down again and stared at Onna. The girl's parents were not there. Her father had been a soldier in Lon Nol's army, but he was never really a part of Onna's life. (He survived and made it to Seattle, where he later died.) The girl's mother, Nheth's sister, fled the Khmer Rouge early on. No one remembers the exact year she fled, maybe 1977. She invited Nheth to join her. There was a big group of them going, maybe seventy or seventy-five people. Nheth thought about joining them. But in the end he decided to stay, as there were too many people depending on him to risk his own death trying to escape.

He learned later that most of those who fled with his sister were gunned down. Later still he found out that the handful who survived made it to Thailand, where they were jailed and beaten before eventually being released. His sister was one of the lucky ones who lived, but he didn't find that out until even later.

Onna and her brother were as good as orphans, but the family didn't see it that way. Nheth looked after all of them: his wife and four children, his mother, his niece and nephew, his widowed sisters. His father was no longer around; his two older brothers had moved away. Nheth was the only man left, so it fell on him to look after the women and children.

The soldier wandered off again, came back, sat, and stared at Onna some more. They knew who he was talking about when he asked, "Can I have her?"

The answer came back, quick and sure. "No," said Onna's grandmother. She had taken care of Onna and Onna's brother since her daughter had fled. The soldier nodded. They thought he would leave then. Instead, he stayed. He continued to stare at Onna.

Finally, he spoke. "Don't stay," he said. "Just go."

Then he led them out of Cambodia and into Thailand. Touch was just a baby; Puthy was fourteen.

Stockton, California, January 2016.

The little girl whose good looks saved the family is now forty-one years old. Onna wears stylish jeans and a black shirt with "Bebe" written on it in rhinestones. She moves with familiarity around her aunt and uncle's cramped second-floor apartment, located in the same complex where the family lived when they first arrived in the United States. Nheth Hak and Mom Khat, seventy-three and seventy, respectively, live in a "gated" community in a rough area of Stockton. One of the gates is always open; the other has a sign on it in Khmer. Most of the residents are elderly; many are Khmer. The complex is next to the train tracks, with cargo-laden trains passing by just beyond the complex's back outer gate.

It is a cold winter day, but inside the apartment it is warm, too warm. The living-room window is cracked slightly to let out some of the heat. Nheth sits on a couch beneath the window, looking out from time to time at the apartment complex's internal walkway and quasi courtyard. His niece and wife sit on the floor. It is a comfortable living room, with lots of rolled-up rugs, blankets, and cushions. On one wall are family markers: wedding and graduation pictures, a college diploma. On another wall is a long mirror with the price—$3.96—still scrawled on the glass. There is a big U.S. flag and a smaller Cambodian one, posters written in Spanish with pictures of American presidents, a clipboard, a bag of vitamin C, several hats, and a brush. On the big flat screen television, the Dallas Cowboys are playing against the Washington Redskins.

When the Khmer Rouge came to power, all Nheth could think was that someone had to come and help. He didn't voice his opinion, didn't share it with anyone. Even talking with his wife and niece in a small group, as he is now, wasn't allowed then. But he thought it. It wasn't his faith in humanity that kept him believing that someone would come and rescue the Cambodian people from the Khmer Rouge; it was the lack of humanity and extreme perversity of the Khmer Rouge. It was just too much. The killing was too harsh; the chaos, too extreme. The Khmer Rouge rebels didn't listen to one another. They fought among themselves. He knew there had to be a group waiting in the wings to replace them.

"I am hoping that someone behind the Khmer Rouge will one day, eventually, rescue us," he says. He speaks in Khmer, with Onna translating. He understands some English but isn't fluent, while his niece switches between the two languages easily.

The rescue didn't happen quite how he had hoped, but the Khmer Rouge were eventually forced from power. The rebels had originally set out to help people like Nheth, people from impoverished agricultural backgrounds.

The life of a farmer was hard; that's what Nheth remembers. He left school in seventh grade to carry dirt. He carried it by the bucketload while balancing a stick on his back with a bucket hanging off each side. Each trip earned him 10 Cambodian riels. Whoever was ruling—the French, the Cambodian royal family, the Japanese—didn't make much difference to him. He was born at the end of World War II, the third of three boys. He has three sisters as well. He doesn't mention their birth order. He grew up in Takeo Province in the southwest near the border with Vietnam. His family did not own land, so he farmed for others.

Nheth moved to Battambang in 1961 to work for a wealthy landowner. He made 300 Cambodian riels a month clearing and maintaining the land, taking down trees and bushes and burning them, and weeding a cotton field. His pay included food and lodging in a worker's dormitory. His extended family and fiancée followed later. His future wife, Mom, was only fifteen years old when they got engaged. They waited until she was eighteen before marrying. After Mom gave birth to their first child, a girl named Sophal, they moved out of the workers' shack and into their own home.

"A lot of kid follow," says Nheth. He speaks the words in English and follows them with a chuckle.

Nheth is quick to smile and laugh. He has a gentle manner, similar to his son Puthy, who looks just like him, except for being taller and younger. Sophal is fifty-two now and lives in Philadelphia. After Sophal came the three boys: Puthy; Chamroeun, now forty-three; and Touch. Two more girls came later: Nalin, now thirty-four, and living in Southern California; and Lisa, twenty-seven, who lives in Stockton. It is Nalin's California State University–Chico diploma that hangs on the wall.

The birth of the children and the harvesting of the crops marked their years. Mom worked alongside her husband in the fields. Together they collected and chopped firewood to bundle and sell. Life was lived day by day. Except with the war going on, fighting between various sides meant none of the children went to school. Nheth wasn't really sure what either side was fighting for. He just knew that in 1967 King Norodom Sihanouk—at the time the head of state, not actually the king—started to tighten his grip. During the crackdown over the next two years, it became more difficult to travel. Roads were closed, and if you were caught where you weren't supposed to be, you were killed.

The cotton fields where Nheth worked were located deep in the forest west of Battambang, but that was also where the communists being persecuted by the government were hiding. It was too risky to work in the forests, so he switched to working in the rice fields located closer to the village. As fighting between the Khmer Rouge and the government soldiers intensified, it became harder and harder to avoid them. Nheth was forced to help carry injured soldiers from where they had been wounded back to their hiding places. Most of those he helped were Khmer Rouge. It had nothing to do with their ideology; they were just closer to where he lived. Besides, Lon Nol's troops had cars. Nheth was called to help maybe once or twice a month. He never refused. "If I don't go, they kill me."

The excursions took away from his work, but he didn't complain. The landowners had long since fled. He worked now to support his family; that was all. Between 1971 and 1972 the Americans bombed the mountainous area near the Vietnamese border, the area closer to where Nheth and Mom had grown up. The bombing actually began in 1969 and lasted four years. As noted previously, during that time the United States dropped more than 2.7 million tons of bombs, killing anywhere from 150,000 to 600,000 civilians. In Battambang, the campaign didn't affect them much. Then, in April 1975, the Khmer Rouge took over. Bombs fell for three days and three nights. War broke out everywhere, says Nheth.

"It doesn't matter where. They would just drop bombs."

When the Khmer Rouge came in, the soldiers didn't care who you were; if you interfered, they shot you. The Khmer Rouge soldiers looked as though they were only thirteen or fourteen years old, says Mom, who is small, plump, and tan. Both Nheth and Mom use their hands when they talk. They are animated with anger, eager to express the emotions they couldn't reveal at the time. Back then, whatever the Khmer Rouge asked them to do, they did it. They pretended to like the Khmer Rouge. They kept their mouths shut, never complained, and neither asked for nor ever offered information.

"During that time they turn you into the dumbest person ever," says Nheth. "Even though I know how to read and write, I have to pretend I don't know."

One of the first things they were asked to do was leave the village. Everyone had to evacuate the towns, villages, and cities and relocate to isolated forests and fields. Nheth and his family ended up in a rice field five kilometers from the closest main road. The regime purposefully isolated the population, restricting the people's movement and placing them in work camps or cooperatives. It was essentially a prison state. After the country was split into zones, they were abolished, reorganized, and renamed at the whim of the ruling central government. Zones were further divided into regions, districts, and subdistricts and villages. In the area around Battambang, where Nheth and his family were living, people were sent to two main areas. Nheth and his family were sent to an area about thirty kilometers from Battambang. They were plopped down in the forest and told to construct a home.

"You can't cross over to anywhere else. That's your area," says Nheth.

The regime drew a border that they couldn't cross. The groups were later enlarged, first to thirty or eighty families and then to a hundred families. None of it was stable, says Nheth. Everything could be—and usually was—changed at the whim of the leaders. They put you in one small group for three months. Three months later they would change their minds and put you in a bigger group.

"They don't have a plan," says Nheth.

Just as San Tran Croucher's family experienced, when their groups were enlarged, meals were communalized. Families could no longer eat together; now they had to eat in a canteen. With communal eating it was no longer possible to cook whatever small animal or insect they could catch. The communal rice pot contained more water than rice, says Nheth. People belonged to work groups, usually arranged by sex and age, not families.

Nheth's group was working on building Kamping Pouy dam, which was constructed from late 1976 to late 1977. To meet the production goal, workers had to work day and night. Tens of thousands of them died of malnutrition, disease, overwork, and mistreatment during construction. A number of similar projects were built with sheer manpower, little more, and often fell apart almost as soon as they were constructed. Nheth mainly carried dirt for the dam, as did his oldest daughter. Puthy remembers carrying rocks weighing as much as ten pounds.

Mom worked in a rice field. After the rice was harvested, her women's group was tasked with separating the grains from the plants. They would stomp on the plants and then sift the result to further separate the grains. Each woman had to fill two huge fifty-pound sacks a day. It was hard, hard work, and you had to finish it. If you didn't, then you didn't eat, says Mom. "They starve you."

The soldiers would take you from the group and give you a different job and a lot less food. And beat you. Both Mom and Nheth mention the beatings. Sometimes the beatings were accompanied by a scolding, a warning. Sometimes, if they really hated you, says Nheth, then they just killed you. Both of them saw it happen.

"If someone that they dislike did something wrong in your group, they pull that person out and kill them in front of you," says Nheth. Bullets were too valuable, so they usually used a shovel-like tool to hit the victim on the head or a machete-like weapon to "chop them."

The younger children, those too young to be of any use, were left in the care of the elderly. Touch was just a baby, but Mom was only able to breastfeed him once a day, as the rest of the time she had to work. She was so exhausted and hungry after giving birth that she once had a serious fall while carrying dirt up a hill. Resting wasn't an option. If you were too sick to work, then you would be followed to make sure you really were ill. If you went to the canteen first before the others, you might be killed for faking an illness.

They were all hungry all the time. But the youngest children, Chamroeun and Touch, suffered the most. When they cried with hunger, Mom would lie to them, promising them: "Tomorrow you will get this. Tomorrow you will get that." It was all she could do to quiet them. The next day she never had anything more to give them.

The rice they harvested went to China. If you asked for even a pinch of it, they smacked it out of your hand. The same went for salt. There wasn't enough of anything. One pair of clothes each, no more. "It's worse than homeless," says Nheth.

The hunger was the hardest, then the fear. The only thing that kept them going was the children. They didn't think they would survive, but they hoped their children might.

The Khmer Rouge fled about two and a half weeks before the Vietnamese arrived. The people were free. Nheth and his family headed into town with everyone else. What wasn't already destroyed was taken. Whoever arrived first grabbed what they could. It didn't matter whose house it was or whose belongings they were taking; they just took them. Nheth and his family didn't take anything. All they had before was a small, one-room bamboo shack with a dirt floor. Now they had nothing. They needed food, but working in the fields was risky; out there they could be captured or killed. Nheth stayed in town and made buckets from aluminum sheets taken from roofs. He had only two tools to work with—an ax and scissors. He made four buckets a day. He didn't sell them; instead, he exchanged them for rice, getting five small cups of rice for two buckets.

"And then those small cups of rice, you don't make rice," says Nheth. "We cook it into porridge so it would be enough for everybody."

Then the drought came, and there was no more rice. Nheth had heard that they were giving out rice in Thailand. He had ventured to the border area before to bring back rice and hear the news. Early on, before the United Nations took over, he heard that some Cambodian refugees who went to Thailand were dumped in the Phnom Dangrek mountain range, where there were a lot of land mines. No one had cleared the land mines, and many people died. The Thai government didn't care. This is how he remembers it.

"People before us," he says, "they didn't make it."

That is essentially true, but it is a little more complicated than he remembers. At first Thailand let the Cambodian refugees in, but in June 1979 the

Thai military forced more than forty thousand refugees back to Cambodia. It is estimated that at least 10 percent of them died. Later Nheth heard there was a new camp, Khao I Dang, which the United Nations was helping coordinate. It sounded better, safer, so the family walked to Thailand.

In Thailand they were loaded onto trucks—ten families to each vehicle—and driven to Khao I Dang. It wasn't until they pulled into the camp and saw foreigners and UN workers giving out food and supplies that Nheth relaxed. "That's when I realize we are safe," he says.

He remembers a lot of little things: the time they arrived, 3:00 p.m.; the number of their section or community, five; the wealth of things they were given, such as rice, wood, bamboo, blankets, pots, mosquito nets. For the first time the children were able to go to school. Nheth became a community leader, a role he would continue in the United States. Life wasn't perfect—bandits came into the camp almost nightly—but they never harmed or killed anyone in the family.

Nheth pushes his cuticles back. "We were okay in Khao I Dang."

They stayed about two years. In October 1980 they were sent further into Thailand to Sa Kaeo II. Another Sa Kaeo refugee camp had been pretty much controlled by the Khmer Rouge. Among those who crossed into Thailand were members of the Khmer Rouge and civilians they had forced to flee. Nheth remembers seeing elite members of the Khmer Rouge at Khao I Dang. In some ways life was easier when the Khmer Rouge were around. At Sa Kaeo II, the Thai guards were rough, says Nheth. The guards would put their dirty feet in the water the refugees drank, would refuse to let them sell anything, and would keep them from learning English. They would also beat them up. At Khao I Dang, he says, they were treated better. Nheth thinks this was because the Khmer Rouge were around, and the Thais were scared of them.

Nheth stops; he wants to clarify a point. He wants to make it clear that life was different for the elite Khmer Rouge and those who worked for them. There are those in the United States, the elite Khmer Rouge, who say it wasn't bad in Cambodia under the Khmer Rouge. And it wasn't, for them. It was hard living with them, first in the refugee camps and now here in Stockton. In the camps there were a lot of Khmer Rouge leaders.

In his position of authority at Khao I Dang, Nheth could have hurt them, but he let it go.

Even in this complex in Stockton, there is an elite Khmer Rouge leader, says Mom. "But if they don't hurt you, you don't hurt them," she says.

And though the Khmer Rouge did hurt the family back then, these people are from a different area.

"Those from our area, we know where they are," says Nheth. "But what can you do?"

They stayed at Sa Kaeo II about a year, during which time Nalin was born. Then they were sent back to Khao I Dang. At some point they found out Onna's mother had survived and was in the United States. As early as 1981 she tried to bring her mother and her two children to the States, but her mother refused to leave without her other children. So they stayed until Onna's mother could sponsor all of them. Nheth remembers the interviews, being asked if he had relatives in a third country. There was a test, lots of questions, and then one last camp in Chonburi, where they went toward the end of 1984.

At Chonburi the workers taught Nheth's family what it was thought they would need to know for their journey. They were told about airplanes and houses, taught how to turn on lights and flush a toilet. They learned that you put meat and vegetables in different parts of a refrigerator. They had electricity for the first time at Chonburi, but camp officials controlled it so they never got to practice flipping an actual light switch.

The first three months after they moved to the United States were the hardest. They had to figure out what to buy at the store and how to get there. They were eligible for government assistance, but they had no idea how to fill out the forms. Onna's mom had sponsored them, but she was not literate in English. She lived in apartment 22, in the same complex where Nheth and Mom still live. After they settled in, Nheth, his wife, and kids moved into apartment 43; another sister moved into apartment 65.

Nheth and his wife recently moved to apartment 24. The living-room window opens directly onto a walkway, and neighbors frequently peek in. Now after greeting Nheth through the open window, an elderly woman enters the apartment. She greets Mom, takes some rice from the rice cooker, and then leaves. Every once in a while a man comes out of another room, crosses through the living room, and steps outside to smoke. He is never introduced. Later I learn he is Chamroeun, the middle son between Puthy and Touch.

As he was in Thailand, Nheth is civically active here. When the apartment complex fell into disrepair—flooding, overcrowding, general filth—he was part of a group known as the Asian Pacific Self-development and Residential Association, which purchased the apartment complex from the U.S. Department of Housing and Urban Development for a dollar in 1993. Afterward the group worked to renovate Park Village and establish social service programs. Nheth was president of the organization for longer than a decade.

Before the apartment dwellers started their own non-profit, there weren't really any groups helping them figure things out, he says. When he first came to Stockton, Nheth had no idea how anything worked. An American neighbor tried to help him occasionally, but mostly he was on his own. In 1987 or 1988 he was accused of receiving an overpayment of food stamps or something along that order; he still doesn't fully understand it. He could choose between jail and community service. He chose the latter. He picked up trash, pulled weeds.

At the time there was supposed to be a government-approved organization helping refugees. And there was, at least on paper, says Thang D. Nguyen of Boat People SOS, an organization that works with Vietnamese refugees. But for refugees with relatives in the States, the sponsoring organizations leaned more on the U.S.-based relative to take care of the refugees, says Thang. This relative often was also a refugee who had simply arrived earlier and had limited knowledge of English and the American legal, social, and educational system. As noted, Nheth's sponsor was his sister, herself a refugee who spoke limited English and was still learning the U.S. system.

The government encouraged Nheth to work, but being already in his fifties, he struggled with the language despite taking regular English lessons. When asked what he wanted to do, he said he could push carts at the grocery store. He was judged too old for the job.

Because so few educated people had been able to survive the killing fields, the members of the Cambodian refugee community in the States tend to be less educated and have fewer transferable skills, says Thang. Their decreased job opportunities, in turn, cause them to struggle more than other Southeast Asian refugees.

Nheth's family survived on government benefits and income from their eldest daughter, who was too old to attend school and so went to work. The rest of the children went to school. In 1989 Touch and Nalin attended Cleveland Elementary School. Onna was in eighth grade at Hamilton Junior High School, but the school bus dropped her off at Cleveland in the afternoon so all the kids could walk home together.

"When we heard the shooting at Cleveland, everybody rushed over there," says Nheth. He recalls the police had the area surrounded. The parents crowded around, trying to figure out where the surviving kids had been taken. After about an hour they were allowed in. Nheth rushed into the cafeteria where Nalin and Touch were.

Touch was different after the shooting—scared, emotional. His parents wonder if he might have reacted differently if he hadn't spent his early years under the Khmer Rouge. They wonder how he was emotionally affected as a baby by seeing his parents so infrequently and by only receiving breast milk once a day.

As for Puthy, could the years of starvation and hard labor under the Khmer Rouge have contributed to his kidney failure? There were no childhood vaccines when Puthy was a baby, and the water they drank under the Khmer Rouge and even later in the refugee camps in Thailand was filthy, stagnant. There is evidence that Cambodian refugees suffer higher rates of hypertension and diabetes, two of the main causes of kidney disease in the United States, than the rest of the American population.

They don't talk about Chamroeun. Only Onna mentions him. She says he is "not fully there" and describes him as though he's a baby her aunt and uncle have to take care of. She tries to stay close to help, but with Chamroeun it is hard.

With Touch she doesn't have to try; they were always close. Just four years his senior, Onna was the first one he called when he was in trouble. His parents didn't always know what happened. In September 1995 she was the one who went to get him from the back of a police car when he was first in real trouble. He had been visiting a friend in a nearby apartment complex known as Manchester. There was a shooting, and he ran, making the police think he was involved.

Before the school shooting at Cleveland, Onna remembers Touch doing well in school. He was good and didn't hang out with a bad crowd. Onna, Nheth, and Mom—all three of them say the same thing: "We don't know how he fall off into that part."

They have ideas. The neighborhood wasn't the best. Nheth remembers a drive-by shooting at their apartment complex. They all remember the American godfather who they thought would keep Touch on the right track. Maybe it was after the man's death that Touch went astray.

"There were things we thought," says Onna, but nothing they knew for sure. "Maybe he didn't want us to know."

After Touch married and moved to Florida, they heard he was a bouncer at a nightclub. Whenever he would visit, he would tell them everything was fine, and they believed him. In the summer of 1998, when he came back for a family wedding, he got a ticket for driving under the influence. They thought that was his only real legal trouble. In June 2005 at Nalin's wedding, he told them everything was good. They didn't know any different until he was arrested that November. In 2006 he told Nalin and Onna that Immigration and Customs Enforcement had talked to him and that he could be deported. The younger generation tried to protect Nheth and Mom from the details. When Touch talked to them, he always told them not to worry. When he talked to Onna, he told her what they did to him in prison and what he had to do to survive.

"I always have to tell him to just walk away or whatever and push him to continue with his schooling in there," she says.

He worked on getting his high school equivalency certificate, read books, wrote to family members. Onna and Nalin tried to help him with his divorce, to determine what prison programs he should participate in, and to look into his immigration status. Sometimes he would call and ask Onna what she had for dinner. Then he would tell her what he had and what he tried to make with it. When his daughter visited family in Stockton in 2009 or

2010, all the young women in the family—lots of pretty women with long, straight dark hair—took a picture and sent it to Touch. Onna still has it on her phone. Onna and Touch would tango together on FaceTime.

"I'm not sure how he did it," she says. Cell phones aren't usually allowed in prison.

When Touch was released, Onna went to Santa Ana and cooked him all the foods he missed while he was locked up. When he was fighting to delay his deportation, they held a rally for him in Stockton. The deportation weighs on him, she says. Sometimes he calls Onna after he gets off work and is tired, feeling ready to give up.

"I tell him, if we don't speak out, we're not going to be heard, right?" Onna says. "That's why we do what we do."

Nheth is afraid for his son. He has been back to Cambodia twice. When he went in 1995, he says there were still Khmer Rouge soldiers around, and he was too scared to leave town. The second time, in 2010, was better; he went to Battambang and Angkor Wat. Even so, Cambodia isn't like the United States. There you can't say what you want to say as you can here, as Touch does. There it is corrupt; the people are different, he says. Touch doesn't know how their minds work. The family has no land, no house, no business there. There is nothing for Touch to do there; he can't even farm or fish.

"Life there is hard, and without a good job, I don't know how you survive," says Nheth. "So by sending him there, he's not going to survive."

Nheth still has nightmares about Cambodia, about the killing fields. He sees himself in the fields, with the Khmer Rouge still in control. When he wakes up, he tries to think good things and meditate for several hours before lying down again.

Two decades after their resettlement, 62 percent of surveyed Cambodian refugees who had lived through the Khmer Rouge suffered from post-traumatic stress disorder and 51 percent from depression, a rate six to seventeen times higher than the U.S. average, according to a 2005 article from the *Journal of American Medical Association*. Those surveyed came from a representative community sample of Cambodian refugees in the largest community of Cambodians in the United States.

In her 1998 dissertation, Professor S. Megan Berthold found that the parents' mental health conditions were largely associated with their experiences in the genocide. In contrast, the mental health of those who were adolescents in the mid-1990s and were at least five years old when they came to the United States were strongly associated with the community violence they experienced in the States. Among the adolescents, more than 80 percent reported having seen or heard gunfire while at home, and only 54 percent were confident they would still be alive at the age of twenty-five.

It comes as little surprise then that a third of these adolescents showed symptoms of PTSD. The number of violent events they were exposed to significantly predicted their level of PTSD, according to Megan's dissertation findings.

Other researchers have examined non-Cambodian adolescents exposed to violence in the United States and concluded that those with PTSD were at risk of reduced academic achievement, more delinquent behavior, impeded or truncated moral development, and greater aggressiveness. This fits well with Touch's background.

The PTSD findings among the older generation fit just as well with his parents' nightmares. Since the Khmer Rouge came into power, his mother says she has never had a happy dream.

"I always see something bad," says Mom. "I always see that moment where I work hard and see my children sick."

PART 3

YEAR OF THE MONKEY

16

TWO CITIES TANGLED TOGETHER

Song is in a wheelchair. He has had another stroke, his third. "A lot of people could not afford second stroke," he jokes.

Physically Song could "afford" three strokes, because the last one was small and did not cause serious brain damage. He is lucky in that sense. Financially he can't really afford this one. He spent a month in the hospital, racking up $180,000 in medical bills. After his first stroke in 2010 he spent three years in a nursing home. The second stroke occurred only last summer in 2015. The third stroke happened over the winter. They are coming closer together now. He keeps a paper about high blood pressure pinned to his office wall and a basket full of prescription medications within arm's reach. On his computer screen he is engaged in various conversations on Facebook. It is spring 2016 and he is dying—and full of ideas.

His schemes seem outlandish, out of step with reality. He is communicating with a stranger who says he has money stashed in an unstable country, and Song can have the money if he helps the stranger retrieve it. Song knows it is too good to be true, and yet he has printed copies of the certificates the man sent him, meaningless pieces of paper with the names of make-believe companies and figures with far too many zeros. He talks about using the funds to start a charity in Cambodia. He needs money for another project as well, a documentary he wants to make about Lon Nol's escape from Cambodia. The man who originally promised to help fund the documentary has gone missing, and there is no script, just the short newspaper article Song wrote about that fateful April day in 1975. Nevertheless, Song sees the project as ready to go; he just needs a little funding.

It all could be written off as the musings of a lonely old man except when Song talks about what he knows, the Cambodian community, his people. When he does, he makes sense, or as much sense as can be made of the divided community. Right now, tensions are high everywhere; the community is "boiling." And it starts here in Long Beach.

To understand the current conflict in Long Beach, though, you have to know the people's historical connection with Cambodia. And to understand modern-day Cambodia, you have to look to the influence of the refugee community in Long Beach. The two are more knotted together than linked. Leaders in the Cambodian community in Long Beach became leaders in Cambodia, leveraging the prestige earned in one place to advance themselves in another. At the center of this group is San Croucher's middle daughter and Sithy's younger sister Sithea San or, more precisely, Sithea's husband, Richer San. Song knows the family; he was friends with both Sithea and Richer when they were in Long Beach. They were kind to him, and he respects what they did for the community in helping to found Cambodia Town, even though he refers to it as little more than a few signs and a shop or two.

What happened when they returned to Cambodia in 2012 is different. That was the year Song's friend Eng Lykuong, a popular Phnom Penh dentist, invested in an agricultural development company that failed to get off the ground and lost $1 million. Two years later, in September 2014, Richer and three other prominent community members—a former ambassador and author, a New York State assemblyman, and the former head of a large non-profit—were accused of luring Eng into the phony business deal. Richer, who has not been convicted, maintains his innocence. The accusations have hurt his reputation in both Cambodia and Long Beach. Added to that is his association with the country's ruling Cambodian People's Party, a relationship highlighted by a certain guest invited to Long Beach's Cambodia Town 2016 New Year's parade in April.

Richer and Sithea are on the board of the Cambodian Coordinating Council, the non-profit organization in Long Beach responsible for hosting Cambodia Town's New Year's Parade. For the parade's tenth year, Hun Sen's eldest son, Lt. Gen. Hun Manet, was invited to the parade. Song believes Hun Manet's appearance was part of the CPP's efforts to improve its connection with the Cambodian diaspora, especially with the younger generation. Whatever the reason, it didn't work. A number of Long Beach–based Cambodian American groups spoke out against Hun Manet's proposed appearance at the parade. Their complaint was as much against Hun Manet as his father and the party both men represent. The protesters spoke out against Hun Sen's Khmer Rouge ties and the CPP's corruption and oppression. They urged officials at city hall and even the mayor to pressure the Cambodian Coordinating Council to cancel the invitation to Hun Manet. In the end, Hun Manet himself announced he would not attend the parade, although he still planned to visit Long Beach.

While Song has his issues with Richer, he likes Hun Manet and Hun Manet's father, Hun Sen. When Hun Sen was in Palm Springs last month, Song went to see him. Afterward he wrote about his visit with Hun Sen and posted it on Facebook. In response, he says, a prominent member of the local Cambodian community wrote bad things about him on Facebook. The two know each other from the Lon Nol years when they both worked for Lon Nol. They always got along fine—until now. The Facebook fight isn't what has Song angry, though.

Song is upset because he wasn't invited to participate in the parade. He is upset because when he went to see Hun Sen in Palm Springs, he says the people in charge didn't give him a name tag. He is upset because he isn't being treated as an important person, a former minister in three separate governments. He feels he should be the parade's grand marshal; instead, the grand marshal is a woman who works in the film industry. The slight is a continuation of the mistreatment he believes he has received from people such as Richer and Sithea when he visited Phnom Penh a year or two ago. While he was there, he said the power couple he once considered to be his friends did not drop by. He believes they expected him to come to them, but that is not how it works in Cambodia, he says. He is old and infirm and without a car. They are younger, have an expensive car, and live in a big home; so it is their responsibility to come to him.

The snubs are part of a bigger problem, one that will only get worse as he continues to deteriorate. To them, he is "irrelevant." He understands this. What he doesn't understand is why. He believes he still has some political influence. He thought about attending the parade, sitting in his wheelchair and watching from the sidelines, but he says his friends advised him not to. It is a question of his honor, his dignity; without that, he says, "you have nothing left."

The last time Chanphirun Meanowuth Min took part in the parade he was with Song, and Song was the main attraction. That was a few years back. This time he is simply representing his framing shop. It is the Friday before the Sunday parade. It is supposed to rain this weekend, but if the sky is clear Sunday, his friend is going to let him use his red 1955 Porsche 550 Spyder. If it rains, he'll have to drive the framing shop's van instead of the classic convertible. He says he is participating more to show his support for the community than to advertise his business. But taking part in a Cambodian community celebration can't hurt business.

Many Cambodian American homes feature Cambodian landscapes, and someone needs to frame them. At present a large canvas painting of Angkor Wat occupies the front of the shop. Chanphirun is stretching the canvas for a customer. Others hire him to frame the paintings they bring back from trips to Cambodia. The quality of these paintings varies greatly. In Cambodia some sell for as little as $100. But a tube of acrylic paint can cost $40. So to keep their costs down, the artists use cheaper paint that flakes and cracks.

Chanphirun has been known to do some painting of his own. It doesn't happen often. A pencil etching of his mother has been awaiting paint since 2006. He based the etching off a photo, not his memory. It is displayed in the front of his shop. In the back room is a nearly life-size photo of Max as a baby. On occasion, Chanphirun has been known to refer to the child in the picture as Matthew before quickly correcting himself. When he was a baby, Max worked as a model briefly after being "discovered" by a talent agent when he was at the mall with his parents. His big break was a diaper commercial, which Chanphirun never got to see. Max made $100 an hour for the shoot, but given that both parents were required to be there, it didn't make sense for them monetarily. So Max's modeling and acting career never really went anywhere. They still keep him listed with several agencies, but now that Max is older, Chanphirun worries that he would need to speak more English than he does for it to work. He has blown-up shots in his shop from Max's professional posing days.

Chanphirun also keeps a photo album from his own most recent birthday bash. It was his sixty-first or sixty-second birthday. He isn't really counting. He had a big party at a Cambodian restaurant on Anaheim Street. One of the guests was a photographer who put together a photo album of the event: Chanphirun smoking a cigar, Chanphirun with a group of women, Chanphirun with his wife, Chanphirun with a group of men. There are dozens of different people in the photos, maybe a hundred; but all of them are "just friends," says Chanphirun. "I don't have relatives."

Chanphirun's relatives are all dead, making New Year's an especially important holiday for him. He believes New Year's is about people you love who have gone, not the living who are still with you. Traditionally you leave food out for your ancestors or give food to the monks to give to your ancestors. The Chinese tradition is to give away money in the belief every dollar you give away will come back to you a hundredfold. The idea strikes Chanphirun as Christian. A lot of religions are similar.

"But you have to be careful who's believing what," he says. "Sometimes they misread the fine print."

His own belief about the year of the monkey is straightforward: don't leave food out. His reason for taking part in the parade was just as simple: a friend suggested it. Like Song, Chanphirun uses jokes to lighten the heaviness of history. He tries to get along with everyone, understanding the necessity of compromise and the difficulty of living purely by ideals. They have that in common. He doesn't know Hun Manet, but he does know the military leader was just a baby during the time of the Khmer Rouge. His father may have been Khmer Rouge, but Hun Manet was too young to have participated in the government or the killing fields. As for protesting Hun Sen's membership in the Khmer Rouge, Chanphirun believes if anyone has the right to be mad, he does.

"I'm the one should be getting mad," he says, "because Pol Pot kill all my family."

And yet he is not angry that Hun Manet was invited to the parade. The reason others are upset, he believes, is not because of the Khmer Rouge connections of Hun Manet's father but because they didn't share in the profits when Hun Sen made money from destroying Cambodia's forests. He goes deeper into conspiracy and history from there until the conversation turns to the Vietnamese, as it so often does when talking about Cambodia.

Two days later on Sunday, April 10, Chanphirun is in a gray Porsche convertible. It isn't raining, but with the storm clouds in the sky, his friend nixed the use of his Spyder. He still decided to accompany Chanphirun, and they both sit in this other Porsche. The sports car belongs to Chanphirun, who still shows flashes of his former self—the boy who once had the best car because his uncle was a ruler, the young man who ran with men who cared more about their wheels than their responsibilities.

David Ros opts for a simpler means of transportation, Alaysia's skateboard. He isn't in the parade; he's helping get participants signed up and registered. He explains that with the last float, the royal court, most of the shirtless men with swords walking alongside the float are missing, casualties of the Hun Manet controversy. Solomon is dressed similar to his father, in jeans and a patterned button-down shirt from Cambodia. He gets around on his scooter.

As the floats line up, waiting to move forward, old women make themselves comfortable on bus stop benches. A Latino man walks up and down Anaheim Street, selling blow-up sharks and cotton candy, while a black politician throws out a few words of Khmer. Little girls twirl parasols, makeup caked on their faces. A cluster of teenagers dressed in long, tight traditional skirts lounge outside a beauty salon while checking their cell phones.

The parade itself kicks off around 10:30 a.m. with "fireworks," or tubes that make a little blast and let out confetti. The monk who opens the festivities talks of peace. A woman walking alongside holds a poster: "No CPP bloody hands in our country."

Chanphirun drives by toward the beginning of the parade; his place is number 13. He is sorry Hun Manet couldn't be there.

"I have done wrong in the past. Thank God, he give me second chance, and I corrected," he says. "Everybody deserves another chance."

17

NEW YEAR, SAME PAST

These are the things Jennifer Diep remembers about communism: no toothbrush, no toothpaste—"never brush my teeth all those four years"—no shampoo, no clock, no time, no date. Nothing, nothing. Oh, and being hungry—starving, actually.

San Tran Croucher's youngest daughter is sitting at a picnic table in Long Beach's MacArthur Park, where the 2016 Cambodian New Year's parade finished. It has now transformed into an extended party. The overcast morning has turned into a warm afternoon, but Jennifer is dressed in knee-high black boots and a long-sleeve denim dress with a red scarf around her neck. She is forty-five years old and ill; recovering from surgery, she can barely lift her arm. Jennifer looks up at the sky. She is lithe like her mother, with bobbed hair and long bangs. When she was a child in Cambodia, she went by the name Sithea Vy. Back then she never looked at the sky.

"If I look at the sky, I look at the trees to see if any fruit I can pick and eat," she says. "If I look at the ground, I make sure anything's down there I can eat: insects, vegetable, grass. Anything you can cook that won't poison."

Back then, she says, you knew it was morning when the sun rose. That was the only way to keep track of time. Night came when it was dark. The insects bit so hard then it was impossible to sleep. All of them—Jennifer, Sithy, and Sithea—had lice, so their mother cut their hair off. But Jennifer's head still itched and she scratched it until it bled. Then the scabs became infected, and the infection attracted mosquitoes. The mosquitoes came during the day when she worked in the field.

Working in the fields was what she spent most of her time doing. She had other tasks as well. They all had different roles at different times and were sent to different locations to perform different jobs. And yet each sister also had her own role within the family to be fulfilled on the occasions when they were together. They divided the tasks by their natural abilities. Sithy was good at "outside stuff": foraging for food, making trades, securing sustenance of some sort. Jennifer was good at "inside stuff": making a shelter from whatever was on hand, making secret fires to cook forbidden food. Sithea was good at being sick.

"She almost lost her life," says Jennifer. "She is ready to go, bottom line. She only skeleton left."

Jennifer and Sithy had close calls too. There was the time Jennifer got lost in the fields and was almost caught by Khmer Rouge guards, and another time her clothes blew away after she washed them, leaving her completely exposed to the elements. Sithy was routinely beaten and forced to watch the murder of her comrades. But neither of them ever came as close to dying as Sithea did. Sithea wasted away on two separate occasions and passed so close to the other side, even her sisters feared sleeping beside her. During the Khmer Rouge years, all Sithea ever did was come close to dying. That was Sithea's role.

After the Khmer Rouge was ousted, the sisters' roles reversed. Sithea became the strong one, the successful one they could all depend on. Sithy became the sick one, continuously suffering from seizures and near disasters. Jennifer's role is less well defined. The baby before the Khmer Rouge came to power, she neither stood out for success or failure under the Khmer Rouge. The same is true now. She is also the one who chose to carry her birth father's name, Diep. She doesn't blame him for being absent when the communists took over; she considers him lucky to have avoided the torture the rest of them endured.

She changed her name to Jennifer at school in Long Beach because no one could pronounce Sithea Vy. Her sisters had shorter names; only she had a two-word first name, which she made into one, Jennifer. She couldn't have chosen a more American one if she tried, naming herself after celebrity Jennifer Lopez. Sithy never officially changed her name, but she also has an American version, Sandy.

Like her eldest sister, Jennifer never finished high school. Unlike Sithy, though, she managed to do okay for herself work wise. She has worked as a data entry clerk, as a secretary, as an accounts payable clerk, and, most recently, as a card dealer. She got into the last occupation thanks to her husband, who is also a dealer. They have one child, a teenage boy whom Jennifer has pushed into participating in the parade today. She wants all Cambodian American kids to participate so in the years to come they can keep the parade going after the older generation is no longer able to do so.

Jennifer and her sisters were just children when they started performing traditional Cambodian dances in refugee camps. The Khmer Rouge tried to destroy Cambodia's traditional dance culture along with other art forms and nearly did so by killing most of the country's artists. The dances were revived in the refugee camps to keep them from completely disappearing. The people carried the practice over to the United States, and San's daughters continued dancing for a while after moving to Long Beach. Then Sithy had a baby, and Jennifer got into different things. Only Sithea stuck with it. Through junior high and high school, Sithea kept up the traditional dancing. Culture was always and still is important to her. She is the reason Jennifer and Sithy and their families are here today.

Despite still being in recovery from her surgery for breast cancer, Jennifer is responsible for dressing and undressing performers, fastening and unfastening large dangling necklaces and extensive bracelets, and removing towering crowns. Jennifer locates a golf cart to drive her several blocks away to the office, where the performers are changing into their street clothes. Ten minutes later she arrives and gets to work.

Inside the small insurance office, shimmery skirts and tops are strewn across desks. Parade participants were outfitted in traditional clothes, wearing pinks, greens, and reds. The women's backs were bare, the men's chests were exposed, and their arms were covered in fake gold jewelry. The highlight was the Cambodian royal court, which included a queen, Sithy's daughter, Lauren Thor. Her outfit required balancing an almost foot-high crown on her head and tottering around on four-inch wedge heels. Sithy was her daughter's royal assistant. Now Sithy sits near the door, eager to exchange her traditional blue dress for jeans and boots.

"Somebody have my shoe, I can't wear," she says, trying to locate her footwear amid the jumble of personal belongings stored in the office.

Jennifer has made her way over to an office desk and is now busy unpinning some sort of decoration from a young man's costume. Sithy focuses on her own costume, having told the performers she had helped dress to simply undress and leave their costumes in the office. She trusts they will do that—either that or she simply doesn't care if they don't. Jennifer is more attentive, taking her responsibility to heart and making sure the performers remove the jewelry with care and package the costumes back up for next year.

Sithy has located her missing shoe and changed into regular clothes. Next year, she has decided, she will ask to dress only the women. She says they are easier to deal with. This year, though, she is done. She leaves Jennifer to deal with the details and, along with her boyfriend, KC, and a few others, climbs into their SUV and heads back to the park and the festivities.

KC is doing the driving, leaving Sithy free to talk in her rapid-fire way. She talks about work, life, love, and everything in between. She has a new job cleaning the facilities and packaging croissants at a croissant warehouse: "$70 a day after taxes, make good money and they pay me every week, better than over there." By over there she means the factory where she used to work for $300 a month cleaning the floor and earned a bit extra for folding clothes. She says the clothing factory didn't always pay her on time, whereas now she receives an official paycheck every week. She found out about the job at the croissant company through the same friend she had helped earlier by sharing her work at the factory with her. What seemed a foolish kindness at the time has proved beneficial in the long run.

Between when she quit or was let go from the clothing factory—it isn't clear which—and when she started packaging croissants, Sithy had trouble paying rent. She and KC ended up moving in with Lauren, Lauren's fiancé, and their three children. Sithy hopes it is temporary, as all of them are crammed into a three-bedroom duplex. But it isn't the first time she has stayed with Lauren, and it probably won't be the last. Of all Sithy's children, Lauren is the one who spends the most time with her mother. In the family, Lauren is the one who gets along with everyone and tries to smooth the edges of rough personalities. In that way she is like her grandmother San. It was Lauren who let Sithy stay with her when Sithy got out of jail. It is Lauren who accompanies Sithy to court, and it was Lauren who participated in the parade today alongside her mother. Now back at the park, Sithy looks for her eldest daughter.

Lauren, who is thirty-one, has San's delicate features coupled with curves, which today are emphasized by tight jeans and a fitted top. She is with her fiancé and their three daughters: ten-year-old Jocelyn and seven-year-old twins Madelyn and Makayla. Jocelyn and Madelyn keep to themselves, but Makayla walks around with her head in the sky. Smiling at every adult face she sees, her attention focuses completely on whomever she encounters. It is this "jolliness" that endeared her to Tom and made him feel protective of Makayla, who has special needs. Although Tom came into San's life after Sithy was already grown and should officially have been Lauren's grandfather, both Sithy and Lauren consider him a father figure. Lauren does because he raised her; Sithy, because he tried to support her as much as he could. Now that he is gone, Sithy regrets the things she didn't do, such as showing up last Thanksgiving after promising Tom she would be there. Lauren just misses him.

The loss has been hardest, of course, on San. Soon San hopes to move into the back unit of the duplex where her daughter and granddaughter are living, a building she owns. She plans to make the move once the family currently living in the back unit finds a new place to live and she sells her house. It will be good for her to be back in Long Beach with her family. She was supposed to be with them at the parade today but canceled yesterday, saying she felt sick. She seldom feels good these days, constantly calling Lauren out of loneliness, although in truth the two have always spoken frequently. Lauren calls her Mae Yiey, meaning literally "mother grand-mother." Lauren says, "Me and her, we're closer than me and my mom."

Now that she is a mom herself, Lauren is continually impressed by how much San did for her and her siblings. The ice skating lessons were not just expensive but also time intensive, with practices before and after school and competitions at five o'clock in the morning. Lauren doesn't even want to schlep Jocelyn to gymnastics, yet San had her and her sisters in ice skating so long Lauren mastered all her double jumps. She doesn't remember Sithy playing much of a role in her life back then. Even today Sithy is more like a sister than a mother.

Sithy says the same thing, complaining that when she goes to a party, her daughter warns her, "Mommy, don't drink." Both her daughter and her mother tell her she is too open and free with words, telling people everything, never holding back. She tells Lauren, "You are my daughter; I know what I'm doing."

Lauren does credit her mother with doing better since she has been out of prison. Sithy has been drug free. She is still less cautious than Lauren would like, still talking too openly, but she isn't getting herself beat up or getting mixed up with gambling and drugs like before. They are closer than they have ever been. While Sithy was behind bars, Lauren even took her young daughters to visit her. When Sithy came out, Lauren let her move in with her and her family. Sithy is getting to know her grandchildren, cooking for them, playing with them. The part Lauren worries about the most if her mother is deported is how her children will react. The girls went from not knowing their grandmother to shouting "Gram's home, Gram's home" every time they hear the gate open.

At the park, while Lauren is talking, Sithy is sharing a sandwich with Makayla. The little girl follows her grandmother with huge eyes and an eager smile. KC is off somewhere else. He also had a role in the parade as a member of the royal court. Sithy goes back and forth on their relationship, talking one minute about a recent fight and the next about how she hopes to marry him in a traditional ceremony before her mother dies. She knows marriage to KC wouldn't be without its complications. She acknowledges, "Honey, he on life parole" of at least several decades. But, she explains, parole is better than probation. With probation they can check on you without notice; with parole they let you know before they check on you. Parole is in fact an early release from prison, while probation happens before or instead of incarceration. The exact conditions for each can vary. The main drawback for Sithy and KC is that KC can't travel without permission. That means if Sithy is deported to Cambodia, then their relationship would be difficult to maintain.

Sithy's next court date is coming up on May 31. Lauren plans to go with her. It isn't a trial but a hearing at which they will announce when the trial will be. On her end, Sithea is trying to do what she can to help. She has government connections in Cambodia, the same politicians the protesters in Long Beach are speaking out against. Nevertheless, they are the ones in power, and Sithea is trying to work them, not just for her sister, but for all deportees of her generation. She is realistic; she knows it won't help to simply ask the Cambodian government not to accept deportees. Instead, she wants to rectify the agreement Cambodia has with the United States by having the Cambodians specify a certain arrival date in the States that would make immigrants and most of the refugees who arrived as children in the 1980s ineligible for deportation. The 1 Love Movement and Southeast Asian Freedom Network are currently focusing on the same tactic.

The one warning Sithea says the government gave her when she brought up the issue was to make sure the Cambodian American community would speak with one voice. Now she fears the disruption caused by those protesting Hun Manet's participation in the parade may have hurt the cause. Hun Manet was never going to be grand marshal, as some reported, she says; he was simply going to walk in the parade. After the Long Beach community protested his involvement, he decided not to participate in the parade, but he still came to Long Beach to visit. The protesters then spoke out against his presence, shouting defamations outside the restaurant where he was Saturday night and gathering at the park at the end of the parade route with their signs and slogans.

Lauren saw one poster with Hun Manet, "and then my aunt, my uncle and then another couple and then, like, faces crossed out, talking about they're communist." It didn't make sense to Lauren, as the communists had almost killed her aunt. Sithea is a businesswoman, a believer in democracy, so Lauren wonders why the protesters were calling her a communist.

Sithea attempts to laugh it off, saying of her name, "[It is] very famous. You Google it, you can see it." Her irony comes as somewhat of a surprise. Slim like Jennifer, Sithea somehow seems physically small and weak. In reality she is a tightly coiled spring of anger and energy. It is mid-afternoon and the festivities are wrapping up now, but Sithea is keeping busy, overseeing the packing up of items at the various booths and displays. Although most people have changed to more casual clothes, Sithea still wears the same long, traditional red dress she wore for the parade.

Her style is businesslike and traditional; she wears glasses and her hair short. Jennifer's style remains somewhere between the two extremes of her big sisters'. None of them are timid in their speech, but Sithea uses her education and social standing to add weight to her arguments. She and her husband are trying to do something nice for the community, she explains. What did the protesters do? They never do anything—volunteer, donate money—they just protest when someone tries to do something for the community, like the parade. Because of all the protests, there were fewer attendees and volunteers at the parade, so the royal court had to walk instead of ride on a float.

Sithea believes the protesters are not protesting her connection with the government back in Cambodia as much as her success. The Cambodian American community in Long Beach has a history of pulling down anyone doing something for the growth of the community, she says. Their actions this time have left her "really disappointed for our community." They want democracy in Cambodia, she says, but the democracy they practice here only applies to those who agree with them. Everyone else is labeled a communist.

When the topic turns to her husband's court case, she is more reserved. She sticks to the same line they have held throughout: "He's just an employee; he works for the company." She won't say much more because the case is still in court. It isn't as easy for others to brush off their misdeeds, especially here in Long Beach. That is one of the problems with the community, according to Sithea. Cambodia has moved on, taken things forward; the educated class speaks English better than some of those in Long Beach. In Cambodia, if you have a skill, if you have money, if you can take care of yourself, then you do well. Sithea works as a consultant for an information technology company.

She believes with Sithy's limited education her only realistic option in Cambodia would be farming. Then there are her sister's seizures; Sithea thinks the current health care system in Cambodia is lacking.

She still remembers when Sithy started having seizures in the refugee camp, how she had so much energy nobody could hold her so she would fall to the floor, how she struggled to breathe, and how the doctors didn't know what to do with her. The seizures prevented Sithy from attending school in the United States, an environment in which Sithea excelled and prospered. Sithea pushed herself to get educated; she didn't need her mom telling her how important education was because she knew. The same was true for her commitment to the community; it came from something inside of her. She formed friendships with people who shared her values. Sithy's friends belong to a different crowd. Their educations, the friends they spent time with—that might be how the sisters diverged. It isn't clear what happened, says Sithea, just "somehow [in] this environment I can cope better than my sister."

She acknowledges she wasn't always the successful one. During the killing fields she was the weak link, and her sister Sithy helped them survive. That may have left Sithea less traumatized by the killing fields than Sithy was and thus able to use them as inspiration. Whenever Sithea has a challenge, she thinks, "If I survived the killing fields, this is nothing. I can overcome." That is what she and her husband do, she says. They don't use their experience to hold them back in sadness and trauma but to spur them forward. That doesn't mean it has stopped haunting her. She has dreams sometimes, wakes up sweating in the middle of the night, and has to remind herself that it's okay and that she is not living in that time anymore. It doesn't stop her from growing. But it stops others, and she notices this more in Long Beach than in Cambodia.

"Sometime I come, I see my community here, it's really sad. They still the same," says Sithea. "They not grow, some of them."

She includes her older sister, Sithy, among this group. "She still stay in the past."

18

GIRLFRIENDS

David was supposed to be a half-naked guy. Of the hundred or so volunteers who didn't show up to walk with the royal court in the Cambodian New Year's parade, he was one of them. A few of his friends were going to participate as well, but they weren't even awake when David went knocking on their doors a bit before eight o'clock in the morning. They also weren't really into the shirtless thing.

David had other reasons for dropping out of the royal court. After helping with the parade registration in the morning, he decided to watch the parade instead of participating in it. His decision had a lot to do with his mother, Chanthaveth Ros, who hates the Cambodian People's Party and was disgusted when prominent CPP member Hun Manet's name got linked with the parade. Even after Hun Manet announced he would not walk in the parade, Chanthaveth still didn't want her son to be involved in the festivities.

So David wasn't a half-naked man. Instead, he remained behind the scenes, spending a few hours checking everyone in before the parade kicked off at ten o'clock. Even in the background, though, he was noticeable, rolling along on his skateboard, and that was part of his plan. It is important for him to be seen helping out, for those involved in the anti-deportation movement to take part in community events. It is also important for them to interact with the current Cambodian government. The night before, David met with Hun Manet's people. He lowers his voice as he says this, as if his mother might be listening. He is beginning to think the CPP members aren't all bad—at least not the younger generation.

It is late afternoon, and David is hosting a small barbeque in the swath of shared concrete that his home and several others face. Too small to be called a courtyard, there is enough space for a grill, some lawn chairs, and even a table, although the table is actually in David's single-car garage, which has everything but a car inside of it. Two men are smoking weed in the open garage; another is seated in a lawn chair by the front door, his wife at his side. There are more women inside the house and several young kids running around shooting each other with toy guns. At least two of the men in attendance are in a similar situation to David's, yet neither of them is active in the anti-deportation movement. Most of the really active people are women, says David. The little gathering he is hosting is actually for two female activists, at least one of whom recently returned from Cambodia, where she was promoting the cause. David believes men don't get involved because if they do care about the issue, chances are they are deportable, and they think that by exposing themselves they will get picked up faster.

"They don't want to bring attention to themselves," he says. "Everybody's just trying to stay low."

David recently started thinking about doing the same thing, yet he is still committed to the cause, and that requires putting himself out there. Knowing Hun Manet was going to be in town, he tried to secure a meeting with him. When that failed, he relied on friends to help him get into an event Hun Manet held the night before the parade that was geared toward getting the younger generation involved with the party. David was able to talk to a man who promised to deliver his message to Hun Manet. David gave the man a flash drive with the campaign launch video on it and a copy of the agreement between Vietnam and the United States that the campaign would like the Cambodian-U.S. agreement to mirror.

"I rolled it all down to him, about the family situation, this thing needs to be revised, and so forth," says David.

When the man told David that Hun Manet already knew all of this, David said he was aware of that, "but I want him to know it in every city he goes." The plan was for a member of the movement to give Hun Manet the same message in each Cambodian American community he visited, continually reinforcing how important the issue is. As the Cambodian government has the power to change the situation, the activists are upping their pressure on it to do something.

David says some in the movement have even joined the CPP to effect change from within. David refers to this phenomenon as "taking one for the team" because few in the movement support the CPP and thus must sacrifice their own beliefs to help the cause.

But some are now deciding the CPP isn't as bad as they were led to believe. They report that a younger element in the party has more progressive thinkers who want to steer the country toward development and away from corruption. This younger generation, the ones like Hun Manet, don't want the old ways, but out of respect for their elders they are playing along with them while they are still alive. That is what David has heard, and it makes sense to him. After all, it is the older generation that keeps David from joining the party to help advance the cause. One member of the older generation in particular—his mother—is stopping him. Joining the party, he says, would break her heart.

"She's in bad health, and to know I joined a party she adamantly is disgusted about . . ." He doesn't finish. His mother has warned him over and over again that because he is a deportee, he is particularly vulnerable should he become close to the party. She tells him the party can use him, manipulate him, and blackmail him very easily. "Or they could just deport you and kill you over there."

He has to be careful. It is as though he is walking a tightrope; he can't lean too far to either side or he will fall. That means he also can't take part in the parade protests even though he supports them and in the long run believes they will prove beneficial. The unrest, he believes, will help the Cambodian leaders see how disgusted Cambodian Americans are with them. Once they realize that, David believes he will have an advantage because he can tell them it will improve their image if they help change the deportation agreement. From what he has heard, the team of activists that recently returned from Cambodia did a pretty good job of convincing the government that how deportations are conducted needs to change. But he hasn't had the full update yet. That will come after the guest of honor,

Mia-lia Kiernan, cofounder and organizer of the 1 Love Movement, arrives, and they meet with other leaders in the movement.

In the kitchen, David's girlfriend Debbie Keodara is making a special fish dish for one of the guests of honor. "This is going to stink," she warns.

She is by herself in the kitchen, chopping, sprinkling, and stirring. It is Debbie's first time making the Cambodian fish dish, and she is not sure how it will turn out. She points out she is Laotian and more comfortable cooking Laotian food.

"Me and my daughter are like, she [the guest of honor] better be pretty because this thing stinks," says Debbie.

She is wearing a loose white tank top and a tight pair of black pants. Debbie has a small muscular build. In a week or so she will be forty-one years old. She has been with David seven years, and in all that time "there is never one day something doesn't happen that I don't think about it [his deportation]." When she first started dating David, things were pretty casual, and she wasn't too worried about the fact that he had been in prison. Three or four months later, when he told her he was deportable, things were more serious, and it was "too late." She was "too old" to do anything but stay. She took a chance with him, hoping and praying things might change; yet she also was aware they probably wouldn't. Whenever he was out, she called to check on him to make sure she knew what was going to happen.

She tries not to think about his deportation, yet she also knows there will come a time when she has to face it, and she needs to be prepared. She lives in a weird sort of denial that reality keeps interrupting, preventing any sort of lasting comfort. When a stranger knocks on the door, she is scared to open it. She knows agents can come for David at any time, not just when he goes to check in. She doesn't watch the videos the other deportees post after they arrive in Cambodia. It would be too sad for her.

Debbie is chopping onions now. The brown rice has already been roasted and blended. She calls out to David as he passes, "Babe, did you grab my lime?"

David points out the lime on the counter, the one he picked from his mother's tree. David is the one who saves. Debbie is the spender—at least she would be if she had any money, but she doesn't. David is the family's main financial support; Debbie only works in a day care part time. At present, David is on temporary disability, though, and receiving only two-thirds' pay. His right hand has some sort of tendonitis, aggravated probably from the constant and repetitive movements of connecting blood lines and sanitizing dialysis equipment. The pain he worked through before has come back to haunt him. He hasn't worked since January but hopes to be back on the job by summer. Debbie is confident he will be. Since she has been with him he has always had a job, always been the one who supported the family. Her own income is not even enough to buy her makeup.

"It's a joke," she says, without laughing. Debbie's humor is so subtle and delivered so flat that it is easy to miss. The pain underneath is evident. She doesn't try to hide it, admitting that she is lonely and depressed in Long Beach, a place she finds too crowded. She grew up in Seattle, Washington. When David gets deported, that is where she plans to return: to her friends, to her family, to the Lao people who live there.

Debbie was two years old when she left Laos and fourteen when she came to the United States. The years in between were spent in Thailand, waiting for an older brother who had been arrested in Laos. After escaping imprisonment in Laos, her brother hid in the mountains. Her late father, Khamsaen Keodara, would not leave his son behind, so they waited. A high-ranking military man in the Laotian army, her father brought many other people to the States as well. She says he was able to do so because of the support he had shown the Americans during the war. Debbie likes to brag that half the Laotians in the United States got here by using her father's last name. He would tell the Americans, "Oh, that's my family," and they would bring them. When he died four months ago at the age of eighty-six or eighty-nine—different sources list different ages—hundreds of people attended his funeral, she says.

Talking about her father is the one thing that seems to make Debbie happy. She keeps a photo of him in his younger years on the wall. He was a good man. She doesn't say if he was a good father. David is. He takes Solomon everywhere with him. Debbie says, "They want to be twins." Solomon is a complete "daddy's boy." If his dad isn't there when he wakes up, he starts to cry. When David is gone, she plans to tell Solomon his daddy is out of town until she thinks he is old enough to understand. "I'm just going to keep lying to him," she says.

It seems as good—or as bad—a plan as any. Her daughter knows more. Alaysia knows that the activists who come over to meet with David are there because they are all in danger of being sent to Cambodia. She understands this could happen to David. She doesn't know it is because he committed a crime, but she does know not to tell her little brother. Beyond that, Alaysia doesn't ask questions. She is a quiet child. Like her mother, she doesn't have a lot of friends in Long Beach. She does well in school, helps care for her younger brother, and keeps the secret with which she has been entrusted. Because she is Laotian like her mother, there is no question of their following David to Cambodia. They don't have citizenship and don't speak the language.

Debbie has said all she has to say, so I tell her I am going to track down David and follow him around for a while. She calls out after me, "It's not good to follow him. He's going to take you back to Cambodia."

It is a good joke, only she isn't laughing when she says it. She isn't even smiling.

David is outside with Sam, a father of three outfitted in black-and-white tennis shoes with blue laces. Sam is light skinned and tall with tattoos all up and down his arms and neck. His eldest child is seven years old; his youngest, three months, which is only one month older than Sam was when he came to the States in 1980. Sam served eight years in prison for "having a possession that wasn't mine" and has been out since 2008. He is a truck driver now, living in Anaheim. Growing up he had no idea what his parents went through in Cambodia; they were good at masking it. He would hear tidbits of stories and would think whatever they went through was their thing. He was American; what happened to his parents in Cambodia didn't concern him. It wasn't until later that he understood there was more to it than that.

"Me, this generation, I just feel like I'm caught in this middle," he says.

Mia-lia arrives around 5:30 p.m. She isn't ready to reveal what happened in Cambodia just yet. Touch texts David saying he won't be able to make the meeting; he couldn't get a ride.

Two days earlier, when I saw him at his brother's house in Santa Ana, one of the first things Touch said to me was, "Where's the car?"

It was eight o'clock in the morning, and he was headed to the gym, a routine that usually requires a bike. The street was quiet, with everyone already having gone to work, and the trash collectors had yet to empty the trash cans neatly positioned in front of the sidewalk. Exercising is something Touch began behind bars after he decided he didn't want to come out of prison looking like some fat "Oompa Loompa." There also really wasn't much else to do. Working out became a way for him to keep his mind off things and get rid of his frustrations. It still does that. It is also one of the ways he stays healthy so he can meet all the medical requirements for the kidney transplant.

The gym is only about a five-minute drive from Puthy's house. Outside Touch stops a guy exiting the massive structure.

"Yo, how you doing?" Touch asks. "You done?"

The guy slaps Touch's hand in greeting and offers a half-complete thought: "Maybe Tuesday."

"Maybe Tuesday, huh?" Touch smiles and keeps walking.

Inside he heads upstairs, past row upon row of stair climbers and elliptical machines. The music is loud; the mirrors, large. After leaving his trademark hat in the locker room, Touch sits down on a large mat to stretch. A father and son are sparring in the nearby boxing ring. Touch's own family doesn't have big plans for the weekend; most of them will attend the New Year's celebrations in Stockton next weekend. Touch plans to join them, as he did last year when he counted at least twenty big statues at the Stockton celebration and maybe triple the number of people in attendance than when he was a child. The Stockton festivities include a concert and blessings. Monks and parents dole out the blessings. In return those receiving the blessings give the monks food. In Touch's family, they also give their parents money.

Touch has already secured permission from his probation officer to travel to Stockton next weekend, and he hopes to do the same at the end of May for Memorial Day weekend. His daughter, Priscilla, will be sixteen on May 24, and he wants to hold a Sweet Sixteen party for her in Stockton. On both occasions he will travel with Puthy, who tries to squeeze trips in between dialysis sessions.

Puthy is doing better now; he is no longer losing weight after having given up the foods that were causing him trouble. Touch is learning more about his brother's body, about the difficulties of finding a donor pair for them. Puthy has type O blood, which means he is a universal donor and can donate to a person with any type of blood, but he himself can accept a kidney only from someone with type O blood. Because a type O donor can donate to anyone, Touch can't see a situation where that donor would donate to a stranger like Puthy over donating to his or her own family member. Touch has type B-negative blood. The only reason he is helpful to Puthy is that he does not have high blood pressure, so he could conceivably donate a kidney in a paired kidney exchange. He is the only one in their family who could do this, as everyone else has high blood pressure, which precludes kidney donation. His thirty-year-old sister, his thirty-five-year-old sister—all of them have high blood pressure. "Everybody," he says, "except me."

"Seems like God put some purpose . . . ," he says, not quite completing his thought.

Done stretching, Touch stands up and puts on his gloves. He walks past the cardio machines and toward the free weights and the guys in tank tops with heavily tattooed biceps just like his. On Touch's right bicep is a cobra; on his left are cards and dice and "Asian Boyz." He had all of them retouched while he was in prison, where "it's cheaper, way cheaper." Touch lays his towel on a bench and puts a 25- and 45-pound weight on each side of the bar. His goal is to bench press 275 or 300 pounds, but he is stuck at 245. He tries to push his limits but not when he is by himself as he is today.

His usual gym partner, Danny, Puthy's college-age nephew, is absent. Danny lives in the same house as Touch; his parents co-own the house with Puthy and Puthy's wife. Touch's brother has no children of his own. He says Puthy and his wife wanted children, but they were never able to conceive. When Touch suggested they adopt, he says, Puthy told him it wasn't the same. Now Touch thinks it is probably for the best. A child is a lot of responsibility, and he thinks Puthy is too weak right now to handle that.

Touch has a lot going on as well. In between his trips to Stockton, he needs to check in with Immigration and Customs Enforcement. It was

January when he last checked in, and the agency gave him until April before wanting to see him again. He is hoping he will have the enrollment papers from the kidney program by then so he can get his official additional two-year stay of deportation. He has done pretty much all he needs to enter the program as a donor: has had all the blood tests—one time they took twelve tubes from him—and has seen numerous doctors. He tells them all over and over again that he is not being forced into helping his brother in any way. He has had an electrocardiogram and an X-ray. He also had to do "some sort of running test" and made it to level 5 when some people don't even make it past level 3.

They haven't told him the final results yet, but they found plaque in his arteries, just a little bit. They also told him his cholesterol is a little high. He knew about the cholesterol from prison. The health care system behind bars is pretty good, he says. The copayment to see a doctor is only $2, although as wages are only about $18 a month, it doesn't end up being that cheap. Touch got extra money from his brother. Puthy sent the money, but Touch isn't sure if the funds themselves came from his parents or from Puthy. Touch never asked.

He moves on to the incline press machine, puts a 45- and 10-pound weight on each side. He has a pair of wireless headphones and tends to listen to the music from when he was young, nineties stuff: Dr. Dre, Salt-n-Pepa, East Coast, West Coast. He listens to them all but not the new stuff, with rappers talking about millions, not $20 anymore.

"And that's something I can't relate to," he says. "They from the bottom like everybody else. Make it to the top, so they forgot where they came [from]?"

Touch never forgets. The Asian Boyz gang tattoo is still on his bicep. He is Facebook friends with the guys he grew up with, guys who have been deported back to Cambodia. When the activists were in Cambodia, they paid a visit to Battambang and held a party for the deportees there. His friends posted pictures on Facebook, and one of them even called. Touch asked him about the party, the meeting, what was being said. His friend said what the deportees always say: "We're going home!"

"I guess he was drunk," says Touch. "That's the only answer I got from him."

He hopes it is true. He hopes they can change things before his time comes up again. In the meantime, he is free; at least ICE says he is free, and he believes he is free in spirit. But in real life he isn't. It is hard to be free when he has no future here.

He has been lifting for about an hour now. He usually ends his workout with a quick mile run on the treadmill. But it's Friday, the end of a long week, so he skips it and heads to the Fantastic Café for a late breakfast instead. It is an old-style diner in a newer neighborhood, its walls covered with pictures of young white guys dressed in military uniforms from maybe half a century ago, its booths occupied by Latino families. Touch seems to have forgotten his borderline high cholesterol and orders scrambled eggs, hash browns, and steak. At least his toast is whole wheat.

He is working on getting his driver's license. It has been longer than a decade since he drove, and it is strange to be doing things over again, as if he is being reborn. It is good actually to have the chance to redo things. Only he is finding there are some things he can't do over, such as be a father to his daughter. She should be a sophomore in high school, but credit wise she is still a freshman. Before he was locked up, he always pictured her graduating from high school, no problem. He saw himself giving her the love and support she deserves and being there to teach her as a parent is supposed to teach a child.

"But I fail," he says. "I fail when I got put away for nine years, and I knew that."

He switches gears then, as he stops blaming himself and puts it on his ex-wife. Things aren't good between them. He blames her for Priscilla's doing badly in school, for Priscilla's getting into boys too young, for keeping Priscilla from him. Sympathizing with him was easier when he was taking some of the responsibility and not loading it on a woman who isn't there to defend herself and had to raise a daughter alone for almost a decade.

The idea of separating from his family again haunts him. It is the pain of separation that keeps him from dating. When his friends and family ask him why he isn't dating, he tells them he can't cope with the sadness that will come when he is deported. It bothers him, though. He spends a lot of time thinking about it; he just can't figure out how it would work. He tries to work out a scenario. He tells the woman his name, goes on a first date. They talk, they get along, and they go on a second date.

"And you like, 'Hey, I'm getting deported. How you've been?' How she going to feel?"

That's where he gets stuck. If she wants a serious relationship, then she probably doesn't want to deal with deportation. So she is going to back out right then.

"So what good am I?" Touch wonders. "I'm like a sitting duck, just waiting for something to really happen to me."

19

A PARTY AT OAK PARK

Cleveland Elementary School, Stockton, California, January 17, 1989.

Nalin Hak is jumping rope when she hears it.

Pop! Pop! Pop!

She stops jumping and turns to look where the noise is coming from, the playground. Nalin is in the first grade. Usually she swings on the monkey bars in the middle of the playground during recess. But today she and her cousin decided to jump rope behind a tree on the edge of the playground. It is only a few weeks after New Year's Eve, so the noise seems familiar.

"Who's setting off firecrackers?" Nalin wonders.

One of her friends, a little girl who often plays at her house, is on the monkey bars. Or at least she was. Now all the kids on the playground are running. Nalin looks at her cousin.

"What's going on?" she asks.

"I think someone's shooting at us," says her cousin.

Nalin knows to run to her classroom in an emergency. This is an emergency, and Nalin is a good girl, so she does what she has been told. She runs toward her classroom—right through the path of the gunfire. Somehow she makes it to the hallway safely. She looks down and sees an injured girl crawling on the floor.

Five children are killed that day. Three of them are from Nalin's Oak Park neighborhood. One of them is her friend on the monkey bars.

Oak Park, Stockton, California, May 2016.

For a decade, every year around the anniversary of the shooting, Nalin had the same nightmare. Like so many dreams, her nightmare is a disjointed series of images that don't connect: she is going to school, she is behind a tree, there is gunfire, she starts running—nobody is there. On the ten-year anniversary of the shooting, one of the girls who was injured during the shooting wrote an article about the massacre for the high school newspaper. When Nalin read the piece, she cried. For the first time she mourned her dead friend. For the first time she processed what had happened. She allowed herself to grieve. After that she never had another nightmare.

Maybe it was easier for her to acknowledge the loss and move on because she was so young when it happened. In some ways, she says, she didn't really understand what was going on. Her brother Touch was older, in fifth grade. Nalin thinks that might be why it affected him more. She knows everyone has a different way of mourning, of processing information. Touch simply "never talked about it."

Nalin Chhim is thirty-four now, an accountant, a wife. It is the Sunday of Memorial Day weekend, and the family has gathered to celebrate her niece Priscilla's sixteenth birthday. They are set up at a cluster of picnic tables in the same park where Priscilla's father, Touch, hung out when he was a kid, the same park near where the city's seventh homicide of the year occurred two months ago. At least half a dozen other parties are taking place today in Oak Park, a flat grassy field with groups of trees and tables that occupies several blocks in central Stockton. Most of the gatherings feature bounce houses, balloons, and a mix of generations. The men tend to congregate around the grills; the women, in the shade of the oak trees.

Touch is on his feet, checking in with family and friends. He has replaced his trademark hat with a baseball cap. In his khaki shorts and button-down purple shirt, he is hard to miss. Nalin, a lone figure tucked away on a woven mat under the trees, is more difficult to locate. She is heavier than her slim brothers, not as flashy as her female cousins. Quieter and less outspoken than her charismatic older brother, Nalin didn't know a lot of people growing up. But plenty of people knew her. Touch made sure of that. He had a lot of friends, and he told all of them that Nalin was his little sister, the sibling just below him. That is what Touch is like, says Nalin—warm, loving. He is also outspoken.

As a kid Touch resembled a typical American teenager, challenging his father's rules. Only he wasn't a typical American teenager; he was something in between, a child on the verge of adulthood who was trying to balance two very different cultures. Touch and Nalin were forced to please two divergent sets of authority: at school they were told not to speak Khmer, not to act Cambodian; at home, their father scolded them for acting American. Nalin gave in to both sets of authority, playing smart American student during the day and obedient Cambodian daughter at night. It wasn't an easy concession to make.

"I wanted to play soccer," she says. "I wanted to do a lot of the American stuff, but my dad's like, 'You're a Cambodian girl. You're not supposed to do that. You're supposed to know how to cook and clean.'"

She laughs. "But I don't know how to do any of that," she says.

She does know how to fluently read, write, and speak Khmer. She attended a Khmer class when they were kids. Touch didn't go. Nalin was curious about her culture, about the history of Cambodia. Touch, she says, wanted to assimilate; he wanted to be American.

Their father didn't understand his youngest son. Nheth belonged to a different world, a world in which he was respected, honored, and followed. It was a limited world, restricted mostly to the Cambodian American community. Outside of those boundaries he flailed. He struggled to learn English, misunderstood the laws, and was unable to find work. It was scary and dangerous out there, an unknown he couldn't protect his children from.

Back then in their neighborhood, says Nalin, "wherever you go, you hear someone got shot, got robbed." Their dad wanted them to stay home after school. He was scared of what might happen to them if they were away from home. The shooting at their grade school probably didn't help. Nalin sees this; she knows the emotional baggage her parents came with and the lingering stress that comes from growing up in a virtual urban war zone. Touch talks about it sometimes, but a lot of his friends shake it off. They say it wasn't that bad; it didn't affect them that much.

That's Curly's attitude. The nickname comes from his long wavy hair, an attribute that combined with his substantial build and tan skin leads some to think he is Polynesian. But there is no question Srim "Curly" Chrim is

Cambodian. The first thing he says when I mention the deportation issue is, "I'm already safe." It turns out, though, Curly is also facing deportation. Sixteen years ago Immigration and Customs Enforcement detained him after he finished serving time for a probation violation. In all the years since, Cambodia has never issued him travel documents. The way Curly sees it, if they wanted him, then they would have taken him a long time ago.

They have taken plenty of other guys he grew up with. Still others, like Touch, are waiting to go. Some of them are at the picnic today; he sees others around town with bulky ankle bracelets. The situation is all too familiar. Yet Curly shrugs off any suggestion that their upbringing might have been difficult, might have played into their current troubles. He downplays the inner-city violence, the poverty, and the untreated trauma. "It was all right, I guess," he says of adjusting to life in the United States.

His wife, Emily Chrim, insists it wasn't. "It's not fine," she says. "They think it was. But as an outsider, I can tell you that a change in life like that has not allowed them to grow up the way you would have if you were born here."

A white girl from Florida, Emily has straight, light brown hair and a spattering of freckles on her face. Curly, Touch, and their friends don't see things the way she does, she says, because it was just how they grew up; they're used to it. They adapted and so believe it is okay, but the adaptations have cost them and are still costing them. In school, even when they understood English, their teachers continued to treat them as if they didn't until the kids started to doubt their own mastery of the language. To this day, she says, Curly, now thirty-seven years old, gets nervous when he has to speak English with anyone in an official position.

To fit in they stuck together, with many forming gangs. Their parents didn't interfere because as refugees they didn't understand what they were dealing with. Curly never joined a gang, but Touch did. He was part of the Oak Park crew, the Asian Boyz. Almost everyone at the picnic was Oak Park except, of course, Emily. Although she has lived in Stockton for six years now, Emily still has the ability to see things as an outsider. To her the designation "Oak Park" doesn't mean anything. Maybe at first the term didn't mean much in Stockton either. Back then most of the Cambodian refugees settled in an apartment complex near Oak Park. Over time some of them moved to an apartment complex a few blocks away on Manchester Avenue, and they started referring to the complex simply as "Manchester." Emily doesn't quite understand why the two Cambodian American groups became rivals, but they did. The Oak Park group had its gang, and the Manchester kids had theirs. Or maybe each had several. Emily isn't sure of the details. She just knows the two areas became rivals, and the only reason her husband didn't end up taking sides is because he spent time in both areas and so had to maintain neutrality.

Curly doesn't talk about this; neither does Touch. None of them do. But their actions and references add more weight to Emily's argument than the words they never speak. Decades later they still reference Manchester and Oak Park as if they are different cities, not different apartment complexes just blocks apart. Touch still has Asian Boyz inked on his bicep and won't go to Manchester. The older generation is just as stubborn. Several times Curly and Emily offered to move Curly's mother to a nicer place, but she doesn't want to leave Manchester. It may not be a nice neighborhood, but it is her neighborhood and where she is comfortable.

Curly and Touch tried to escape it. Curly went to work in Alaska for a bit; then he tagged along with Touch and Touch's wife when they moved to Florida. It was in Florida that Curly met Emily. She was fourteen at the time; he was older than eighteen. Because they had their first son before Emily turned sixteen, Curly got in trouble with the law. He got five years' probation and a lifetime on the sex offender registry. Emily is thirty-one now, and they are married with three sons. But Curly can't volunteer on his youngest son's field trips or coach his eldest son's football team. He violated his probation several times—it wasn't hard to do—so he also served a bit of time. After his last stint behind bars, ICE locked him up. Now a deportation order is hanging over him.

Emily was just a teenager back then, so she didn't grasp everything that was going on. Now she does. A year ago she became an immigration attorney.

For the first six years Curly was good. He checked in with ICE every month, then every three months, and followed by every six months. He had been extended to annual check-ins by the time he moved back to Stockton with his wife and kids in 2006. Soon afterward a letter arrived at his mother's home in Stockton telling him to check in at the nearest ICE office. He got scared. He missed his first check-in, then his second, then his third. Ten years passed without his entering an ICE office. Then, last month, he decided to check in again so he could get a work permit. He had been working without one as a truck driver, but now he needed one. Emily went with him. Nothing much happened. They didn't hold him and didn't penalize him for not checking in for a decade. They just updated his papers and let him go.

Emily and Curly used to joke that the Cambodians don't want Curly. After Emily ordered Curly's immigration papers, she decided the joke was actually true: the Cambodians don't want him. Of course, it doesn't say this in his file. It only says something about his being removed is not in the foreseeable future. That comes from the American side. It has led Emily to conclude that the Cambodians get to pick and choose who they take and that her husband falls under a category they don't want—sex offenders. She also thinks those who have been released from detention following prison are unlikely to be taken. The people getting sent back are largely those who are being detained now, not those who were detained years ago, then released, and told to check in. Early on, or soon after Cambodia began accepting deportees in 2002, some of those who had been out for years were taken, but Emily believes that happened because Cambodia hadn't considered them previously. Now once people are released, she doesn't think it is likely they will be taken. It is just a hunch, though.

Even if it is true, it doesn't help Touch. He already has a date set; his travel documents are ready. There is another difficulty with Touch's case. He has on his record an aggravated felony, which means after deportation he virtually would be barred from the United States for life. Curly does not, so after ten years he can apply for a new green card, as can those already deported to Cambodia. The thing is, although they are eligible to apply, whether they actually will be granted a green card is up to the discretion of U.S. Citizenship and Immigration Service.

The deportees without aggravated felonies do have a chance, though, unlike those such as Touch with aggravated felonies. The only solution Emily can think of for the latter group is to try to get post-conviction relief. For it to work, an attorney has to argue that a client's previous attorney did not explain the immigration consequences of their plea. If the judge agrees, then the client is eligible to withdraw the guilty plea. When the case is reopened, the attorney negotiates an "immigration neutral plea," so his or her client pleads to a code that is not an aggravated felony. The conviction remains and the punishment would have already been imposed and served, but the client would not face a lifetime ban.

As a lawyer, that is what Emily would tell Touch. As his friend, her advice would be different. "I want to tell him, 'Who cares, just stop checking in,'" she says. "'The worst that's going to happen, they're going to deport you,' which they're going to do anyway."

She knows how difficult that living without papers would be. She did it with Curly for a decade, fearing every knock at the door might be ICE coming to take away her husband. She has stood by Curly through a lot, and most of the time Touch has been there with them. When Curly was locked up for violating probation, Touch would give Emily money and help her with the children. He also was the one who got into crystal meth with Curly. It was not long afterward that Touch was locked away for nine years. Emily and Curly tried to help him out when he was locked up by checking on Priscilla. They still try to bring her to events when they can, but her grandmother doesn't always allow it.

The grandmother is at the party now. She makes a point of saying hi to Emily, mentioning how she has three teenagers under her care at present. She has helped with Priscilla since Priscilla was a baby. When Priscilla was just a few months old, Touch and his wife sent her to their parents in Stockton. Ever since then Priscilla has gone back and forth between her parents' place in Florida and her grandparents' in Stockton. The most recent move came last July when Priscilla was sent to live with her mother's mother in Stockton.

Priscilla doesn't hide the reason for her latest relocation: she was failing ninth grade. She is proud of how she has improved academically since being in Stockton, and in her sophomore year she received an A, two Bs, and a C. It still leaves her behind credit wise, though, and she is hoping to make up some of the courses over the summer. She also wants to get a job. A lot will depend on what her grandmother allows her to do. Like everyone else, Priscilla mentions how strict her grandmother is with her, but she doesn't voice it as a complaint so much as a fact. She has a sweet childish voice and matching deep dimples on either side of her face. In a light pink slip dress and laced-up strappy sandals, she flits around the event, careful to please both her mother's Laotian family and her father's Cambodian crew. That is how she refers to them—her Laotian family and her Cambodian family. Always separate. The division is no doubt because of her parents' divorce, but her words make it cultural.

Her dad tells her she has her mother's personality. She admits that may be true; after all, she spent most of her life with her mom. In looks though, she is certain she resembles her father. When they stand next to each other, the resemblance is clear; the smile is the same. Both father and daughter are pretty much all smiles today, especially when a massive pink sheet cake is brought out around 4:00 p.m.

"Why is it so big, Dad?" Priscilla asks.

Touch doesn't answer and just places two large candles on the cake—one shaped like a one; the other, a six. With the candles lit, he puts his arm around his daughter so family and friends can snap cell phone pictures of them. Standing side by side, it is evident how much time Touch missed in his daughter's life. The girl beside him is almost as tall as he is. Touch moves away, takes a picture of her. Her aunts and uncles, cousins, nieces, and nephews take their own shots, calling her nickname—"Cilla!"—so she will look their way.

"Okay, are you done?" she says at last.

Touch hands her a knife, and she cuts the cake. She is wearing a designer Michael Kors watch, a pricey piece of jewelry her father gave her. It wasn't what she wanted for her birthday, but she professes to like it. She accepts the gift with openness and honesty, the same way she has accepted her father's reinsertion in her life. She calls the watch nice but doesn't hide the fact that she didn't ask for it. Likewise, she accepts her father's efforts to reconnect with her but admits that for most of her childhood he was locked away.

She doesn't remember anything much before her father went to prison. What she remembers is receiving phone calls from a father who wasn't there. Seeing everyone else with a dad, she would wonder, "Where's my dad?" When she got to be a teenager, it felt odd, weird, as if she didn't really have a father.

"And then, once he got out, I saw him, I started crying," she says. "I was just like, 'Wow, like, you're my dad.'"

He has tried hard to be a dad and do the things he thinks dads do: take her shopping, give her money, try to find ways to see her, and spend time with her. Yesterday she spent five hours with him and the rest of her Cambodian family. Touch is making an effort, but he doesn't always get it right. Sometimes he says stuff that hurts her feelings, things a father shouldn't say, she says. Usually it is about her not spending time with her Cambodian family, and she thinks that is unfair. The only reason she doesn't spend more time with them, she says, is because her Laotian family won't let her. With practice, with time, she figured her father would improve.

Then she learned time was something he didn't—they didn't—have. She couldn't believe he was going to be deported, taken from her again. She wants him close to her. Sending him away again would "break my heart," she says with a teenager's flare for the dramatic. Yet she knows it will happen and just hopes, like her father, that it will happen after she graduates from high school. She hasn't told him what she wants to do after that, about the career path she has chosen for herself—prison counselor.

She has introduced her father to her boyfriend. Dennis shows up after her Laotian family has gone. He is quiet. He is a good Christian boy, says Touch, who neither approves nor disapproves of the relationship. It is early evening now, and people are packing up their chairs, their mats, their children. Touch is sitting by Emily, his button-down shirt unbuttoned, revealing a tank top underneath. They talk about Priscilla's boyfriend. It has been more than half a lifetime since Emily married, but she remembers her teen years well. She warns Touch that he will push Priscilla away if he doesn't let her date who she wants.

"She staying with you tonight?" Emily asks.

"She's going back. I can't have her stay," he says.

Someone asks the question on everyone's mind: "Because her grandmother won't let her?"

"No," says Touch, "because Daddy's kind of drunk." He smiles, continuing to sip a beer.

Tomorrow, after Puthy has dialysis, he and Puthy will drive back to Santa Ana. Then Touch will be back to his regular life, his night-shift job, his role of kidney donor. He has finally been cleared to officially enter the UC-San Diego Health program. They gave him the paperwork, and he took it to ICE so he could get his official extension. Only he has not been given the official extension; he isn't really sure why. So he is waiting again, waiting on ICE and, now, waiting on Puthy. Once Touch was cleared, Puthy learned the doctors wanted him to redo his medical tests. Three years have passed since he first underwent medical tests to make sure he was healthy enough to receive a donated kidney. Puthy understands it has been a long time and that they need to redo the tests. He just doesn't understand why they didn't tell him that while he was waiting on Touch, why they couldn't have tested him while Touch was being tested.

The delay means more time on dialysis, more time sitting still for three hours and fifteen minutes three times a week. Not moving, just waiting. If he moves, the machine beeps. Some dialysis centers have a small TV. Other centers have internet access. Usually Puthy sleeps for the first hour. Then he sits and waits. It isn't the easiest thing, staying in one spot for so long. It is boring. He won't let anyone go with him, knowing they will be even more bored than he is. It is tough, but he has no choice; he has to do it. Family members who want to go with him have a choice, so he refuses to let them waste their time alongside him.

"Over here, my mom want to go with me. I say, no, it's not a good thing people just sit down three hours and watch," he says. "Nothing to do in there."

It is a hot day, but Puthy is wearing jeans and a long-sleeve shirt, the only one present wearing so much clothing. He is thin and tired; the trips to Stockton are hard on him. Tomorrow will be even worse, having to drive back to Santa Ana right after undergoing dialysis. He does it for his brother and his parents, for his family. It was his money that went to Touch when Touch was in prison. Touch never asked and he never told him, but most of the time Touch was locked up, that is where the money he received came from. Puthy sent money to Priscilla during that time too, when it was her birthday, when she needed some things. He still gives her things—an iPhone, an iPad.

Chamroeun—the third brother, the one born between Puthy and Touch—is here too. He is the only man present not wearing a shirt. He stays with the men the whole time. A woman, probably a relation, passes by and pulls his jean shorts up a little higher on his waist. He seems not to notice. He is never introduced, only pointed out. Nalin mentions his alcoholism and how he dropped out of high school. He speaks English, but his accent is so thick it is difficult to understand him. He has emotional problems and anger issues. "I don't know what he's holding," says Nalin.

When her mother talks about the Khmer Rouge years, she describes Chamroeun as looking like the famous images of starving African children with bloated bellies. She talks about how he was so hungry he would eat dirt. When she was young, Nalin didn't believe all the stories her parents told her. She thought they were exaggerating, that they were just telling stories about how hard they had it as all parents do. When she was in high school, she decided to research the Khmer Rouge for herself. Then Nalin realized everything they had said was true. They actually went through all of that; her brothers actually experienced all of that. The stories about their pushing logs out of the way so they could drink from a watering hole at night only to discover in the light of day that the logs were bodies—that was true. Her parents, her brothers, her older sister—they survived that horror.

Later she would learn her husband had lived that way as well. He is older than she and remembers being eight years old in Cambodia and having his mother taken from him. He never heard from her again.

Nalin has made two trips to Cambodia—one in 2010 with Puthy and her parents and one in 2013 with her husband and his family. On the second trip she remembers how afraid her husband's family was in Cambodia of asking questions, how they wouldn't ask for something they wanted in a shop, and how meek they were when people were rude to them. Nalin didn't understand their hesitancy; as an American she is used to speaking up.

In Cambodia she discovered that when you're poor, you don't have a voice. That is one of the things she worries about with Touch. He will be poor when he returns to Cambodia. It will be difficult for him to find a good-paying job as he doesn't speak the language well and has limited skills. Nalin knows she would be better off over there. She is an accountant—her skills are almost always in demand—and she is fluent in written and spoken Khmer. Her husband could manage as well, and being older than she, he is closer to retirement age. She and her husband have talked about it. When Touch is deported, they have a plan: they will go with him.

20

JUDGMENT DAY

Every once in a while Sithy looks back at her family from her spot at the defendant's table. Her mother, San, seated on the edge of the last row in Courtroom C, looks small and frail in a slightly too-big black suit. Sithy's daughters, Lauren and Laurel, in leggings and nice tops, squeeze in next to Lauren's three daughters, the younger two with bows in their hair. They all drove together from Long Beach, leaving at 6:30 a.m. to make sure they arrived at Los Angeles Immigration Court by 8:00 a.m.

All they need to do this August morning is offer proof that Sithy's abusive ex-boyfriend is working for the government in Cambodia. That is how Sithy's lawyer, Kim Luu-Ng, explained things to them. Now at a little past eight o'clock, Kim passes a picture of Sithy's ex in his military uniform to the prosecuting attorney, Rebecca Stern. Kim waits as Rebecca examines the photo.

After a minute or two Rebecca looks up. "I need a few minutes," she says.

Sithy glances at her family. She is dressed in a form-fitting skirt and business jacket; her long hair is down. Her life is looking pretty good these days. She has her driver's license now, and after today her deportation nightmare should be over. Except now there seems to be a problem. Sithy watches her mother and daughters exchange worried looks. She sees her grandkids fidget expectantly. Only Kim remains calm. Kim approaches the prosecutor's table and explains the picture that shows her client's ex-boyfriend in his Cambodian military attire came from Facebook.

Rebecca is not swayed. The photo has no context; it is just a print of a single photo. She wants to see the photo on the Facebook page on which it appeared.

Kim apologizes. "I will take care of it," she says. "Just give me a few minutes."

Sithy and Kim gather their things and make their way into the gallery. Another lawyer and his client replace them at the defendant's table. In the back of the gallery San looks lost. She searches for an answer on her grandchildren's faces. They are just as baffled as she is. Kim told them that the case would go smoothly, that the government agreed not to deport Sithy as long as Kim produced proof that Sithy's ex-boyfriend was in Cambodia working for the Cambodian government. But the prosecutor today is different, and she is demanding more detailed proof.

Kim hustles Sithy out of the room. She motions for Lauren to follow. Just before they exit, Kim reaches out and pats San's shoulder. "It's okay," she says.

Then she is gone. San is left sitting on a half-empty row, waiting to see if Judge Rose Peters will deport her daughter to Cambodia.

Kim had a rather strange path to immigration law. She started as a litigator in a big law firm. Then she moved to Legal Aid. Now she has her own private practice as an immigration attorney and co-owns a restaurant with her husband, who is a chef. She is on numerous boards, is always rushing to meetings, and takes calls while driving from one place to another. It is all "very LA," but there is something else as well: Kim is a refugee. Her family fled Vietnam almost forty years ago.

Kim has successfully defended around two dozen Cambodians in deportation proceedings. The cases, she says, are "very, very difficult to win." A few weeks before Sithy's hearing, as Kim drives to a meeting, she explains that each deportation case and argument is different, but torture is a common theme. An earlier case ruling established that if you can make a compelling humanitarian argument regarding torture or persecution that happened many years ago, then you will be allowed to stay based on what happened all those years ago. The problem is that in immigration court, precedents don't always mean anything, says Kim. Immigration judges often make very, very bad decisions.

"They don't obviously weight the evidence correctly. They don't take into account all the evidence that was presented," says Kim.

When it comes to cases of long-ago torture, Kim feels judges rarely find the arguments persuasive enough, at least in the case of Cambodians. The genocide Cambodians experienced, she believes, is not treated the same as the Jewish Holocaust and not seen with the same severity. Kim admits her point is just a theory; it is not as if Jewish Holocaust survivors are lining up to claim asylum based on torture they received in Europe decades ago. But if they were, she thinks they would be more likely to be granted asylum based on their suffering than Cambodians would on theirs.

Not all of her clients are direct survivors of torture. Some are the children of torture survivors, or secondary survivors of torture. The argument she uses for this younger generation relies on evidence that suggests many survivors of torture suffer from severe post-traumatic stress disorder, making them unable to live a normal life. In this state they no longer possess the skills, desire, or mental capacity to raise their children properly. Thus, for these children, "even though they were not direct victims of torture, they secondarily suffered from the effects of torture," says Kim. Those are some of the points Kim uses in her strategies for her clients.

Unfortunately, not everyone has a lawyer fighting for them. Most don't. Immigrants in deportation or removal proceedings are not entitled to a government-provided attorney. To fight their cases, they must have money to hire a private attorney like Kim, must be lucky enough to have an organization that will help them, or must have a lawyer who will take their case pro bono.

"So if you're poor," says Kim, "chances are you'll get deported."

And if you have an aggravated felony, as Sithy does, you will be deported for life. That is why the stakes are so high in Sithy's case. If she doesn't win now, then she will never be able to return to the United States. Those with lesser crimes are sometimes deported for a decade, but in reality, though, that term is often for life as well, says Kim. That is because if they have a drug crime, which many of them do, then they are effectively banned for life. Under federal law, taking part in selling any amount of drugs qualifies as an aggravated felony. Those who have committed other crimes can apply for waivers but not drug offenders. It doesn't matter much, though, because waivers are very, very difficult to obtain.

"So practically speaking, given the average impoverished Cambodian national that gets deported, unfortunately the possibility of coming back is quite slim, whether it's because of the permanent bar or whether because it's just too difficult," says Kim.

Kim wins because some of her clients can qualify for asylum, or legal protection granted to those who fear persecution in their home country given their race, nationality, politics, or membership in a social group. Others, like Sithy, are not eligible for asylum because their felony convictions are deemed too serious. In their cases, Kim goes for relief under the United Nations Convention against Torture and Other Cruel, Inhuman, or Degrading Treatment or Punishment, which prohibits the return of someone to a country where he or she could be tortured. The UN General Assembly adopted the Torture Convention in 1984, and it entered into force in 1987. Sithy suffered torture under the Khmer Rouge, and because her abusive ex-boyfriend now works for the Cambodian military and has threatened her, she could suffer torture if she is deported.

San and Sithy both provided detailed statements documenting the torture Sithy suffered under the Khmer Rouge. Dr. Rose Marie Durocher, a therapist who treated Sithy at the Program for Torture Victims in Los Angeles, submitted an eight-page psychological evaluation. According to Durocher's evaluation, Sithy is plagued by constant worries that distract her from the present. This may explain her inability to focus and her habit of jumping from topic to topic in conversations. Sithy worries about re-triggering painful memories, about her future, and about her own life as a "nobody." In addition to her painful past, the document notes Sithy's low self-esteem and ends with the doctor's warning: "It is my professional opinion that deportation of Ms. Yi to Cambodia would be disastrous, as it holds for her only traumatic reminders of the years of captivity under the KR [Khmer Rouge] and the horrendous killings to which she was witness."

Back in Courtroom C, Judge Peters has called a short recess. Kim and the prosecuting attorney stand off to the side, discussing Sithy's case. Rebecca wants to know how long it has been since Sithy used drugs. She seems concerned that Sithy is no longer in substance abuse treatment or counseling.

Sithy whispers in my ear that she couldn't continue the counseling because she is working seven days a week now. She grabs my hand, squeezing it tight. Despite all she has been through, Sithy is a warm and trusting person.

The prosecuting attorney glances our way. Then she approaches. She greets San first, asking if she is the mother. San nods. Words tumble out. San says something about Tom. She is crying now, and so is Lauren. Rebecca asks someone to bring them tissue. A box appears, and San, Lauren, and Sithy each take a tissue. San talks about not wanting Sithy to leave. Rebecca is reassuring, without making any promises. Then she heads back to her spot at the prosecuting table.

"That is the most compassionate ICE attorney I have ever met," says Kim. She seems to relax for a minute.

Then court starts up again, and she is reminded of what she is up against. After the original photo was deemed unsatisfactory, Lauren and Laurel searched Facebook to try to find another post proving Sithy's ex was in the Cambodian military. They found a post where he had asked for help with a report he had to write for the Royal Cambodian Air Force. Laurel dashed off to a photocopy shop to print copies of the Facebook post. In the meantime, the court hears two other cases, both involving men from Mexico.

The first man is young, maybe in his twenties. His lawyer seems unprepared and filed the needed paperwork only a few days earlier, making it impossible for the judge to receive it in time. The prosecuting attorney calls the man an "enforcement priority" because of his domestic violence charges. Sithy's family members nod their heads at the mention of domestic violence. The outcome does not look promising. The next case is also an "enforcement priority" because of the man's multiple offenses of driving under the influence. This man is older, in his seventies, and has been in the United States longer than forty years, minus a short two-hour stint in Mexico twenty years ago when he was deported. His lawyer asks for a continuance on his U visa application for victims of violent crimes who agree to help the government fight crime. The prosecuting attorney opposes the continuance, arguing that the proceedings have been dragging on since 2013. The judge sides with the prosecutor and orders the man's voluntary departure. He has until October to leave the country.

Kim's legs are crossed; she swings her top leg rapidly back and forth. She looks at her cell phone and then at her watch. She has to catch a flight to Seattle at 2:00 p.m. She is younger than Sithy but older than Laurel and Lauren. She wears a stylishly loose blue dress, and her long hair is pulled back in a bun. Everything about her says efficient. She types a question on her phone and shows it to Sithy.

"When was the last time you used drugs?"

Sithy reads the text, turns to look at her family. She counts with her fingers and then types "six" and hands the phone back to Kim.

"Six years since you used?" Kim types back.

Sithy nods.

Kim swings her leg again. She checks her watch, scans her phone. She types another question for Sithy.

"How old are you?"

Sithy looks at her mother. Kim shows San the phone. No one seems to know Sithy's exact age. They decide on fifty. Kim swings her leg, checks her watch. The door opens, and Laurel is back with the printouts. This time she made sure to print the whole page so everyone can see the name on the Facebook account and that the message was posted on Facebook. She also reprinted the picture of the ex-boyfriend in military uniform, this time showing it in context on the Facebook page. She has made three copies: one for Kim, one for the prosecuting attorney, and one for the judge.

The man sentenced to go back to Mexico thanks the judge and exits with his attorney. Sithy and Kim step forward. Kim gives Rebecca a copy of the new documents and then takes a seat next to Sithy at the defendant's table. All eyes are on Rebecca as she looks over the documents. Judge Peters explains that the court requested an interpreter for Sithy, but the interpreter did not show up. Kim and Rebecca agree to proceed without one. Rebecca begins.

"The government requested evidence to confirm the respondent's abuser is in Cambodia and in a position of government. That was last time. They supplied the documents to corroborate this today. There was a prior arrangement that if this evidence was given, the government would withhold removal on the basis of the Convention against Torture."

Kim asks permission to approach the bench. She hands the judge copies of the documents.

"Is it okay to mark them exhibit R?" asks Judge Peters.

Kim and Rebecca answer in the affirmative.

Judge Peters reads her judgment: "Order of removal withheld under the Convention against Torture."

Lauren turns to her sister. "Thank God," she says.

Sithy turns to face her family. She is not smiling. Her brow is furrowed; her eyes, wide. Lauren nods at her mother, smiles. Then she mouths the words "case closed." A smile slowly appears on Sithy's face. She turns back in her seat, embraces her lawyer. They stay there a minute, Sithy holding tightly onto Kim. Then they stand up and head into the hallway with the rest of Sithy's family.

As they leave Rebecca smiles. "Good luck to you," she says to Sithy.

As soon as the door shuts behind them, Kim lets out a sigh of relief. There is nervous laughter followed by smiles and hugs. San leans against Kim.

"Kim, I couldn't sleep," she says. "Tom maybe help me up there."

"I haven't slept for three nights," Kim replies.

They both laugh and hug. It is all still sinking in for Sithy.

"I was waiting to hear, 'Okay, case closed.' I don't know, they talk something else. I look around, everybody smiling, but I still scared. I said, 'What happened?' They mouth, 'Case closed.'"

Only when Lauren nodded at her, smiled, and mouthed those words did Sithy understand she was safe. For a minute everyone is reminded of how hard it is for Sithy to navigate in this world, how little of the language and laws she understands. It is easy to imagine how she ended up pleading guilty to a drug charge while alone in a court without an interpreter or her family.

Kim is careful to explain everything to both Sithy and Sithy's family. She hands Sithy the paper that granted her relief under the Convention against Torture.

"This is your legal status now," she says. "You can never lose it."

She also can never leave the country. That is part of the deal. Sithy doesn't mind; since coming to the United States she has rarely been outside Long Beach. Kim explains that Sithy may need to show the paper that proves she was granted relief under the Convention against Torture to ICE and that ICE may still require Sithy to check in. She will need a work permit, which she can use as her identification. She is not a legal permanent resident; instead, she is to have permanent residency under color of law status. The important thing is, ICE cannot deport her.

"Congratulations!" says Kim. Then she adds a warning: "You cannot get arrested ever again."

"Yeah, Mom," says Lauren.

The family celebrates back in Long Beach at Sophy's Thai and Cambodian Cuisine restaurant on East Pacific Coast Highway. San and her granddaughters order a number of Cambodian favorites while Sithy goes off to try to find a place to charge her cell phone.

Mary Blatz shows up a few minutes later. A large white woman originally from New York, Mary is the connecting link in many of the successful Long Beach cases. She isn't a lawyer, but she knows good lawyers, and when members of the Cambodian community come to her for legal advice, she knows what to tell them and where to send them. She also has a habit of getting more involved than is probably healthy.

Blunt and outspoken, Mary came to Long Beach more than twenty years ago as a pastoral director and stayed as a sort of referral agency. The Catholic Church had enough of her and she enough of it, she says, but the Khmer community stuck by her, even making her grand marshal of the 2010 Cambodian New Year's parade. She got involved in citizenship issues after immigration laws changed in the mid-1990s and members of the Cambodian community sought her advice. She, in turn, sought the advice of Catholic Charities and with the group's help figured out how to help members of the Cambodian American community regardless of their faith. It was a natural step to later take on the deportation cases. In Sithy's case it was Sithy's sister Sithea, the one who helped found Long Beach's Cambodia Town, who first approached Mary.

"They all have somebody deported, the famous ones," Mary says.

She is all too aware that Sithea is more infamous these days than famous.

Mary doesn't talk about this around San. Instead, she asks about Sithy's case. "Did she win withholding of removal, which means they stop the removal?"

"Yeah, she can stay here," replies Lauren. "With Convention against Torture."

"That's good," says Mary. "I heard some more people are winning from Convention against Torture."

San's cell phone rings. "Yeah, the case is over, Jennifer." All their phones are blowing up with calls from family and friends wanting to know the outcome of Sithy's case. Sithy returns and sits down next to Mary.

"You have a very nice mother; she saved you," Mary says. "And she told me you saved her in Khmer Rouge. In Khmer Rouge you are the hero."

Sithy places the credit back with her mother, explaining how San made sure she learned to cook and sew when she was young and that both things helped her survive under the Khmer Rouge. San tells a story of fishing with Sithy on a rare Khmer Rouge holiday. All the fish kept coming to Sithy, so San finally asked to switch places with Sithy. They swapped places, and for a little while a fish or two came to San. Then they stopped biting on her line, and all the fish once again went to Sithy.

"I have no idea why," says San. "Sithy put bait for me and everything, but fish does not come for me."

They don't talk about how she later raised Sithy's children. Soon San will move back to Long Beach and live in the duplex with Sithy, Lauren, and Lauren's fiancé and daughters. San doesn't like the noise of the inner city, but the silence in the old house she used to share with Tom is worse. Before she leaves the restaurant, she pays the bill and slips Mary some extra money.

The white woman is the last to go. She has been involved in the fight against deportation for some time and keeps track of the current movement through David Ros. She thinks it is smart what they are doing in trying to get Cambodia to change the memorandum on repatriation. It all seemed promising, but because of recent political events in Cambodia, she isn't sure what will happen. There are some things she knows probably won't work, such as bringing back those who have already been deported. The organizers, she says, "are very idealistic, like more than me."

Mary, at sixty-five years of age, is older than they are, but she isn't too jaded to believe in a better future. As if for proof she explains that she recently married—for the first time. And after hearing about Sithy's success, she wants to try to find a lawyer to help David Ros fight his deportation under the same grounds. Then there is the new group she just found out about from a friend of hers—noncitizen veterans who are now being deported for sometimes minor crimes. As members of the U.S. military, they can qualify for citizenship under the right circumstances, but for these people, their paperwork was not completed, often due to no fault of their own. Now they are facing deportation. It is like the Cambodians all over again.

"I hate this," says Mary. "So I keep fighting."

PART 4

YEARS TO COME

21

BLOOD-KILLER

Seattle, Washington, June 25, 1991.

There was no party the night David killed a man. There was no jibber jabbering that turned to threats. Not much in David's account of what happened that night matches official court documents based on the police report. Instead of going to a party and getting into an argument that turned violent, David pushed his way into the house where his ex-girlfriend was staying and pulled a gun on the man who greeted him at the door. It is true the first shot was fired while the two men fought over the gun, but the second shot David fired point-blank at another man's chest.

Earlier that night, June 25, 1991, David had called his ex-girlfriend Chanthy Ros (no relation), wanting to talk. He insisted on meeting, and she agreed to meet at a grocery store parking lot near where she was staying. When they met up, they argued. David threatened to kill Chanthy and anyone she was dating. Then he insisted on going to the place where she was staying.

Chanthy's friend Thon Thae met David at the door and extended his hand in greeting. David pushed Thon backward and pulled out a semi-automatic handgun. David accused Chanthy of dating behind his back. Chanthy pleaded with him.

"Shut up, or I'll kill you too!" David said.

Then he pointed the gun at Thon.

That is how the official version reads.

On July 27, 2016, David checked in with Immigration and Customs Enforcement once again. In August he went on vacation with his family. Later in the month ICE agents came to his mother's door. At the time, David was spending a lot of time at his mother's house, but he wasn't living there. He had given ICE his mother's address to buy himself time in case officers ever went looking for him. When they arrived that day, they searched the house and the attached apartment. David wasn't there. His mother gave them his cell phone number.

He found out about the visit from a panicked message his mother left on his voicemail. She was so frazzled she spoke mostly in English, a language she rarely speaks with her family. Only halfway through the message did she catch herself, calm down slightly, and switch to Khmer. She blamed herself for letting them in, in the same way she blamed herself for David's getting in trouble in the first place. When David was sixteen years old and dating an older woman, she did not know what the woman was doing was illegal. All she knew was that she didn't like David living with a twenty-one-year-old woman. That is when she believes David started to go bad, when he stopped going to school and just hung around with his older girlfriend. She doesn't blame just the older woman but also herself, for not being there, for not knowing the law. After she let ICE into the house, she blamed herself for that as well. Luckily, David was out of town at the time, and he stayed out of town as he tried to figure out what was going on. He discovered that he wasn't the only Cambodian deportee ICE had come after.

In late August and early September, activists who were able to communicate with the detainees estimate that between forty and sixty Cambodians from around the nation were apprehended. ICE did not release details about the detainments, and newspaper accounts focused mostly on individual or local cases. According to David, going after so many Cambodians all at once, especially those out in the community, was very unusual. In the past ICE has picked up Cambodians here and there, he said. But the agency tended to focus on those who were already detained or those who had come to check in.

This time ICE contacted potential deportees by letter and phone, telling them to check in on a certain day, which was not their usual check-in day. When the potential deportees showed up, they were detained and then taken to the ICE detention center in Adelanto, California. All twelve detained in

Seattle were later released with ankle monitors, but eight taken in Minnesota were still being detained two months later. There were others, but those were just the ones David knows about personally. From what he can tell, Long Beach was the only place where ICE went after people instead of asking them to come in. Before stopping at his mother's home, agents had picked up a friend of his who was also on the deportation list. His friend had watched from the car as the ICE agents pounded on David's mother's door.

In August I also finally caught up with David's friend Mia-lia Kiernan from the 1 Love Movement. By then the movement had been to Cambodia three times in 2016. The shifted focus on Cambodia and on getting the Cambodian government to revisit the memorandum of understanding is deliberate. After years of trying to change things on the U.S. side and not getting anywhere, the activists needed a new tactic.

"It just became very clear we weren't going to get anywhere on immigration reform [in the United States] as most immigrant rights groups have figured out at this point that immigration reform has just been a struggle to push through, especially for folks with criminal convictions," said Mia-lia. "It feels like not a possibility at this political moment, so we needed to rethink and try something else."

Toward that end they have focused on building up an activist community in Cambodia and on getting deportees to organize on their own behalf. They have also had successful meetings in Cambodia with members of Parliament and with people working in various ministries. But even if they convince the Cambodian government to reexamine the agreement, they will still have to deal with the U.S. government. Mia-lia isn't exactly sure what that will entail, but she anticipates it will be the most difficult part of the process.

With her law background, Kim Luu-Ng has a pretty good idea of what needs to be done and isn't too optimistic that it will happen. The MOU between Cambodia and the U.S. government is an executive action, which means for the United States to change it either Congress must negotiate a new treaty or the executive branch must develop some kind of policy action. Kim doesn't think that either is likely to happen.

Katrina Dizon Mariategue with Southeast Asia Resource Action Center is also skeptical that anything can change legally in the United States, at least not in the current political environment. "Right now with the makeup of Congress and elections coming up, it's just not feasible in terms of a legislative fix," she said.

There are other hurdles as well. Several violent incidents involving foreign nationals slated for deportation to countries that would not accept them have some calling for enforcement of a law that allows the United States to deny visas to countries that do not accept their deportees. In September 2016 Thong Vang shot two sheriffs in Fresno, California. Laos had earlier refused to accept Vang, a convicted felon who had been ordered deported to Laos after serving time for gang-related rapes. This is the environment in which SEARAC is working to change things.

With the twentieth anniversary of the 1996 laws on immigration, there have been some attempts to "fix" the laws, but Katrina views these efforts as more symbolic than realistic. Instead of changing the laws, SEARAC is trying to work with the people responsible for making the final decision regarding deportations—Immigration and Customs Enforcement. "We're looking to engage with government agencies that basically have a direct hand in figuring out who gets deported and who doesn't," she said.

The 1996 laws took away a judge's right to prosecutorial discretion, but as immigration lawyers have explained, ICE does have some discretion when deciding who to deport. SEARAC has been trying to understand more about how ICE uses its prosecutorial discretion to figure out who is getting deported and who is being allowed to stay and why. The first step was meeting with staffs in the three ICE field offices that held the highest number of Southeast Asian Americans in 2015: Los Angeles, Seattle, and Philadelphia. Katrina was surprised to find them open to meeting and happy to explain the process of prosecutorial discretion, which allows them to use their own judgment in deciding whether to detain or deport individuals.

In 2011 at the same time President Barack Obama announced his plan to focus on removing "felons, not families," ICE released guidelines regarding the factors that should be considered in the use of prosecutorial discretion. The guidelines encouraged ICE agents to look at positive factors surrounding potential deportees, including those with criminal records. These factors involved the length of time the potential deportees had been in the United

States, the situation under which they arrived in the States, and their community and family ties. In 2014 ICE released another memo that listed new priorities for removing those considered "criminals." While still allowing for prosecutorial discretion, the new guidelines did not outline the positive factors that should be considered, according to Katrina. Under the new guidelines many Southeast Asian Americans with criminal records were lumped under "Priority 1" removals, or those who pose a threat to national security, public safety, and border security. SEARAC said that based on its meetings with ICE field offices, the offices did not understand how they should weigh positive factors against deportation priorities. As a result, many people who should have benefited from prosecutorial discretion did not, according to an October 2016 SEARAC report. It also found that ICE had no uniform system for collecting data on prosecutorial discretion. Basically "ICE really, really, really likes to deport people," said Jose Magaña-Salgado, who spoke at the event SEARAC held for the release of the report.

As a managing attorney at the San Francisco-based Immigrant Resource Center, Magaña-Salgado has quite a bit of experience trying to convince ICE not to deport people. He explained that ICE is good at putting people into the "bucket" of the enforcement priorities and not targeting the people outside of those priorities. But it is "very, very, very bad at exercising discretion, no matter how compelling, for the individuals that end up in the bucket." In other words, once you are on the list as a deportation priority, it is hard to get anyone to look at the positive factors that might be considered through prosecutorial discretion to get you off that list. ICE has set up a procedure for people to send an email when they have been denied discretion. But according to data Magaña-Salgado received from the Department of Homeland Security, not many of those appeals were granted.

Acting ICE deputy press secretary Sarah Rodriguez would not answer questions regarding the report. Instead, she referred me to a November 2014 memo by DHS secretary Jeh Johnson. It includes a long paragraph on how prosecutorial discretion should be carried out that concludes: "DHS personnel are expected to exercise discretion and pursue these priorities at all stages of the enforcement process—from the earliest investigative stage to enforcing final orders of removal—subject to their chains of command

and to the particular responsibilities and authorities applicable to their specific position."

Unfortunately, the statement does not address the issue of how often prosecutorial discretion is actually exercised. Aside from the paragraph in the memo, Rodriguez's only response was, "That's all we have for you on this."

Katrina with SEARAC has had more luck with those to whom ICE reports. Since its report was released, SEARAC has been working with DHS to come up with a system to better track the use of prosecutorial discretion. Is prosecutorial discretion weighing factors such as whether the potential deportees have U.S.-born children, how long they have been in the country, and if they came as refugees?

If it is, then those factors should count in David's favor. His status as his family's breadwinner might also help his case. On the other side, though, is what happened on June 25, 1991. And what happened that night is hard to overlook, no matter how much good David has done since then.

Seattle, Washington, June 25–26, 1991.

Thon grabbed David's wrist and pushed the gun toward the ceiling. David managed to point the gun downward. Then he pulled the trigger. Thon fell to the ground, shot in the head and shoulder. Hearing the shots, Chanty's friends Pouan Prak and Veasna Mith came downstairs. David aimed once again at Thon as he lay on the floor.

"Don't mess with the BK," he said.

David, aka Bun Ra, is a member of the Asian Boyz gang, which is affiliated with the Crips. BK is Crips slang for "Blood-Killer," or someone who kills a member of the rival blood gang.

Chanthy, on her knees now, pleaded with David not to hurt Thon further.

"What did you do to my friend?" Veasna asked when he saw Thon on the floor.

David turned to Veasna now. "Do you want some too?"

Then he fired his gun again, hitting Veasna in the chest. Veasna collapsed face down on the floor. Ros grabbed Chanthy and told her she was going with him. Outside the house, he let her go but warned her not to tell the police or he would kill her and her entire family. Then he drove away in his car.

A little while later the police stopped him for speeding and running a stop sign. David gave a false name and claimed to have been dropping off a male friend. But he fit the shooter's description, which had been reported to police. His gun was found on another stretch of road where he had tossed it out of the car earlier. The next day David signed a statement in which he admitted having shot the men. Earlier that day, at 3:45 a.m., Veasna died at Harborview Medical Center. Thon survived.

Not many people are left who remember the case. Chanthy Ros, David's ex-girlfriend, was murdered in Tacoma, Washington, in 2000. Nhin Chhay, another ex-boyfriend, reportedly shot and stabbed her in a fit of jealous rage. Chanthy had a restraining order against Nhin at the time. She was thirty-three years old and the mother of young children.

Also in 2000 King County Superior Court judge Jim Bates, who had presided over the 1992 jury trial, died of a heart attack. He was fifty-two. The Seattle Police Department is only required to keep reports for three years and said anything relating to a case that old would have been destroyed. The main detective on the case has since retired, and efforts to reach him were unsuccessful, as were efforts to track down the victims directly. Alan Lai, who was the Seattle Police Department's victim assistance coordinator at the time, no longer works for the police department and said he does not remember the case or have any contact information for the victims. David's attorney at the time, Peter Connick, would not speak about the case.

Assistant Prosecuting Attorney Timothy Bradshaw is now Judge Bradshaw. He did not have a specific recollection of the surviving victim or of the deceased victim's family, but he did remember David.

"I thought he was violent and cold," said Bradshaw.

22

THE PASTOR

Nathan Ros doesn't have clear memories of Cambodia or Thailand. His earliest real memory is of the plane ride to the United States when he was six years old. It was his first time on a plane and his first time eating cheese: "Didn't like it." He laughs, then adds: "I love cheese now."

He loved Oklahoma as well, although not knowing the culture made for some strange experiences. Take restrooms. He doesn't remember having them in the camps, at least not the kind they had in Oklahoma City with flush toilets and toilet paper. Nathan learned about all of that along with his brother, David, who was just two years older than he was. In elementary school the brothers did almost everything together. They held hands when they walked to school together. Even today their voices are eerily similar, but the paths they took are not.

What made one brother devote his life to serving his community while the other brother did everything he could to destroy it initially? I wanted to know if Nathan had any insight into how and why he and his brother had chosen such different paths in their youth—and he did.

After Oklahoma they lived in other cities, such as Chicago, and other states, such as Massachusetts. Along the way David became a teenager and started "going astray." It began when he was in junior high school and no longer wanted to hang out with his younger brother, who was still in elementary school. Nathan remembers his brother being sent to juvenile hall and then to California to live with their grandmother.

In 1991 Nathan's mother moved the rest of the family to Long Beach to be near her aging mother and stepfather. Nathan thought it was a bad idea.

Like his brother, he had started getting into trouble in junior high, hanging out with the wrong crowd. His mother had put him in a private school in Massachusetts, which helped somewhat. Back then Long Beach was known to be gang infested. If he had been getting in trouble in Massachusetts, where the gang presence was nothing compared to that of California, he figured he didn't stand much of a chance in Long Beach.

He was right. His first experience was getting jumped by a gang while he was out skateboarding. He had seen the gang's graffiti, but being from a small town in Massachusetts, all ESL meant to him was a school program, English as a Second Language. He thought the graffiti was done by people particularly proud to be in ESL classes. He learned otherwise when members of the Latino gang East Side Longos demanded to know where he was from. Over the years he has learned that "where are you from?" is code for "what gang do you belong to?" But back then he thought they just wanted to know where he was from. So he told them Massachusetts. He laughs now, but it wasn't funny when he was getting beat up. He was scared to walk more than a block from his home. He could see the appeal of joining a gang for the camaraderie, the protection. He has seen it at work.

"I've been a youth pastor for twenty-one years, and I've worked with a lot of teenagers. And you know why these kids turn out that way," he says.

Only Nathan didn't turn out as they or his brother did. For that he credits the grace of God. And on the human level, he credits his church, Cambodian Baptist Church, which has been since renamed Pacific Baptist Church. Nathan had attended church before moving to Long Beach, but that was just something the family did on Sunday. The Cambodian Baptist Church was where he went every day. At church he learned not only the importance of sports but also how to dress, how to look like a man, how to date, how to treat a wife, and how to manage finances. His pastor was a father figure, a man whom Nathan credits with pouring his life into Nathan and the other youth.

"The guys that grew up going to that church, the majority of us, not all of us are preachers or anything like that, but we have families. We're responsible people," says Nathan.

Founded in 1989 by Pastor Joe Esposito and his wife, Mary, the church also had a small private school, and Nathan's mother sent him there. She had learned from her experience with David. She did not want another of her sons to attend public school, where he would be subjected to the gangs' influence. She knew Nathan needed to be separated from the negative influences and provided with positive role models. By this time, David already had a lengthy juvenile criminal record. It was too late for David but not for Nathan. It was through the school that Nathan got to know the church and all its activities. He was still in the neighborhood, but at the church he was insulated from some—certainly not all—of the violence.

"We've had gang fights in our church, people getting shot. Our pastor had his house garage blown up," says Nathan.

The church was targeted because it tried to pull people out of the violence. When a child is headed down the wrong path, explains Nathan, the church helps place the child in a special home or treatment center. At the same time, it requires that the parents attend church and receive training and counseling so when the child is returned, the family has better coping skills. That is what happened with Nathan's then future sister-in-law: she was placed in a home, and her family was counseled by the church. Somewhere along the way Nathan met her sister and married her. He went on to work for the church and to raise four children of his own.

The church school now costs $4,230 a year. That is more than when Nathan was a student but still relatively affordable for a private school. The church keeps the price low because the families it serves have limited income, and it understands the importance of getting the kids in school to save them from the gangs. Because once they end up in gangs, says Nathan, "most of them end up in jail or doing something that they'll regret in life," such as killing a man and spending almost two decades behind bars. That was the path David took, and Nathan believes he would have gone down that path had his mother not taken him out of public schools.

"If it wasn't for our church and the grace of God, I'd be in same situation [as David] because I was headed down that road," says Nathan. "Same road my brother went to."

Now Solomon and Alaysia are in the same school Nathan attended. And they love it. They come home singing "Jesus Loves Me" and other songs. At least

Solomon does. Many of his cousins are there as well. He and Alaysia have discounted tuition because they are included on David's sister's account, and the school drops the price for each additional child a family enrolls. Still money is tight. Debbie quit her part-time day-care job and is now working full time dealing with orders for a company that sells batteries. They gave up their apartment and moved into the separate three-bedroom apartment at David's mother's house. It is the same place where Immigration and Customs Enforcement agents came looking for David several months earlier.

Even now, months later, sitting in his mother's Long Beach backyard, David is uncomfortable talking about the detentions. He feels guilty for having missed them. His friends and counterparts in the movement tell him he didn't do anything wrong, assuring him that you're not required to be home all the time. They tell him ICE has his phone number, and the agents can call him or come around looking for him again if they want. He does not have to turn himself in. He knows all this, but it still bothers him, worries him. All this time he has known what he is facing and that one day he will be deported and separated from his son.

"But it never hits," he says, striking the table for emphasis, "until you're actually in that position."

After he learned that ICE agents had come looking for him, he considered turning himself in or self-deporting. He has a friend, a guy who had lifetime parole in the United States, who did that. The guy was so scared of slipping up and ending up back in prison that he told the Cambodian consulate he had a family emergency in Cambodia and that he needed to go there. He was allowed to go but could not come back to the States. The advantage of self-deporting, says David, is that you don't have a record as a deportee in Cambodia and can create a new identity for yourself there. That hasn't been much of a help for his friend. He isn't doing well and regularly calls David and other friends asking for money. He physically isn't able to do labor anymore and has found the transition more difficult than he anticipated.

But his friend's struggles aren't what kept David from self-deporting. It was video calls with Solomon and Alaysia. While he was out of town, he kept in touch with the kids through video chats on his phone. Every time he saw Solomon, his son would ask, "Daddy, when are you coming home?

Daddy, where you at?" Then he would say, "Daddy, I miss you." Debbie would get on the phone and tell him that Solomon cried for him every day. Even his neighbor reported that Solomon was constantly crying for David. When David thought about his son growing up without him, he cried. And he decided he couldn't leave them. Self-deportation was not an option. In time David returned to Long Beach and moved his family to the three-bedroom apartment at his mother's house.

He hasn't been able to go back to work, and at this point he won't be able to go back to his same job. He hired a lawyer to go after his boss and make sure his treatment, which now will include surgery for tendonitis, is paid for out of her company's workers' compensation policy. With his experience and certification, he should be able to get a similar job elsewhere; the demand for a skilled worker who can repair and maintain dialysis machines is high. But as soon as employers see his background, he knows most will lose interest. That has always been his biggest problem—his background.

"My crime is not just like something that goes away after seven years. It stays on your record for the rest of your life," David says.

As he talks he pushes back his cuticles. His prison weight-lifting physique has softened, and his son jokingly tells him he is getting fat. Solomon has climbed into his dad's lap and draped his arms around his neck. He uses his father as a sort of jungle gym, sliding on and off of him at regular intervals. Every once in a while he interrupts to ask for something. "Daddy, can you get my motorcycle?"

David walks to the side of the house and retrieves a child's bicycle that has extra plastic around the seat and handlebars to make it look like a motorcycle. Solomon struggles to reach the seat.

"I bought it for him a little bit bigger," says David. "I anticipated him growing too much."

He watches his son struggle with the bike, which has training wheels on it. David got it for him last Christmas when he was still working and not on disability. By this Christmas he had hoped to be working with a friend in a new business venture. The friend promised to fund a junk-hauling business, and David has been researching how much money they can make and how in demand they will be. It sounds promising, only the friend and the business opportunity are not in Long Beach; they are not even in California. David was planning on moving, but then Solomon started attending the new school and is enjoying it so much that David is reluctant to remove him.

If he did move, David says he would tell ICE, but it would also be a good time to just disappear. His next check-in with ICE is coming up in January. He is supposed to bring a letter that shows he has contacted the Cambodian government to help facilitate his deportation. ICE has been urging him to do it for some time, but so far he has avoided it. Now he feels he has to have something for ICE. He plans to get the letter, whether he checks in or not, but he isn't sure if he will check in. After ICE came looking for him, he is worried that when he checks in next time, the agents will detain him.

The various advocacy groups he knows that are fighting the deportations have pledged to help him if he is detained when he checks in, but he is not convinced they will be able to stop his deportation. He knows people have been advocating hard for the release of those who were detained in August and September, but many of them are still being held. A friend who is also active in the fight told him that if David checks in and is detained, it is highly unlikely anyone will be able to get him out. In a text message he told David: "From a friend to a friend, I'm telling you don't check in."

Despite all the work the 1 Love Movement has done in fighting for the deportees' right to return, David understands once he is deported there is little chance of his coming back to the United States. At least when he is over there he will have a friend, Chandara "Zar" Tep. David knows Chandara from his violent teen years. It was Chandara's gun that David used to kill a man.

Touch has a friend in Cambodia as well, his childhood friend Sarith "Rith" Chan. Sarith has his own house and a business driving people around in his *tuk-tuk*, a three-wheel mechanized taxi. When he was first deported he struggled, making just $5 a day in fares and losing $2 to the police for tickets. Then he figured out how to attract foreign customers, especially English speakers who felt at home when they heard his American accent. In addition to transporting people, he started serving as their guide and increased his daily earnings to $40, which is not bad in a city where a one-bedroom apartment goes for about $120 a month. Now he has a van to take larger groups. He has made a life for himself; all that is missing is a family. Touch tells him he should get married, but Sarith says he doesn't want a woman to steal his money. He complains that in Cambodia it is different. There is no dating like in America; instead, you move straight to engagement and paying money to the woman's family.

"He said, 'Uh huh, I'm not going to give $5,000 for her. I don't even know her,'" says Touch.

Touch is wearing shorts and a baseball hat, enjoying the unseasonably warm fall weather. Puthy has on pants. He laughs about the payments, explaining that if the girl's family is rich, they demand more money. If the girl comes from a poor family, it is better, he says; you only pay $1,000 or $2,000.

"But when go rich family girl, you make big mistake," says Puthy. "You need a lot of money go there."

Sarith had a girlfriend in the States but not a wife or children. Six months or so after he was deported, he no longer had a girlfriend, either, as the distance took its toll on the relationship. He has kept up with his childhood friend, though. He calls Touch on his cell phone and video chats with him when he is waiting for a passenger. He sets up a hammock in his tuk-tuk so he can relax. He'll be swinging there and pass his phone to a boy walking by on the street and tell him to say hi to his friend in America. He tells Touch not to worry; when Touch is deported to Cambodia, he can live with him. Sarith will put him to work driving the tuk-tuk or the van.

"He said, 'Whenever you touch down, you got my number. Don't worry about it,'" says Touch. "I was like, 'Yeah, we'll see.'"

23

FRIENDS AND FAMILY

Battambang, Cambodia, January 2017.

I meet Sarith Chan the day before his engagement party. I don't mention what Touch told me about Sarith and his reluctance to settle down. I don't have to. Rith, as he likes to be called, spells it out almost immediately. He has been "skating the marriage thing" ever since he started dating his girlfriend two and a half years ago. Now, with his parents in town, they have decided it has gone on long enough. He will be married next month before his parents return home to the United States.

Rith still seems a bit surprised by it all. "I think I'm a player for life," he says and laughs.

He is dressed in a T-shirt, a pair of baggy shorts, and a baseball hat. By Cambodian standards he is tall, which is the first thing I notice about him. The next thing I notice is how much he sounds like Touch. It is not his accent but his way of talking, especially the slang he uses, that reminds me of Touch. One of the things that struck me the first time I was in Cambodia in 2014 and made me want to write this book was that the deportees I met there sounded similar to my high school classmates in California in the 1990s. The Cambodian refugees I went to high school with picked up the West Coast slang. Davery was one of them. We ate lunch together, suffered through French together, and generally tried to survive high school together. Then we had the popular kids to deal with—and the violence.

At school there were boys who lit girls' hair on fire, dealers who passed drugs and money back and forth during class, and episodes of explosive anger that outshone any actual learning taking place. I only remember hearing gunshots during class once, as some boy shot at a girl's feet to impress her. But outside of school hours, there were other incidents: a school dance derailed when someone chased the principal with a gun, reports of a couple shot on a nearby street, and numerous rapes in the dark hallways when no one was around. Our high school wasn't the worst; in some ways it wasn't even that bad. But it wasn't in the suburbs. It was a city public school in the early 1990s.

I escaped to college in San Diego while Davery stayed in the neighborhood. She was the one who told me about the Cambodian Americans being deported. I was a journalist by then and interested in the story. I traveled to Cambodia in 2014. I wanted to write about female deportees, and that is how I met Mikki. She was a mess: alcoholic, incoherent, unstable. At the end of our interview she asked me for money to take a bus to Battambang in the northwest of the country. I gave her a few dollars, not because I thought she was actually going to buy a bus ticket, but because she sounded and looked so similar to the girls I had grown up with. And because I could go home and she couldn't.

Now, three years later, I am in Battambang again, this time with Rith. A provincial capital of fewer than two hundred thousand people located in the country's rice bowl, Battambang is slower paced than the Cambodian capital of Phnom Penh. The tuk-tuks, motorcycles, and scooters that zip around the crowded streets of Phnom Penh are less numerous here, although still abundant. The street vendors sell grilled rats in addition to sweet corn. Many of those who made it to America as refugees came through refugee camps in Thailand, a destination they often reached via Battambang. If the deportees have family left in Cambodia, this is often where they will find them. About half of those deported to Cambodia live in four northern provinces, including Battambang Province.

I have been here three days, and Rith has been avoiding me the entire time. Finally he has agreed to meet for breakfast at a café that serves biscuits and gravy, which is what Rith orders, along with scrambled eggs. He is nervous, guarded. Even the simplest questions prove complicated, like about his age. And yet his easygoing nature makes it hard for him to remain quiet for long.

"It's weird because I been growing up, my green card, my ID card, said 1979, so the whole time I'm thinking it's 1979," he says of his birth year. "But when I come to Cambodia, with my family, it's a different story."

One of his aunts told him she thought he was born in 1977. Another said 1978. The second aunt offered more details: she has a daughter the same age as Rith and used to breastfeed both of them; that is why she thinks he was born in 1978. He is no longer sure who to believe. What he knows is that he was born in Battambang, that his family escaped to Thailand, and that in 1981 they went to Ohio. From Ohio they made their way to California—first to San Jose and then to Stockton's Oak Park. That is where his memories begin. That is where he met Touch. They knew each other in the late 1980s but didn't become friends until they found themselves in the same gang as teenagers. Rith had been around gangs his whole life. Family, friends, his older brother, a cousin—they all were involved. At first it was just hanging out, drinking, smoking weed. But then the violence began, says Rith. He dropped out of high school, got arrested for joy riding, moved to Washington State, returned to California, and then moved back to Washington.

It is a familiar story, one told and one lived by many of the refugees. Families moved to escape bad situations, but they often ended up in the same kind of neighborhoods and facing the same kind of problems, said another deportee Van Veth. I had met Van a few days earlier, before I met and talked to Rith. Nheb Thai, Rith's cousin, introduced us. It isn't unusual for more than one family member to be deported; there are cases of brothers being deported, although cousins seem to be more common. Rith's brother never made it this far. He was shot to death in Stockton. Rith was in his mid-twenties at the time and had been recently released from prison after serving time for assault. He was living in Washington State but had come back to Stockton to visit.

"I used to love the city [Stockton] to death until my brother got murdered, and I don't love that city no more," says Rith. "I don't even think about that city no more."

He didn't think much of Battambang when he first arrived in Cambodia in 2012. He wanted to stay in Phnom Penh, the big city where things were happening and where he spent his first month living with his aunt and uncle. Then his mom came and took him to Battambang. She showed him a piece of land she owned in the city next to where her sister lived and told him she wanted him to build a house there.

"When I seen the land, nothing but a banana farm, I was like, 'Hell, no,'" says Rith.

After breakfast we drive to the land, which now includes Rith's two-story home. The house is surrounded by a high gate, something Rith's local family were against. He built it anyway. They, in turn, continue to try to walk right into his house, twisting and turning his doorknob in exasperation even though he has told them he locks his door and that they should knock when they want to visit.

It wasn't until Rith started talking to his relatives that he realized how gruesome things had been under the Khmer Rouge. He knew his father had been in Lon Nol's army that had fought the Khmer Rouge. His relatives told him that at one point a local official had warned his grandmother to get her son-in-law, Rith's father, out of town quickly because the Khmer Rouge were going to kill him. That is when his family fled to Thailand.

His parents are visiting here now. I thought I would want to ask his father about those years, to learn more about the family's escape, but now it no longer seems necessary. He survived. His eldest son was later murdered in the United States. His surviving son had been out of prison for the better part of a decade when he was deported to Cambodia. I am not sure that anything more needs to be said.

I smile at Rith's father and lean down to pet Spike, Rith's pit bull. Rith's tuk-tuk is parked alongside the house, a van behind it. The tour-driving business began as a joke. While Rith's father was previously visiting him in Cambodia, he jested that Rith should buy a tuk-tuk to make some money. Then Rith's mother commented that if Rith had a tuk-tuk he could drive her to temple. It wasn't until his parents left that Rith started thinking seriously about buying a tuk-tuk and earning a living transporting people around.

He began by parking on the street and waiting for customers. When that failed to result in enough fares, he tried to snag customers as soon as they arrived in town by meeting them at the bus station. From there he was offered a job driving foreigners to and from work and taking them sightseeing on weekends. Soon he had developed his own day tours and started booking customers through a local guesthouse. The majority of his customers are backpackers who pay $8 to see local attractions such as the bat caves, a bamboo train, and a winery. Not long ago he ditched the tuk-tuk and bought the air-conditioned van, which he now uses on all his tours. In Battambang he has been able to find a niche for himself, as have several other deportees who have tourist-related businesses here. It hasn't been easy, but they are starting to see some success and are now in the position of being able to aid new arrivals. When Touch comes, Rith plans to help him get on his feet.

That is what Sna tried to do for his friend Rath Koy. Sna lives about fifteen minutes outside of Battambang City. On the morning I visit, a small group of deportees is gathered on a wooden platform in his backyard, lounging in the shade of a tree. Food, weed, and beer are all on offer. A pit bull and chickens wander around. Everyone is speaking English, except the Cambodian workers who are constructing a first floor below Sna's traditional raised wooden home. Sna is wearing an LA Dodgers jersey, with his long hair back in a ponytail. He was born in a refugee camp in Thailand and raised in Santa Rosa, California. He is thirty-six years old and has been in Cambodia eight or nine years now, first in Phnom Penh and then here in Battambang, where he has family. He remembers how disorienting it was at first, how confused he was by squat toilets with water hoses for washing instead of toilet paper for wiping.

"I walk into restroom, 'What the fuck?'" says Sna.

The others laugh, remembering their own confusion upon seeing the porcelain pits with feet markers. Sna continues, "I like, 'Oh, all right, where you wipe your ass? Where's the paper at? Oh, okay, let me try to figure this out.'"

They are laughing hysterically now. Sna sums up: "I figure it out fast." The others nod in agreement. In many ways the deportees have more in common with each other than with their local relatives. When Sna moved houses, it was Garfield, a tall deportee from Long Beach, who helped him carry his furniture across a field. When Sna's childhood friend Rath Koy asked if he could stay with Sna, the answer was "anytime." They had met in kindergarten, both arriving fresh from Southeast Asia and speaking barely any English. They went to elementary school together, got in trouble together, and were locked up together. Sna was deported to Cambodia first. Rath came to Battambang because of Sna. He stayed in Sna's house for a while. Then Rath married Sna's cousin and moved to his own place. Sna can still see Rath's home from his backyard. But Rath no longer lives there.

They all remember the time Rath ran into the street, right into traffic. They recall mornings when the first thing he would do was smoke cigarettes and drink rice wine.

"He said he wanted to go back home," says Sna. "I said, 'Man, this is home.'"

Rath could never see it that way. His exile friends have photos from his funeral on their cell phones. His lifeless body is laid out, with his skin still taut, his hair still thick, his build still firm. Everything about him emphasized he did not die of old age or natural causes. Instead, he drank himself to death. He simply "wanted to die," says Sna.

This form of suicide is not officially recognized by the humanitarian organization that helps deportees, the Returnee Integration Support Center. Sarith Keo, RISC's codirector, lists only two official suicides among the deportees—a hanging and a drowning.

Bill Herod, who advises RISC, would add around ten more. Among the unofficial suicides are a diabetic who stopped taking the insulin he needed to survive and several deportees who, after being told they would die if they didn't stop drinking, did not stop drinking and died. There have also been drug overdoses. In the fifteen years they have been arriving here, 26 of the 538 deportees have died. At any given time about a dozen of them are in jail. Then others just disappear. No one seems to have heard much from Mikki since I saw her three years ago. Neither Sarith nor Bill know how to find her, and I do not attempt to look. Instead, I meet with a female deportee who can be included as one of the exiles who has made the most of her banishment. Only twelve women are among the exiles; Sophea Phea is one of them.

The first time we met in 2014 Sophea agreed to be interviewed but did not want her name used or her features revealed in a photograph. She was doing okay at the time, working at a restaurant, but admitted sometimes when the loneliness got bad she drank too much. Now she is teaching at an English-language school, making foreigner wages for the first time. Foreigners working in Cambodia typically make more than locals do, but because deportees no longer possess American papers, they are usually treated and paid as locals.

When Sophea's grade school students ask her when she is going back to the United States, she tells them she doesn't know. In truth, while she would like to visit, she no longer wants to return. Life is better for her here. She is doing things she never would have done in America, such as traveling to Japan, Burma, Thailand, Singapore, and other Asian countries. The hardest part is being separated from her family, including her thirteen-year-old son. Last year he came to visit. It was awkward. When Sophea left the States, he was eight. Now he is taller than she is.

"I didn't know how to treat him," she says. "I didn't know how to be a mother to him."

When he was visiting, her son would get angry and complain that she was babying him, but she was just trying to make sure he was okay. Her brother and sister, who were also visiting, told her she needed to discipline him. She didn't know if she had the right to do that. Plus she was scared that if she did put her foot down, her son would accuse her of not having been there for him. He would be right. When he was not even a year old, Sophea was arrested for about $3,000 in credit card fraud. Between serving time, being held in immigration detention, and finally being sent to Cambodia, Sophea hasn't been much of a mother.

Staying close to her own mother was easier. Her mother even came to Cambodia to visit. It was the first time she had been back since watching Khmer Rouge soldiers murder her parents. Sophea and her mother spoke on video phone almost every day. When her mother went into the hospital, Sophea was watching on video phone when prayers were said for her mother and at the end when they pulled the plug. Then she shut off the screen and found herself alone in her apartment in Phnom Penh. Separated from her siblings and the rest of her family, she had to deal with her grief alone. That is one thing that does not get easier—the loneliness. Many of the deportees marry soon after arriving, she says, so they can have a sense of family. For the women it isn't so easy. Culturally Cambodian women are expected to be more demure than their American counterparts are. Sophea has found dating difficult. She knows finding any surviving members of her mother's family will be even more trying. She has friends here but no family.

Bill Herod doesn't think that is necessarily a bad thing. Cambodian relations have little idea what it is like for the deportees, he says. Their worldview is extremely limited and does not include an understanding of what it means to be a refugee or prisoner in the United States.

"There's just no way that a farmer in Battambang can understand what it's like for a Khmer family to be thrown into Chicago and living on welfare in the midst of gangs from Asia and South America," says Bill.

There is also sometimes resentment because the deportee had a chance to make a good life in the United States and blew it. For all these reasons Bill decided having distant relatives in Cambodia wasn't worth much. "In fact," he says, "sometimes it was more of a problem."

Friendships among deportees can also prove damaging. On the same street where Rith and I ate breakfast, two deportees had a recent disagreement that ended with one stabbing the other. Those who know them say they were friends. One was in the process of starting a non-profit library program. He is dead now. The other is on the run.

24

EXILE

Phnom Penh, Cambodia, January 2017.

Bill Herod is drinking coffee at an art café in Phnom Penh when the text arrives.

"Morning, Bill. Did you have breakfast? I'm at jail."

That is the basic content of the message. The sender is a deportee. The recipient, Bill, is the man you see if you want to understand deportees in Cambodia. An American with white hair and a black eye patch, Bill has been helping deportees since they first began arriving in 2002. When Bill asked the Cambodian government what its plan was for the deportees, he was told, "There isn't any plan." The non-profit sector didn't have a plan, either, so Bill helped set up an organization. Several reinventions later, it is known as the Returnee Integration Support Center.

The work begins when RISC meets the deportees at the airport and continues indefinitely as they struggle to transition to life in Cambodia. Staff members help deportees obtain the government documents they need, such as driver's licenses and passports. RISC aids them in finding family, housing, and employment; visits deportees who wind up behind bars; and pays for medicine, medical treatment, and job training. The staff members also regularly field calls on their personal cell phones. Even Bill, who is officially retired, still gets distressing messages such as the text he received this morning.

From the café balcony where Bill sits near Independence Monument, it is hard to imagine how different things were a little more than twenty years ago when he came to Cambodia to work in the non-profit sector. At night the park across the street is overtaken by skateboarding teenagers, dancing middle-aged women, and picnicking families. Restaurants are lively, and food vendors set up shop anywhere there is space to set down a few plastic chairs. Motorcycles, tuk-tuks, and cars constantly jockey for position on the congested streets.

Yet a closer look reveals the Friendship Monument that commemorates the relationship between Cambodia and Vietnam, including Vietnam's ten-year occupation of Cambodia after overthrowing the Khmer Rouge regime. Another memorial is dedicated to victims of a grenade attack that occurred during governmental turmoil in the 1990s. There is no need for a reminder of the Khmer Rouge, as Prime Minister Hun Sen, one of its former members, has a house across the street.

Almost forty years after the fall of the Khmer Rouge, a reality television show is still trying to reunite families whose members lost track of each other during the genocide. Not everyone is ready, or able, to look for their families. One woman I meet was separated from her family as a toddler during the forced exit from Phnom Penh. She has never been able to search for her mother or siblings because she has no idea who they are. She doesn't even know what her real name is; she only knows the one given to her by the family that eventually took her in.

Dr. Sotheara Chhim believes many Cambodians suffer from a uniquely Cambodian trauma syndrome similar to post-traumatic stress disorder called *baksbat* (broken courage). A member of the first generation of psychiatrists working after the Khmer Rouge, Sotheara came up with criteria for diagnosing baksbat that include three things: physical and psychological distress, submissiveness, and loss of self.

"I think this is like a society disease," he said when I met him at his Phnom Penh office. The concept of baksbat dates to the Thai occupation of Cambodia in the fifteenth century and has passed through the generations until the Khmer Rouge subjected the country to even more baksbat, said Sotheara. Today he believes most Cambodians suffer from baksbat, which makes them similar to the three monkeys who see no evil, hear no evil, and speak no evil.

"They feel as if they are blind," he said. "They see something, but they pretend as if they don't see. They hear, but they don't hear. So their response is just to shut up."

This distress is prevalent in the country to which the deportees are sent. In addition to the trauma their families suffered under the Khmer Rouge, they suffered a sort of cultural bereavement in the United States. After finally adapting to life in the States, their being sent to Cambodia creates a sort of reverse culture shock or cultural bereavement, said Sotheara. He has treated some of the deportees and believes they would have been better off in the United States. Because of a lack of human resources, Cambodia's mental health service is based purely on the biomedical model, he said. In other words, medication is prescribed, but patients have very limited access to any other kind of service that would help with recovery. One hospital has inpatient mental health facilities, but it has fewer than a dozen beds and strict admittance criteria. With no better option, families have been known to chain up mentally ill members. Bill remembers seeing signs of chaining on one deportee.

Cambodia knew it was not prepared to accept deportees and resisted accepting them for several years before finally succumbing to U.S. pressure. Now the government wants to renegotiate the deal. Its inspiration is 1 Love Cambodia, the group founded with help from the 1 Love Movement, the organization David Ros is involved with in the States. In the fall of 2016 the Cambodian government set up a task force to reexamine the memorandum of understanding with the U.S. government regarding the deportations. While reviewing the repatriation agreement, Cambodia requested that the current MOU be suspended, a request the United States denied. Since then Cambodia has not issued any travel documents, essentially stalling deportations. Cambodia's actions have brought hope to 1 Love Cambodia.

Bill and his RISC colleagues are less enthusiastic. In the fifteen years he has worked with deportees, Bill has seen them have two main reactions to deportation. Some accept their situation and make the most of it, getting a job, marrying, and having kids. They view deportation as a chance to make a fresh start. Then there are those who live in denial and never adjust, eventually succumbing to alcohol or drug abuse and often ending up in jail or dead. In 1 Love's fight to end the deportations and secure the right for deportees to return to the States, Bill fears the 1 Love representatives and members are focusing on leaving instead of helping the deportees make Cambodia their home. Instead of fighting for the right to return to the States, he wants the 1 Love Cambodia members to visit their fellow deportees in jail, intervene when a deportee is headed down the wrong path, and generally focus their energy on succeeding in Cambodia instead of seeking something he is afraid they will never attain.

Bill is sympathetic to their cause. In the past he even tried to fight for changes, such as asking the U.S. government to stop sending mentally ill deportees to Cambodia or at least to include their medical records when it does send them. But he doesn't believe ending the deportations outright is a realistic goal because, first, those facing deportation are Cambodian citizens under the Cambodian Constitution and international law, even if they were born in refugee camps in Thailand. Second, under international law, Cambodia has a legal obligation to accept the return of its own citizens. These two things "are sort of written in stone," says Bill. That means whether you agree with the deportations or not, they are legally sound.

As for the Cambodian government's actions, Bill wonders whether its motivation is more monetary than altruistic. Knowing how hard it would be to end the deportations, he believes the government may be simply seeking monetary compensation for agreeing to accept deportees. Despite his unease, Bill manages to get me a meeting with representatives of the Cambodian government. Among other things, Bill is credited with bringing the internet to Cambodia. Mean In, who was one of Bill's first internet literacy students, is also the assistant to Chou Bun Eng, the secretary of state for the Ministry of Interior.

I meet with Mean and his boss the day before I leave the country. When I show up, Mean informs me he just told his boss about the meeting five minutes ago. Then he briefs me on the situation. When the first MOU was signed, Cambodia was not ready to deal with the deportee issue, he says. Now the government is ready to confront the issue and has set up a task force to ensure it handles the deportation issue better this time around. His boss then outlines the key things the Cambodians want to change: They want the program to be based on voluntary, not forced, returns to Cambodia.

They want those deportees who are already in Cambodia to be allowed to visit the United States. They also want the U.S. government to support new arrivals financially while they adjust to life in Cambodia.

"The integration takes time, resources, and full support," she says. "We haven't done enough in the past, and we don't want to repeat this mistake again."

Her reasons for these changes echo the arguments put forward by 1 Love: the breakup of families, the double punishment for those who have already served time for their crimes, the violation of human rights, and the deportees' lack of connection to Cambodia. "We can recognize them as Cambodian," she says. "But they do not adapt themselves as Cambodian citizens because they live their whole life [in the United States], they do not stay in Cambodia."

Some can't speak the language or eat the food, adds Mean. They don't even speak English properly; instead, they are using slang, or "homey language," that does not go over well in Cambodia, he says. As they talk, his boss thumbs through a series of papers from 1 Love and various American politicians who support an end to the deportations. What really seems to have caught her attention, though, are the numbers: she has heard there are around 4,000 more who will be deported. Others have reported closer to 2,000, but either way it is far more than the 538 who have already come. Among those already here, there have been suicides, murders, and arrests for various criminal charges. She doesn't want the same thing to happen with a far greater number. Whether the U.S. government will agree to their requests is not something she knows. But, she says, "we have to request."

Mean seems equally ambivalent about the outcome: "We can only ask."

The U.S. side is less talkative. In an email, Anna Richey-Allen, a State Department spokesperson for the East Asian and Pacific Affairs Bureau, said that the government was aware of the Cambodian government's request and that either side has the right to convene a commission to discuss repatriation policy issues. She did not elaborate.

In quieter moments, Chandara Tep seems to understand the futility of the fight, at least when it comes to the right to return. Chandara has a baby face and a handful of nicknames. Zar is the one David calls him. For Chandara the battle is more about those who have yet to be deported, like David, than about those already in Cambodia like himself: "It's just like we don't really matter." That is why he helped form 1 Love Cambodia.

"We just don't want to see people going through what we going through," he says. For Chandara that meant spending the first three months he was in the country in his house, never venturing outside.

According to Bill, that is not that an unusual response. The first few months the exiles are in Cambodia they are in shock, unable to function and orient well. Years ago Bill gave up having an orientation during this initial time, and now he waits a few months later until they are more able to focus. Those who come directly from prison or immigration detention face the additional challenge of overcoming what Bill calls post-incarceration syndrome, which means basically they expect everything to be provided for them, including food, shelter, education, employment, and medical care.

Chandara didn't come directly from prison. Like David, he was out for years, long enough to start a family and plan for his eventual deportation. His wife searched for job opportunities in Cambodia, and Chandara saved money for a house. When he was finally deported five years ago, he bought a five-bedroom house in Phnom Penh. He has been waiting for his wife and three children to join him ever since.

Chandara's story, as he tells it, begins earlier than most. He was born in 1973 and escaped to Thailand with his family before the Khmer Rouge rebels solidified their power. "Escape" is a relative term. His family left Cambodia because his father's siblings had already been killed. On his paternal side of the family were rebel fighters who were slaughtered by others fighting to control Cambodia. His father, he says, was born wealthy and used to commanding people. He once had everything, and after he lost it all and was resettled in the United States, he never recovered. Instead, he sat alone in silence, never even bothering to get his driver's license. It was from his father's loyal followers—former soldiers and bodyguards— that Chandara learned what little he did about Cambodia. His mother's side of the family was involved in traditional medicine, and his family had several wild animals. One story that sticks in his mind is about his mother escaping with him and his siblings and being stopped by Khmer Rouge soldiers. When they asked where she was going, she said to the fields to work. When they asked if the elephant traveling with her was hers, she said no. The soldiers shot it. The family left their sun bear at a zoo in Thailand.

They were settled in San Francisco's Tenderloin neighborhood in 1978. Chandara was five. His memories are of pimps, prostitutes, and low riders. Condoms and syringes littered the sidewalks. It seemed as though his parents were mugged every other day. After a few years they moved to Modesto, about a half hour outside of Stockton. That is where the real trouble started. Chandara and his family had been early arrivals, and Chandara was called on to translate for his more recently arrived classmates. He also increasingly found himself in the role of fighting their battles, sticking up for the Southeast Asian immigrants who did not fully comprehend the English-language taunts being hurled at them. Chandara understood, and because he did, he felt it was his job to defend them. He got suspended from high school and kicked off the football team for sticking up for another refugee, or, more precisely, for breaking the jaw of the boy who was doing the teasing. That is how he tells it at least.

While doing time in juvenile hall for assault, Chandara met a drug dealer and decided that drug dealing would be a good way to make a living. When he got out, he started dealing crack cocaine. Things were going well until, according to his accounting, the shady cop aiding his business started using drugs and stealing from him. There was a shootout. Chandara would eventually be charged with assault with a firearm on a police officer. He met David while he was on the run.

They both were living in Seattle and had friends in common. David lived in an apartment complex across the street from the house where Chandara stayed and where David liked to hang out. Chandara says he had no idea what David was up to the day he brought a gun to a meeting with his ex-girlfriend and ended up shooting two men, killing one. The gun, he says, belonged to him or one of his "homies." The leather jacket David was wearing was Chandara's.

The law caught up with both of them.

After serving a few years, Chandara was released and got mixed up in a blue-collar crime scheme that involved the theft of computer chips. He didn't get caught for that, but he did get caught for possession of a gun and stolen property. After he served his time, he was put in immigration detention from which he was released on $25,000 bail in 1998, he says. Legal permanent residents in immigration detention are not usually eligible to apply for release on bond, and Chandara is not sure why he was allowed out.

The next year he married his prison pen pal. They had two sons, now fifteen and twelve years of age, and a daughter, now ten. Chandara got a job at a sheet metal company and became an expert on the laser machine, a skill that got him recruited by another company, which eventually paid him $30 an hour. He bought a house, a boat, jet skis. His wife earned her master's degree in business management and accounting.

For six years he fought his deportation case in the courts. At the last hearing he attended, he says, the judge told him to come back with a suitcase because he was going to be deported at his next hearing. He never went back. He stayed under the radar for another seven years, working hard to pay his family back the $25,000 it lost in bail money. He looked over his shoulder the entire time.

"Every night I lay down, look at my wife sleeping, my kids sleeping just like, 'Man, I know one of these days that I'm going to lose this,'" he says. "And it finally happened."

Immigration found him in 2009 and held him for ninety days, after which time the agents were forced to release him because Cambodia had not produced travel documents for him. For the next two years he was required to check in regularly with ICE. He sent his wife and eldest son to Cambodia to buy land for the family. The deal went bad; they ended up losing $7,000. Soon after they returned to the United States in 2011, Chandara was deported to Cambodia. His wife came to visit twice. The plan was for her and the children to join him in their five-bedroom home in Phnom Penh. Two years passed and they didn't come. Then his wife stopped talking to him, he says. That was three years ago. He says he hasn't heard from her since. Friends tell him his children are doing well in school, but he says he is unable to talk to them directly.

Two years ago his younger brother was deported. He lives in the country-side with their older sister, who was left behind when the rest of the family escaped. She ended up marrying a Khmer Rouge soldier who later lost his legs and one arm to a land mine. Chandara stayed with his sister briefly when he first arrived but found it too difficult to adjust to country living. He still talks to his sister but is not in contact with his brother.

It is the separation from his wife that really hurts him, though. They were a team, and when they stopped working together, he sunk into a deep depression, drowning himself in alcohol. For the first time in his life, he thought of suicide. He had never contemplated that before, not even when he was in prison and in solitary confinement.

"That's when I felt like I knew how my dad feels, losing . . . nine brothers and sisters," he says. They were all killed.

His dad never spoke about his family. He never spoke much at all, says Chandara. He did drink. What got Chandara to stop drinking and dig himself out of his depression was 1 Love. The movement gave him something to fight for, something to hope for. He may have lost his family, but there is still a chance for the others, for the ones like David. That is what he believes; that is why he is in 1 Love Cambodia.

"1 Love woke me up," he says. "I'm here for a purpose."

25

LEFT BEHIND

Moung Ruessi District, Battambang Province, Cambodia, January 2017.

At first I don't pay much attention to the elderly couple and small boy sitting quietly under a tree. The man has only a few teeth left in his mouth; the woman has small, broken yellow ones. I am in a village about an hour outside of Battambang to meet Khe Khouen, a forty-year-old deportee from Washington State. I look around, searching for a middle-aged woman, but it is the old woman who greets me in English. Her voice is soft and sweet. She smiles, and I catch a glimpse of younger life under her weathered and leathery skin. It is hot, but she wears a scarf around her neck and leggings under her loose dress. She is very thin, too thin, the kind of frail that comes with age or a life that prematurely ages you. She asks if I want to come to her home, and we head there on motorcycles. She rides with the old man, who I later learn is genuinely old, and the boy. I ride behind a man I have paid to take me here. As we maneuver down a dirt road, I realize the woman's voice and her quick show of affection remind me of someone else, Sithy.

Eastvale, California, November 2016.

Sithy is no longer in imminent danger of being deported, but she does not yet have all the papers she needs. The work permit she applied for three months before hasn't arrived. She wants to start driving cars for the transportation company Uber, but without a work permit San is scared Sithy will get in trouble again. Sithy assures her mother that she won't do it unless it is legal, but San knows Sithy is impatient to move on with her life. Working at the croissant factory is physically exhausting, and Sithy wants to find something that pays better. She needs money to pay her lawyer to look into getting her citizenship, a lengthy, risky, and expensive process that would require retrying her case.

Sithy explains that without citizenship she cannot travel, something she and her family both admit she has no inclination to do. But that isn't why she wants U.S. citizenship. She wants it because without it, she doesn't feel safe. She knows how easy it was for her to get on the deportation list before. While she now goes out of her way to avoid people who do things that could get her in trouble—like gambling and drugs—she still feels as if she is on shaky ground. She is right; she is. And in her family, she is not the only one.

San's second daughter, Sithea, the successful college graduate who was making a name for herself in Cambodia, is back in California with her husband. San doesn't mention Sithea, but when San is out of the room, Sithy whispers an update: Sithea's husband, Richer, and two of his colleagues were convicted in absentia in Phnom Penh Municipal Court of defrauding a Cambodian dentist of $1 million. The three belonged to a company that the dentist invested in and are reported to have lived lavishly off of her investment before leaving the company, which never achieved its goals. Richer and his friends deny the fraud charges, saying they were merely employees of the company. In September a fourth defendant killed himself. The following month the surviving three were each sentenced to one year in prison in Cambodia and ordered to jointly pay $1 million and an additional $75,000 in damages. Because all the defendants are currently living in the United States, the dentist, Eng Lykuong, also filed a lawsuit in U.S. federal court.

Sithy is living in her sister's Long Beach home and paying rent so Sithea can keep up on her bills and not lose the house. All three sisters are now living together. While she isn't happy about her sister's situation, Sithy can't help feeling slightly vindicated. Ever since they came to the States, Sithea has been the one her mother always trusts, while Sithy is the one she worried about. Now, says Sithy, "look what happening there."

Not that Sithy's relationship is that much more secure than her sister's. While Richer is facing jail time and a substantial fine, Sithy's boyfriend, KC, is facing deportation. Instead of checking in with immigration, he checks in with his parole officer every month. This and the fact that Sithy has heard that if you are working like KC you are less likely to be deported make her think KC is safe from deportation.

Recent political events may prove her wrong. A few days earlier the country elected Donald Trump—a man who ran on a promise to increase deportations—as the next president of the United States.

Battambang Province, Cambodia, January 2017.

It is not Khe's case that initially makes me think of Sithy. Sna, the deportee with the childhood friend who drank himself to death, also reminds me of her. That is because, like Sithy, Sna beat his case. His ex-wife hired a lawyer who was able to adjust his status to receiving political asylum and to withhold his order of removal, he says. The district attorney tried to appeal, but it didn't work. Sna won. The court let him go—and he went right back to doing what he did before. He hung around with the same people, did "drugs, got pulled over, whatever." He was picked up by immigration again. This time when he tried to fight his case, no lawyer would represent him. They told him he was wasting his money, he already had his chance, and he blew it. He was sent to Cambodia.

I hope the same doesn't happen to Sithy. If it does, I fear her fate could mirror that of Khe.

Khe's house is a single-room, wooden lean-to on the side of the road. In front there is a hammock and wooden platform, both covered by an awning. A puppy scrounges for food on the dirt floor. The old man, Khe's husband, repairs bicycles. The little boy is an orphan who lives with them. Later Khe tells me he is her husband's grandson. She is open and talkative, but her words don't always add up. She admits, "I was selling dope. That's why I got deported." But whenever I ask how old she was when a certain event happened, she offers the same age, thirty-six or thirty-seven. In her version of events, she was working as a card dealer in a casino when a man approached her about selling drugs. He told her she could make more money if she sold cocaine. So she did. She also started using it. The man gave her a gun. When the police caught her, she shot at them. She says she didn't hit anyone. I tend to believe her, as she would probably still be in jail if she had.

Other details are fuzzier. She has a son; RISC confirms this. She has an uncle who lives near her and checks in on her. Her husband is known to drink and hit her. Her memory has been blurry since she arrived in Cambodia in 2009, says Sarith Keo, codirector of RISC. He thinks it may be because of the drugs she took earlier in life. As far as he knows she hasn't abused drugs or alcohol in Cambodia, but she has been taking pills for depression and sleep since she arrived. In the beginning she lived with relatives in Phnom Penh, but after a few months the relatives took her back to RISC, unable to handle her. RISC helped locate an uncle in the countryside, and Khe was sent to live with him. She has been living near him ever since. Sarith tried to help find her work, but she cried all the time and was unable to hold down a job. Sarith makes sure she keeps her monthly appointment with a psychiatrist, something RISC pays for along with her medication. He also fields regular calls from her. She used to call in tears a lot, talking about suicide. Since she has been in treatment, she has been doing better, he says. Still she reports doing "a lot of thinking," which makes it hard for her to sleep. Sometimes she thinks about what others must think of her for leaving her son in the United States. In her mind she sees them staring at her, judging her for leaving her son.

"I think I'm a real bad person that I did that to my kid," she says. "I don't want to live because this is not good, to be a woman and do that to my child."

She hides nothing. She tells her story as she recalls it, her emotions on full display. When I ask what medicine she takes, she shows me the prescription. Her openness and trust leave her vulnerable, and I feel as protective of her as I do with Sithy. Despite their age, it is as if they are children who want desperately to be loved and cared for, lacking the ability to do either themselves. Sarith gives Khe money, but he isn't sure where it goes. She has never been good at budgeting. She tells me she buys rice by the can, lacking enough money to buy a full bag at a time. She doesn't ask outright for money, but her intention is clear. She isn't sure how they will eat tonight.

There was a time when she was healthier, even a little plump. She has a single small photo album from her former life. Inside is a picture of her taken at a wedding reception maybe ten or twenty years ago. In the photo her skin is pale and soft, her body is plump, and her hair is wavy and full. I search for traces of that fresh-faced young girl in the haggard old woman in front of me. I cannot find them. We were born the same year, but my teeth are still intact, my skin is still relatively elastic, my body is thin from working out, not from starving.

I give her money so she can buy a few cans of rice for tonight. I don't know if that is what she will use the bills for, but it only costs me a few dollars. She asks if I want her puppy; he eats too much, she says. Then she asks if I can give her the number of another female deportee, a woman who once made macaroni and cheese for her. No one calls her anymore, she says, not the other deportees, not her family in the States, not her uncle here in Cambodia.

As far as Sarith knows, Khe's uncle still checks in on her, and her mother has come to visit twice. He does not have a current phone number for her elderly mother and did not meet with her the last time she was in Cambodia. Without RISC and her uncle, Sarith says, "I don't know where she go."

Not being able to support herself or hold down a job makes Khe feel worthless. Then she shares something that I remember seeing quoted in Sithy's file, using a word Sithy had also uttered when describing herself to a therapist.

"I feel like I'm a piece of trash," she says. "I'm nobody."

AFTERWORD

The day I leave Cambodia in February 2017 it is announced that the United States will deport more than thirty Cambodians in the very near future. The Cambodian government has agreed to issue them travel documents. The Cambodians are still reviewing the MOU, but in the meantime it is clear the deportations cannot be stopped. Those being deported include people picked up over the summer when Immigration and Customs Enforcement came knocking at David's door. If he had been home, he would probably be on his way to Cambodia now. It is doubtful he will escape next time. During his January check-in with ICE the agent did not mention coming to his home, but in February President Trump vowed to focus on deporting those who already have deportation orders, people such as David who have been living on borrowed time ever since they were released from immigration detention.

David has started therapy. In April he moved to Washington State. He said he did it for Debbie—and for a new opportunity. He didn't mention whether he had checked in with ICE since the move, and I didn't ask.

By mid-May the number of deportees had climbed to 566, yet for the advocacy community there were moments of hope. In March a judge waived Ched Nin's deportation, arguing it would present an extreme hardship on his family. More good news came in June when Puthy received his kidney transplant. In the days before the operation, his brother Touch seemed nervous. He had a car and a driver's license and seemed to have settled down in Santa Ana; now the paired kidney transplant surgery in San Diego threatened to change that. A day after his own surgery, Touch posted a photo of his parents on the beach, with their pants rolled up as they waded in the waves. Touch commented on their smiles and how happy they were now that Touch and Puthy were doing well. The posts that followed were about food—a cookie and coffee on June 13, four days after his surgery, and an omelet on June 14. On the fifteenth he posted a picture of himself standing in front of the pool at Puthy's house with the caption: "Thank God home sweet home!!"

As for the others I met, San has moved back to Long Beach and is now living in the same duplex as her granddaughter Lauren. She bought a ticket to visit her sister in Vietnam but had to cancel when her late husband's family told her she needed to meet with a lawyer first to deal with his estate. One of the two lovebirds she and Tom bought together recently died. Sithy is so far staying out of trouble.

Song, the former politician, had another stroke. Last time I saw him, he was watching a woman's talk show and speaking in a whisper. By September 2017 he was back in Cambodia, talking politics with a reporter from a local English-language newspaper.

After originally agreeing to speak again, Sambath Nhep stopped answering emails and phone calls. Chea Bou also did not answer emails. It is unknown whether the couple's relationship has continued to survive Chea's deportation.

When I saw last Chanphirun, Lon Nol's nephew and an early deportee who managed to avoid deportation, our talk turned to superheroes. Chanphirun had just finished a framing job and was enjoying a drink with his friend Terry in the back of his frame shop.

"The last Superman movie I saw, it reminded me of you," said Terry. "Their planet is about to be destroyed, and Superman's parents put him in a capsule."

Chanphirun sipped his margarita. "In a way, you're right," he said.

Terry continued: "I thought of the part where they are sending off the child, knowing they will never see him again."

Chanphirun took over. "The day I catch the flight, my dad stayed home all day, not work."

It turns out back then Chanphirun was hardly home at all, taking off for a month at a time. He was there, though, in 1973 when Phnom Penh was being shelled with rockets. Much of the city was evacuated, but his family stayed in their house. His uncle Lon Nol, then the prime minister of Cambodia, lived a block away. The rebels were aiming for his uncle's house.

Chanphirun's last day in Cambodia came two years later. He arrived home that day around 1:00 p.m. to pack for a flight that left at 3:00 p.m. His father had been home all day, waiting. They didn't talk much, just "said goodbye; that was it." His mom took him to the airport. She told him to take care of himself.

Then he got in his time capsule and never saw his parents or the country he knew from his childhood again.

He is one of the lucky ones.

In August 2017 the United States announced it would stop issuing visas to citizens of Cambodia and three other countries it considered uncooperative in accepting their deported citizens. In an official statement issued the following month, the Cambodian Ministry of Foreign Affairs and International Cooperation said it had not halted cooperation and was still prepared to accept Cambodia's deported citizens. Not long afterward SEARAC reported that ICE had begun detaining Cambodians again and that the Cambodian government had agreed to interview twenty-six individuals and issue a new bunch of travel documents.

ACKNOWLEDGMENTS

At one point in his or her academic career, almost every American student is asked to bring a baby picture to school. I was given the assignment in my high school French class in 1992. All the students were excited about such an easy task, all except my friend Davery. When Davery told us she didn't have any baby pictures, we didn't believe her. Everyone has baby pictures. Then she told us about fleeing the Khmer Rouge and her homeland, Cambodia. Later she told me about Cambodian Americans who were being sent back to Cambodia. I had never thought of Davery as being anything other than an American. She and I talked and dressed alike, and we both hated French. If it weren't for Davery, I probably would have never written this book.

Ranjit Arab was the first editor to see the importance of such a book, but it was Tom Swanson who saw it through to completion. I consider myself extremely lucky to have landed with Tom and Potomac Books. University of Nebraska Press has been supportive and committed throughout the publishing process. Vicki Chamlee did a brilliant job as copy editor. California Polytechnic State University–San Luis Obispo has also been supportive of the project, and the College of Liberal Arts and the Journalism Department both helped fund my research.

Nothing, of course, would have been possible without the individuals and families who let me peer into their lives. It is not easy to open your past, present, and future to a stranger, and I am incredibly grateful to each and every person who shared his or her life with me. I am especially grateful to the late Tom Croucher, who took the time to record many of his wife's memories. Numerous lawyers, activists, and scholars also took the time to share their knowledge with me. Many of them, especially Bill Herod, went out of their way again and again to find me what I needed.

Friends and family members have been a great support. They include but are not limited to my mother, Karla Van Meter; stepfather, Trevor Pitts; father, Dennis Cengel; Aunt Letty and Uncle Bob; writing buddy Andrea Chmelik; and friend Sopheap Lim. *Time* magazine editors Andrew Katz and Bryan Walsh came through when I needed them, as did Courtney Brooks at *Roads & Kingdoms*. And, of course, thanks go to my three amigos: M, P, and G.

Note on Cambodian spellings: Khmer is written in script; thus, there is not always one correct way to spell words translated from Khmer to English, especially for small villages. I have tried to use the most common English spelling whenever possible. As for Cambodian names, most have been switched to the Western style of first name followed by last name, except in rare cases when that did not make sense.

Memories are not perfect. The scenes created from the Khmer Rouge years are based on my research, the subjects' memories, and a little literary license.

APPENDIX

U.S. immigration law is complex and confusing. While each individual case varies, here are some of the laws and court cases that affect many of those people profiled in *Exiled*.

IMMIGRATION AND NATIONALITY ACT

Created in 1952, the act consolidated immigration legislation in one place. For further reading, see U.S. Citizenship and Immigration Services, "Immigration and Nationality Act," Department of Homeland Security, last updated September 10, 2013, https://www.uscis.gov/laws/immigration- and-nationality-act.

THE REFUGEE ACT OF 1980

Created largely in response to the Southeast Asian refugee crisis, the act increased the annual number of refugees the United States accepted, redefined "refugee" as a person with a "well-founded fear of persecution," and established an Office of Refugee Resettlement. For further reading, see Pub. L. 96-212, S. 643, 96th Cong. (1980), https://www.archivesfoundation.org/documents/refugee-act-1980/.

Refugees are not automatically granted citizenship. After being in the United States twelve months, they must apply to become legal permanent residents. Once they have lived in the country for five years, they can apply for citizenship. For further reading, see Bureau of Population, Refugees, and Migration, "U.S. Refugee Admissions Program FAQs," January 20, 2017, https://www.state.gov/j/prm/releases/factsheets/2017/266447.htm.

THE CHILD CITIZENSHIP ACT

Refugee children can automatically acquire citizenship when one parent naturalizes. This law took effect in 2001. Prior to that both parents had to be citizens for a child to automatically derive citizenship.

For further reading, see Ilona Bray, "Derivative U.S. Citizenship, via Naturalized U.S.

Citizen Parents or Adoption by U.S. Citizen," Lawyers.com, 2017, https://immigration .lawyers.com/citizenship/american-citizenship-derivative-citizenship.html.

ANTITERRORISM AND EFFECTIVE DEATH PENALTY ACT

Passed in 1996 following the 1995 Oklahoma City bombing, the act made it much easier to detain and deport immigrants.

ILLEGAL IMMIGRATION REFORM AND IMMIGRANT RESPONSIBILITY ACT

Also passed in 1996, this act expanded the number of criminal convictions that qualified for automatic deportation and eliminated key defenses against deportation. For further reading on the 1996 laws, see Human Rights Watch, "US: 20 Years of Immigrant Abuses," April 25, 2016, https://www.hrw.org/news/2016/04/25/us-20 -years-immigrant-abuses.

MEMORANDUM OF UNDERSTANDING

In its 2002 memorandum Cambodia agreed to accept their nationals being deported from the United States. For further reading, see SEARAC, "Memorandum between the Government of the United States and the Royal Government of Cambodia for the Establishment and Operation of a United States—Cambodia Joint Commission on Repatriation, Mar. 22, 2002," April 27, 2016, http://www.searac.org/sites/default /files/Cambodia%20and%20US%20MOU.pdf.

ZADVYDAS V. DAVIS, 533 U.S. 678 (2001)

In this 2001 U.S. Supreme Court case, the court ruled that if it is unlikely that a detainee who has already been held six months will be removed in the near future, then he or she must be released. Prior to 1990, six months had been the detention limit, but in 1990 Congress granted an exception for aggravated felons. This term of detention affected many detainees facing deportation, including many Cambodians, after the 1996 acts.

For further reading, see American Bar Association, Commission on Immigration, "A Legal Guide for ICE Detainees: Seeking Release from Indefinite Detention after Receiving a Final Order of Deportation" (Washington DC: American Bar Association, 2006, revised 2017), https://www.americanbar.org/content/dam/aba/publications /commission_on_immigration/legalguide_indefinitedetention.authcheckdam.pdf.

SOURCES

PREFACE

The information about the murder suicide in the Cengel family comes from the author's memories and the article "Man, Tired of Living, Kills Family, Self," *Tipton (IN) Daily Tribune*, May 11, 1953.

Information about the U.S. resettlement of the most vulnerable refugees comes from the U.S. Department of State's fact sheet "Refugee Resettlement in the United States," January 13, 2016, https://2009-2017.state.gov/r/pa/prs/ps/2016/01/251176.htm; and the Rachel Aviv article "The Rights of Refugees Who Do Wrong," *New Yorker*, December 7, 2015. Additional information on refugee resettlement comes from the U.S. Department of State, "U.S. Refugee Admissions FAQs," May 13, 2013; and the United Nations High Commissioner for Refugees, "UNHCR Refugee Resettlement Trends 2015," June 2015, http://www.unhcr.org/en-us/news/agenda/2012/3/559e43ac9/unhcr-refugee-resettlement-trends-2015.html.

The story about Nheth Hak, Touch Hak, and Nalin Chhim comes from personal interviews conducted with them in 2016.

Information about the 1980 Refugee Act comes from various sources, including the book edited by Huping Ling and Allan Austin, *Asian American History and Culture: An Encyclopedia* (London: Routledge, 2015).

Information about PTSD and intergenerational transmission comes from Rachel Yehuda and L. M. Bierer, "Transgenerational Transmission of Cortisol and PTSD Risk," *Progress in Brain Research* 167 (2008): 121–35; and Rachel Yehud, L. M. Bierer, J. Schmeidler, D. H. Aferiat, I. Breslau, and S. Dolan, "Low Cortisol and Risk for PTSD in Adult Offspring of Holocaust Survivors," *American Journal of Psychiatry* 157, no. 8 (August 2000): 1252–59.

INTRODUCTION

Information about the Cambodian genocide comes from numerous sources, including Cambodia Tribunal Monitor (http://www.cambodiatribunal.org/), a group composed of academics and non-profit organizations providing access to the Extraordinary Chambers in the Courts of Cambodia.

Sources for information regarding Cambodian history include: Elizabeth Becker, *When the War was Over: Cambodia and the Khmer Rouge Revolution* (New York: Public Affairs, 1986); the textbook *Ministry of Education Youth and Sports of the Royal Government of Cambodia Social Study* (Phnom Penh: Ministry of Education Youth and Sports of the Royal Government of Cambodia, 2000), funded by the United Nations Population Fund and its Educational, Scientific, and Cultural Organization, http://www.d.dccam.org/Projects/Document_Projects/Cambodia_Social_Studies_Textbook .htm; and concerning Tuol Sleng prison, "Fact Sheet: Pol Pot and His Prisoners at Secret Prison S-21" (Phnom Penh: Documentation Center of Cambodia, 2011), http://www.d.dccam.org/Archives/Documents/Confessions/pdf/FACT_SHEET--Pol_Pot _and_His_Prisoners_at_Secret_Prison_S-21.pdf.

Information about the percent of the population killed in the genocide comes from various sources, including the book edited by Mary Yu Danico, *Asian American Society: An Encyclopedia* (Thousand Oaks CA: Sage Publications, 2014).

Regarding the numbers of Cambodians resettled in the United States and those forced back into Thailand, see Sucheng Chan, "Cambodians in the United States: Refugees, Immigrants, American Ethnic Minority," in *Oxford Research Encyclopedia of American History* (New York: Oxford University Press, September 2015), http://americanhistory.oxfordre.com/view/10.1093/acrefore/9780199329175.001.0001 /acrefore-9780199329175-e-317?rskey=uvGjpx&result=1.

Information on Cambodian refugees comes from Walter Leitner International Human Rights Clinic Returnee Integration Support Center, "Removing Refugees: U.S. Deportation Policy and the Cambodian-American Community" (New York: Fordham Law School Leitner Center for International Law and Justice, Spring 2010), http://www .searac.org/sites/default/files/Removing%20Refugees%20-%20US%20Deportation %20Policy%20and%20the%20Cambodian%20American%20Community.pdf.

Statistics regarding poverty, incarceration, deportation orders, and deportees in Cambodia come from the Southeast Asia Resource Action Center (SEARAC), www .searac.org/.

Information on deportation crimes comes from Human Rights Watch (HRW), "Forced Apart (by the Numbers): Non-Citizens Deported Mostly for Nonviolent Offenses," April 15, 2009, https://www.hrw.org/report/2009/04/15/forced-apart -numbers/non-citizens-deported-mostly-nonviolent-offenses; and HRW, "A Price Too High: US Families Torn Apart by Deportations for Drug Offenses," June 16, 2015, https://www.hrw.org/report/2015/06/16/price-too-high/us-families-torn-apart -deportations-drug-offenses.

Information about the 1996 laws comes from a variety of sources, including Rachel Aviv's article "The Refugee Dilemma: What Do We Owe Those We Take In?," *New Yorker*, December 7, 2015, https://www.newyorker.com/magazine/2015/12/07/the -refugee-dilemma.

Information on San Tran Croucher and Sithy Yi comes from personal interviews conducted in 2015 and 2016 in California; and from San Tran and Tom Croucher, *San's Story of Survival and Persecution*, unpublished manuscript.

Information on Chanphirun Meanowuth Min comes from personal interviews in 2015 and 2016 in California.

Information on Song Chhang comes from personal interviews in 2015 and 2016 in California.

Information about Nheth, Puthy, and Touch Hak comes from personal interviews conducted in 2015 and 2016 in California.

Information from Tracy Harachi comes from a personal interview in Cambodia in 2014.

Information from Bill Herod comes from email and phone interviews in 2014 and 2017.

Information from Nicole Navas, Grace Meng, and Ira Mehlman comes from phone interviews in 2014.

Information about Sambath Nhep and Chea Bou comes from a personal interview with Sambath Nhep in early 2016 in California; and Momo Chang, "Oakland Man Facing Deportation for Nonviolent Drug Crime," *East Bay Express* (Oakland CA), August 12, 2015.

Information from Anida Yoeu Ali comes from a personal interview in Cambodia in 2014.

1. THE DIPLOMAT AND THE DEPORTEE

Information on Chanphirun Meanowuth Min comes from personal interviews in 2015 and 2016.

Information on Song Chhang comes from personal interviews in 2015 and 2016; and Richard S. Ehrlich, "Suicide & Executions: Cambodia 1975," *Columbus (OH) Free Press*, April 23, 2015.

Details of Chanphirun Meanowuth Min's drug conviction come from contemporary newspaper accounts, including Teresa Watanabe, "Cambodians Fear Possible Deportation," *Los Angeles Times*, February 21, 2003.

The description of Lon Nol's exit comes from interviews with Song Chhang; and Song Chhang, "Lon Nol's Helicopter Exit," *Cambodia Daily*, April 2, 2014.

Information regarding the TV journalists killed during the war comes from Song

Chhang and Jim Axelrod, "Fallen Journalists in Cambodia Remembered," CBS.com, June 1, 2013, http://www.cbsnews.com/news/fallen-journalists-in-cambodia-remembered/.

Information and numbers regarding the resettlement of Cambodian refugees comes from Sucheng Chan, "Cambodians in the United States," in *Oxford Research Encyclopedia*.

Resettlement and Long Beach information comes from the Cambodian Community History and Archive Project (CamCHAP), California State University–Dominguez Hills, http://www4.csudh.edu/anthropology/cambodian-community-history-archive-project; Susan Needham and Karen Quintiliani, *Images of America: Cambodians in Long Beach* (Mount Pleasant SC: Arcadia Publishing, 2008); and the 2010 U.S. Census.

Information about deportation comes from the book by Daniel Kanstroom, *Aftermath: Deportation Law and the New American Diaspora* (New York: Oxford University Press, 2012).

2. "IT WAS A MASSACRE"

Information about Puthy and Touch Hak comes from personal interviews conducted in 2015 and 2016 in California; and Paula Wissel, "This Man May Be Deported to Cambodia before He Can Give His Brother a Kidney," KNKX.org, May 27, 2014.

The account of the school shooting comes from an interview with Touch Hak; and Associated Press, "Five Children Killed as Gunman Attacks a California School," *New York Times*, January 18, 1989, http://www.nytimes.com/1989/01/18/us/five-children-killed-as-gunman-attacks-a-california-school.html.

Information on the situation in border and refugee camps comes from Columbia Center for New Media Teaching and Learning, "Forced Migration: Cambodia," October 2007, http://ccnmtl.columbia.edu/portfolio/medicine_and_health/forced_migration.html.

Legal information regarding Touch Hak's case comes from phone interviews and emails with his lawyer, Jacqueline Dan, who works with Asian Americans Advancing Justice in Los Angeles.

Information about Many Uch comes from a phone interview in 2016.

Information on the long-term health of Cambodian refugees comes from Grant N. Marshall, Terry L. Schell, Eunice C. Wong, S. Megan Berthold, Katrin Hambarsoomian, Marc N. Elliott, Barbara H. Bardenheier, and Edward W. Gregg, "Diabetes and Cardiovascular Disease Risk in Cambodian Refugees," *Journal of Immigrant and Minority Health* 18, no. 1 (February 2016): 110–17.

3. THE MOTHER

Information about San Tran Croucher and her daughters comes from personal interviews with them in 2015 and 2016. Additional information comes from legal declarations made by San Tran Croucher, Sithy Yi, and Tom Croucher, and from *San's Story*.

Additional historical details, including the evacuation of Phnom Penh, come from Ben Kiernan, *The Pol Pot Regime: Race, Power, and Genocide in Cambodia under the Khmer Rouge, 1975-79*, 3rd ed. (New Haven CT: Yale University Press, 2008); and Becker, *When the War Was Over*. Information on the U.S. bombing comes from Taylor Own, "Bombs over Cambodia: New Information Reveals that Cambodia Was Bombed Far More Heavily than Previously Believed," *The Walrus*, October 12, 2006. Further information explaining the wide range of civilian deaths during the U.S. bombing can be found at World Peace Foundation, "Cambodia: U.S. Bombing, Civil War, and Khmer Rouge," Mass Atrocity Endings, August 7, 2015, https://sites.tufts.edu/atrocityendings/2015/08/07/cambodia-u-s-bombing-civil-war-khmer-rouge/.

Information about Khmer Krom and Vietnamese relations comes from Shawn McHale, "Ethnicity, Violence, and Khmer-Vietnamese Relations: The Significance of the Lower Mekong Delta, 1757-1954," *Journal of Asian Studies* 72 (May 2013): 2; and HRW, "On the Margins: Rights Abuses of Ethnic Khmer in Vietnam's Mekong Delta," January 21, 2009, https://www.hrw.org/report/2009/01/21/margins/rights-abuses-ethnic-khmer-vietnams-mekong-delta.

4. THE MURDERER

Information about David Ros comes from numerous personal interviews in 2015 and 2016 and court documents.

Background on gang activity comes from Al Valdez, "The Tiny Rascal Gang: Big Trouble," *POLICE Magazine*, January 1, 2000; and Barry Leibowitz, "Asian Boyz Gang Founder Marvin Mercado Gets Life, No Parole from Calif. Judge," CBS News, March 31, 2011.

Information on Tracy Harachi comes from a personal interview in 2014.

Additional information from Walter Leitner International Human Rights Clinic, "Removing Refugees."

Information on deportation rules comes from various sources, including numerous conversations with immigration attorneys such as Jacqueline Dan in 2015 and 2016.

Trial information comes from a phone interview with King County (WA) judge Timothy Bradshaw in 2016. The Washington State Supreme Court ruling concerning murder in the second degree is available at the Washington State Legislature, RCW 9A.32.050, "Murder in the Second Degree," 2003, https://app.leg.wa.gov/rcw/default.aspx?cite=9A.32.050.

5. SITHY AND SITHEA

Information on San Tran Croucher, Sithy Yi, and Tom Croucher comes from personal interviews conducted in 2015 and 2016. Additional information comes from legal declarations made by San Tran Croucher, Sithy Yi, and Tom Croucher, and from *San's Story*.

Sithea San, "Never Give Up," TEDxSoCal Talk, August 13, 2012, https://www.youtube.com/watch?v=xoPvAOI3R8k. TEDx talks are smaller, independently organized versions of TED Talks.

Information on Richer San's legal troubles comes from Greg Mellen, "Long Beach Khmer Leader Jailed in Cambodia," *Orange County (CA) Register*, September 7, 2014; and Simon Henderson and Hay Pisey, "Businessman Freed after Officials Intervene," *Cambodia Daily*, October 21, 2014. Information on his U.S. citizenship status comes from Phorn Bopha and Simon Henderson, "Former US Diplomat Accused in $1M Fraud Case," *Cambodia Daily*, September 1, 2014.

Resettlement and Long Beach information comes from the Cambodian Community History and Archive Project (CamCHAP); Needham and Quintiliani, *Images of America*; and the 2010 U.S. Census.

6. "IT'S NOT WHAT YOU THINK"

Information on San Tran Croucher, Sithy Yi, Sithea, Sithea Vy, and Tom Croucher comes from personal interviews conducted in 2015 and 2016. Additional information comes from legal declarations made by San Tran Croucher, Sithy Yi, and Tom Croucher, and from *San's Story*.

Additional historical details come from Kiernan, *Pol Pot Regime*; and Becker, *When the War Was Over*.

7. THE WIFE WITHOUT A HUSBAND

Information on Sambath Nhep comes from a personal interview in 2016.

Information on Chea Bou and his case comes from a 2016 phone interview with his lawyer, Linda Tam, with the East Bay Community Law Center, Berkeley. Additional information comes from Momo Chang, "Man Facing Deportation for Nonviolent Drug Crime," *East Bay Express* (Oakland CA), August 12, 2015; and Southeast Asia Resource Action Center.

Information on crime in Oakland comes from United Press International, "Killing Lifts Oakland's One-Year Homicide Record to 146," *Los Angeles Times*, January 2, 1987, http://articles.latimes.com/1987-01-02/local/me-1561_1_oakland-homicide.

Information on the larger drug case comes from San Francisco Division, Federal Bureau of Investigation, "Federal Grand Jury Charges Multiple Defendants with

Racketeering, Extortion, and Narcotics Crimes Occurring at and through Two Bay Area Casinos," press release, March 3, 2011.

Information on deportation of noncitizens with drug offenses comes from HRW, "A Price Too High."

8. STEALING FROM THE DEAD

Information on San Tran Croucher, Sithy Yi, Sithea, Sithea Vy, and Tom Croucher comes from personal interviews conducted in 2015 and 2016. Additional information comes from legal declarations made by San Tran Croucher, Sithy Yi, and Tom Croucher, and from *San's Story*.

Regarding San's stay in Boeng Chrang's rice fields, I used San's spelling, but research shows it may have been spelled Boeng Chaeng. Additional historical details come from Kiernan, *Pol Pot Regime*; and Becker, *When the War Was Over*.

9. THE FATHER

Information about David Ros comes from numerous personal interviews in 2015 and 2016.

Information on the long-term health of Cambodian refugees comes from Marshall et al., "Diabetes and Cardiovascular Disease Risk," 110–17.

Kidney failure information comes from the National Institute of Diabetes and Digestive and Kidney Diseases.

Information on Southeast Asia Resource Action Center comes from its press releases, interviews, and website, www.searac.org/.

Information from Many Uch comes from a phone interview in 2016; and Nicole Newnham and David Grabias, "Revisiting *Sentenced Home* and the Case of Many Uch," iTVS, August 10, 2010, https://itvs.org/blog/revisiting-sentenced-home-and-the-case-of-many-uch.

10. AN EDUCATION IN SILENCE

Information on Sithy Yi comes from personal interviews conducted in 2015 and 2016. Additional information comes from legal declarations made by San Tran Croucher, Sithy Yi, and Tom Croucher, and from *San's Story*.

Sithy Yi's PTSD diagnosis comes from an April 2, 2015, psychological evaluation by marriage and family therapist Rose Marie Durocher.

Information from S. Megan Berthold comes from a phone interview in 2016.

Information from Thang D. Nguyen comes from a phone interview in 2016.

The conversion from Thai baht to U.S. dollars used fxtop.com to calculate inflation and then convert the currency in September 2017.

11. A SECOND CHANCE

Information on Chanphirun Meanowuth Min comes from personal interviews in 2015 and 2016.

Information on Terry Min comes from a personal interview in 2015.

The poem on the wall is "Footprints in the Sand" by Mary Stevenson.

Information on Song Chhang comes from personal interviews in 2015 and 2016.

Information on Long Beach comes from the Cambodian Community History and Archive Project (CamCHAP); and Needham and Quintiliani, *Images of America*.

Information on resettlement comes from Sucheng Chan, "Cambodians in the United States," in *Oxford Research Encyclopedia*.

Information on the Hun Sen regime comes from HRW, "30 Years of Hun Sen: Violence, Repression, and Corruption in Cambodia," January 12, 2015, https://www.hrw.org/report/2015/01/12/30-years-hun-sen/violence-repression-and-corruption-cambodia.

12. THE MEDICINE MAN

Information on San Tran Croucher comes from personal interviews conducted in 2015 and 2016. Additional information comes from legal declarations made by San Tran Croucher, Sithy Yi, Tom Croucher, and from *San's Story*.

Information on Khao I Dang camp from Vivian Tan, "Famed Cambodian Refugee Camp Reopens as Educational Centre," UN Refugee Agency, May 31, 2016, http://www.unhcr.org/en-us/news/latest/2016/5/574d5f1b4/famed-cambodian-refugee-camp-reopens-educational-centre.html.

Holding center violence accusations come from Columbia Center, "Forced Migration: Cambodia."

13. EXPIRED

Information about Puthy and Touch Hak comes from personal interviews conducted in 2015 and 2016.

Legal information regarding Touch Hak's case comes from phone interviews with his lawyer, Jacqueline Dan, with Asian Americans Advancing Justice, Los Angeles, in 2015; and on the response letters from ICE (September 8, 2015, and October 27, 2015) to two of his Form I-246 applications.

The information from the United Nations Children's Fund on records in Cambodia came from Ministry of the Interior of the Royal Government of Cambodia, "Recording of Civil Status Focusing on Primary Rights of the Child," paper presented at the Third Asia Regional Conference on Birth Registration—a Child's First Right, Bangkok, Thailand, January 2003.

Information from the Cambodian Embassy comes from a 2016 phone interview. Information regarding ICE comes from a 2016 email.

Information from Michael Chua, the living donor nurse coordinator at the University of California–San Diego Health, comes from a phone interview in 2016.

Information on dialysis comes from Beth Israel Deaconess Medical Center, "The Benefits of Transplant Versus Dialysis," http://www.bidmc.org/Centers-and -Departments/Departments/Transplant-Institute/Kidney/The-Benefits-of-Transplant -versus-Dialysis.aspx.

Information about Puthy Hak and Touch Hak comes from personal interviews conducted in 2016.

14. "NOT HOME FOR THE HOLIDAYS"

Information about David Ros comes from numerous personal interviews in 2015 and 2016.

Information regarding David Ros's meeting with the Cambodian ambassador to the United States comes from personal interviews with David Ros and Mary Blatz, who was also there.

David Ros says there are 2,500 Cambodian Americans still on the list to be deported. This compares reasonably with statistics from Syracuse University's Transactional Records Access Clearinghouse website, "Deportation Outcomes by Charge" (http://trac.syr.edu/phptools/immigration/court_backlog/deport_outcome_charge.php), which lists about 2,400 Cambodians from 1998 to 2016, leaving a little fewer than 2,000 still to be deported.

Information about the "Not Home for the Holidays Event" comes from the event and interviews with individual speakers.

Information from Harene Chau comes from a personal interview in 2015.

Information about Bill Herod's eye comes from numerous articles, including Kit Gillet, "Cambodian Refugees Deported for Crimes in U.S. Long for Only Home They Know," *McClatchy DC Bureau*, July 8, 2013, http://www.mcclatchydc.com/news/nation -world/world/article24750811.html.

Information on the San Bernardino shooting comes from a variety of news accounts, including Sarah Parvini, "For Those Wounded in San Bernardino, a Painful Path to Recovery," *Los Angeles Times*, December 30, 2015, http://www.latimes.com/local /california/la-me-sb-victim-recovery-20151230-story.html.

15. NEVER-ENDING NIGHTMARE

Information from Nheth Hak, Mom Khat, and Onna Oum comes from personal interviews in 2016.

Information about the U.S. bombing of Cambodia comes from Amanda Pike, "Cambodia: Pol Pot's Shadow, October, 2002," *Frontline/World*, PBS, http://www.pbs.org/frontlineworld/stories/cambodia/; and Own, "Bombs over Cambodia."

Further information explaining the wide range of civilian deaths during the U.S. bombing can be found at World Peace Foundation, "Cambodia: U.S. Bombing."

Kamping Pouy dam construction information comes from Lorn Dalin, "A Trip to Kamping Pouy Basin, Battambang Province," *Voices of Genocide: Justice and the Khmer Rouge Famine* (Phnom Penh: Documentation Center of Cambodia, November 20-22, 2013), http://www.d.dccam.org/Projects/Radio/pdf/A_Trip_to_Kamping_Pouy_Basin_Battambang_Province.pdf.

Numbers regarding Cambodians forced back into Thailand come from Sucheng Chan, "Cambodians in the United States," in *Oxford Research Encyclopedia*.

Information on Park Village comes from Jennifer Torres, "Celebration of a Milestone: Cambodian Refugees Mark 15 Years of Life at Park Village," Recordnet.com, October 29, 2008, http://www.recordnet.com/article/20081029/a_news/810290326.

Information on the long-term health of Cambodian refugees comes from Marshall et al., "Diabetes and Cardiovascular Disease Risk," 110-17.

Kidney failure information comes from the National Institute of Diabetes and Digestive and Kidney Diseases.

Information from Thang D. Nguyen comes from a phone interview in 2016.

Statistics on PTSD come from Grant N. Marshall, T. L. Schell, M. N. Elliott, S. M. Berthold, and C. A. Chun, "Mental Health of Cambodian Refugees 2 Decades after Resettlement in the United States," *Journal of American Medical Association* 3, no. 294 (August 3, 2005): 571-79.

Information from S. Megan Berthold comes from a phone interview in 2016; her dissertation, "The Effects of Exposure to Violence and Social Support on Psychological and Behavioral Outcomes among Khmer Refugee Adolescents" (PhD, University of California–Los Angeles, 1998); and S. Megan Berthold, "War Traumas and Community Violence," *Journal of Multicultural Social Work* 8, no. 1-2 (2000): 15-46.

16. TWO CITIES TANGLED TOGETHER

Information on Chanphirun Meanowuth Min comes from personal interviews in 2015 and 2016.

Information on Song Chhang comes from personal interviews in 2015 and 2016.

Information on Richard Yu's legal troubles comes from Greg Mellen, "Long Beach Khmer Leader Jailed in Cambodia," *Orange County (CA) Register*, September 7, 2014.

The controversy surrounding the New Year's parade comes from first-person sources and reporting by Greg Yee and Josh Dulaney with the *Long Beach (CA) Press Telegram*, including "Cambodia New Year Parade Appearance by Military Leader Stirs Controversy," March 19, 2016.

17. NEW YEAR, SAME PAST

Information from Jennifer Diep comes from a personal interview in 2016.

Information from Sithea San comes from a personal interview in 2016.

Information from Lauren Thor comes from a personal interview in 2016.

Information on Sithy Yi comes from personal interviews conducted in 2015 and 2016. Additional information comes from legal declarations made by San Tran Croucher, Sithy Yi, Tom Croucher, and from *San's Story*.

18. GIRLFRIENDS

Information from Debbie Keodara comes from a personal interview in 2016.

Information from David Ros comes from numerous personal interviews in 2015 and 2016.

Information about Puthy Hak and Touch Hak comes from personal interviews conducted in 2015 and 2016.

Information regarding the death of Debbie's father comes from Debbie and various newspaper accounts, including "King County Deaths," *Seattle Post Intelligencer*, August 13, 2015.

19. A PARTY AT OAK PARK

Information about Puthy and Touch Hak comes from personal interviews conducted in 2015 and 2016.

Information from Nalin Chhim, Srim Chrim, Emily Chrim, and Priscilla Hak comes from personal interviews in 2016.

Stockton homicide numbers come from Jason Anderson, "Man Slain in Shooting near Oak Park Stockton's Seventh Homicide of Year," Recordnet.com, March 29, 2016.

The account of the school shooting comes from an interview with Nalin Chhim; and Associated Press, "Five Children Killed."

20. JUDGMENT DAY

Legal information comes from Sithy Yi's lawyer, Kim Luu-Ng.

Information on San Tran Croucher and Sithy Yi comes from personal interviews conducted in 2015 and 2016. Additional information comes from legal declarations made by San Tran Croucher, Sithy Yi, and Tom Croucher, and from *San's Story*.

Information on Mary Blatz comes from a personal interview in 2016.

Information regarding the Convention against Torture comes from Kim Luu-Ng; and Hans Danelius, "Convention against Torture and Other Cruel, Inhuman or Degrading Treatment or Punishment," UN Audiovisual Library of International Law, December 10, 1984, http://legal.un.org/avl/ha/catcidtp/catcidtp.html.

Information on Sithy's PTSD diagnosis comes from a psychological evaluation written by Rose Marie Durocher on April 2, 2015.

21. BLOOD-KILLER

Information on the shooting, including the re-created scenes, comes from the Superior Court of Washington for King County Information docket on David Ros's case.

Information from Mia-lia Kiernan comes from a phone interview in 2016.

Information from Kim Luu-Ng comes from a phone interview in 2016.

Information from Katrina Dizon Mariategue comes from a phone interview in 2016.

Information from Alan Lai comes from email correspondence in 2016.

Peter Connick did not return email or phone messages in 2016. A woman in his office said he was not interested in speaking.

Information on the Seattle Police Department comes from conversations with representatives of the Seattle Police Department and the Seattle Police Guild in 2016.

Information on the SEARAC report comes from its report "Automatic Injustice: A Report on Prosecutorial Discretion in the Southeast Asian American Community" (Washington DC: Southeast Asia Resource Action Center, October 2016), http://www.searac.org/sites/default/files/SEARAC%20SEAA_PD_report_web.pdf; and a webinar release event on October 26, 2016.

Information on Thong Vang comes from various articles in the *Fresno Bee* published in 2016.

Information on the murder of Chanthy Ros comes from various articles in the *Seattle Times* published in 2000; and David Ros's mother, Chanthaveth Ros.

Information from King County (WA) judge Timothy Bradshaw comes from a phone interview in 2016.

22. THE PASTOR

Information from Nathan Ros comes from a phone interview in 2016.

Information on 1 Love Movement comes from its Facebook and fund-raising pages.

Information on Pacific Baptist Church comes from its website http://pacificbaptist .com/ministries.html; and from Nathan Ros in a phone interview in 2016.

Information from David Ros and Chanthaveth Ros comes from personal interviews in 2016.

23. FRIENDS AND FAMILY

Information from Sarith Chan comes from a personal interview in 2017.

Information on Battambang comes from World Population Review, "Cambodia: Population Density," 2017, http://worldpopulationreview.com/countries/cambodia-population/.

Information from RISC comes from personal interviews in 2017.

Information from Sophea Phea comes from a personal interview in 2017.

24. EXILE

Information from RISC comes from personal interviews in 2017.

Information from Dr. Sotheara Chhim comes from a personal interview in 2017.

Information from Chou Bun Eng, secretary of state of the Ministry of Interior of Cambodia, and her assistant In Mean comes from personal interviews on February 6, 2017.

Information from Chandara Tep comes from a personal interview in 2017.

25. LEFT BEHIND

Information from Khe Khouen comes from a personal interview in 2017.

Information from Sithy Yi and San Croucher comes from personal interviews in 2016.

Information about Richer San's criminal case comes from Colin Meyn and Khuon Narim, "Dentist Takes Fraud Case to US Court," *Cambodia Daily*, October 20, 2016, https://www.cambodiadaily.com/news/dentist-takes-fraud-fight-us-court-119504/; and Buth Reaksmey Kongkea, "Khmer-US Businessmen Convicted on Fraud Charge," *Khmer Times*, October 21, 2016, http://www.khmertimeskh.com/news/31109/khmer-us-businessmen-convicted-on-fraud-charge.

Information from RISC comes from personal interviews in 2017.

AFTERWORD

Information on deportations comes from an interview with Bun Eng and Mean, February 6, 2017; and Matt Surrusco's multiple articles in *Cambodia Daily* in January and February 2016.

Information on Song Chhang comes from Ros Chanveasna and Ven Rathavong, "Lon Nol's Last Information Minister Weighs in on Sokha Case," *Khmer Times*,

September 15, 2017, http://www.khmertimeskh.com/news/31109/khmer-us -businessmen-convicted-on-fraud-charge.

Information regarding the U.S. government's announcement comes from Salem Solomon, "US to Stop Issuing Visas to Citizens from 3 African Countries, Cambodia," VOA News, August 25, 2017, https://www.voanews.com/a/us-to-stop-issuing-visas-to -citizens-from-3-african-countries-cambodia/4000227.html; and "Statement of the Ministry of Foreign Affairs and International Cooperation," Phnom Penh, September 14, 2017, https://www.mfaic.gov.kh/site/detail/13592.

INDEX